Beyond the China Sea

Sharon Lockwood

NEW TECUMSETH PUBLIC LIBRARY

PUBLISH AMERICA

PublishAmerica
Baltimore

First printing

ISBN: 1-4137-9256-1
PUBLISHED BY PUBLISHAMERICA, LLLP
www.publishamerica.com
Baltimore

Printed in the United States of America

Dedication

I would like to dedicate this book to those who have played a major role in my life.

First, I would like to dedicate this book to my daughter and best friend, Tasha, who I absolutely love and adore. I would like to take this opportunity to thank you for not only being so supportive over the years, but encouraging me with every wild endeavor I chose to take part in. I am and always will be truly fortunate and thankful to have you in my life.

Second, I have nothing but utmost respect for Dana Pharant and Hazel Soares, two people I am truly honored and privileged to have in my life. Without their continued encouragement, support and influence, I may never have embarked on such an incredible journey thousands of miles away to teach English, nor would I have written and published *Beyond the China Sea*, or my first book, a book of poetry entitled *Metaphorically Speaking Mostly*.

Finally, two people I love and am grateful to have in my life are my parents, Bill and Dorothy, who could never keep up with my spontaneous decisions and adventurous escapades, but raised and nurtured me to become the person I've become today.

Acknowledgments

Special thanks to all those extraordinary individuals I had the opportunity to get to know, understand and became friends with along my journey. I would like to acknowledge and thank all those exceptional individuals who made my stay in China one I will never forget, the most unforgettable experiences of a lifetime. Without a doubt, it is truly one of the most incredible cultures and way of life that one could ever experience. You truly are incredible people, and to everyone, thank you from the bottom of my heart.

This special acknowledgment and thanks also goes to the following people: Brenda Dostie, my best friend of forty years and her husband, Denis, who I love and adore. Thank you both for not only your gracious hospitality during my stay in the serenity of your home in Drayton Valley, Alberta, to complete this book, but for the care package you sent me in China. It was so much better than any Christmas present would have been; to my Aunt Annabell and Uncle Anthony Marsico, thank you both for your generosity and hospitality during my visit to Virginia to register this book, but also for checking on me five out of seven days a week without fail during my stay in China; an extra special thanks to Drew Hewitt, who not only helped me perfect my resume to secure a job in China, but after I lost the first three chapters of this book, Drew played a major role in the retrieval of previous e-mails and the continuation of the book; my friends Dana Pharant, Mary Fraser and Connie Deary, who all replied to some pretty outlandish long letters I sent.

The importance of communication, contact with friends and family from the outside world when living in a foreign country thousands of miles away from home, I cannot stress enough. Having such a dedicated group of readers always anxious to receive the next saga of my Chinese adventure became my motivation, making this book possible. Tasha Lockwood, Bill and Dorothy Braden, Lisa Marsico, Ralf and Rosalba Braden, Tracey Branch, Hazel Soares, Robb Turner, Larry and Sandy Wilkinson, Wayne and Debbie Lockwood, Jim Deary, Steven Moran, Pat Fox, Tim and Candy MacIntyre, Lynn Howarth, Cyndie and Michael Jerome, Rick New, Marge and Gary Mann and Mike Williams.

It is so gratifying having each and every one of you in my life.

When you open your heart and feel,
You will begin to awaken to all around you.
When you feel with your heart,
Only then will the words begin to flow.
When you write what you feel in your heart,
The description will begin to flow
In a direction beyond your imagination.

Table of Contents

Introduction

Teaching English in China can be a very fascinating and rewarding experience, yet at the same time it can also be so intimidating and mind-boggling it will make your head spin.

Although a Communist Third World country, the people, the language, the history and the way of life depict China in its truest form. China portrays many fascinating and remarkable features, yet it can also reveal many strange situations and unfamiliar surroundings that we as North Americans are never faced with.

While living and teaching English in a small city of over nine million in Central China, a language barrier is prevalent and can be a major obstacle for many foreign teachers, and foreigners in general. Even so, culture shock is certain, with transformation proving much more difficult. Immersion in a culture with limited English conversation and interaction has a profound way of putting one's vulnerability to the real test. Those willing to view Asian cultures and lifestyle with an open mind, especially remote areas, stand a much better chance of continuing the journey they sct out on.

In larger cities such as Shanghai, Beijing and especially Hong Kong, English seems to be a bit more prevalent; however, it can still be a challenge to find those who speak it well. For many Chinese learning English, more emphasis has been put on learning to read and write, not speaking. This trend is slowly beginning to change, and as a foreign teacher it can be a very frustrating task at times.

Nonetheless, to walk away knowing you never gave up, yet you made a difference, an impact on those rebellious few, whether it was big or small, brings everything else into perspective, making it all worthwhile. It is an exceedingly different way of life, one very difficult to comprehend unless you live in the center of it and experience it firsthand.

Chapter 1
Shanghai Connections

Subsequent to dedicating five years of skills and talents to being a site supervisor for the same construction company, I was terminated soon after new management took over. It was time to set out and pursue a new direction and my new future.

My goal was to find employment on a cruise ship or teach English overseas. Working on a cruise ship intrigued me the most, yet everything was moving me toward teaching overseas. After completing a short mandatory TEFL course (Teaching English as a Foreign Language) my direction was becoming clear, and I began doing research into my new mission. What kind of school did I want to teach at, and where? I wanted a smaller city, somewhere with plenty of history and culture.

With less than two weeks before my departure to China, my tickets, passport and job were all in order after a few months of careful preparation. Something still seemed to be missing, but what?

After numerous e-mails back and forth to confirm trip details, suddenly there was a small glitch. Because the Chinese were to take care of the visas, an entry visa completely slipped my mind.

May first, also a major Chinese holiday, was fast approaching, which meant I had less than a week to submit, secure and have Chinese authorities at the consulate approve my visa application in time.

There's nothing like a good ol' last-minute challenge to get the blood pumping and send the blood pressure rising. Doubts began to mount as to whether I should continue this outlandish escapade I was about to embark on. On the other hand, however, it would prove interesting, if nothing else. Besides, I already given up my apartment, my life, and had paid for a return airline ticket to China for the next six months, so really I had nothing to lose.

Approving a visa took four to five days. I had exactly five, so before making the hour-long journey to the city, I checked then re-checked everything to ensure nothing was missing.

While waiting in line, I couldn't help but observe the many photos spread across one wall, perhaps pertaining to various Chinese events throughout the years. One photo in particular caught my eye. It was of an Asian man laying face down, a pool of blood at his head. The bottom left hand corner of the picture disclosed an unfamiliar axe with an extremely long handle. Definitely not something I needed to see prior to departure, I thought, as the woman at the counter yelled, motioning me to move forward.

Sliding my documentation through a small slit opening between the sliding glass windows secured along the entire counter, the Asian woman briefly examined my application before holding it up, pointing out a line I had left blank pertaining to the duration of my stay in China.

She slid the application back through the slit for me to complete. After writing six months, I slide it back again. Before responding in broken English with a Chinese accent, she slowly glanced up, scowling.

"Six months?" she questioned. "You want visit China for six months?"

"Yes," I replied.

"Why you want go to China for six months?" she bluntly questioned.

"To travel," I replied, somewhat confused by her interrogation.

"You cannot travel to China for six months!" she exclaimed.

"Why not? I've traveled for six months in other countries before."

"In China?"

"No, Australia and Europe."

She turned to engage in a brief conversation with the Asian gentleman next to her, then turned back to me.

"You get no visa for six months, only three!"

She then grabbed my application, vigorously crossing out six months and replacing it with three before tossing it with others into a stack.

"Come back Thursday," she bellowed. "You pick it up then."

It was definitely not a situation worth arguing about, nor was I in any position to do so. After all, who was I to question the authorities about the legalities of Chinese documentation? Four days later, as promised, everything was in order upon pick up.

The day of departure had arrived, and I stood in the airport terminal with my daughter, pondering the best way to say goodbye to my 19-year-old. Waiting, wondering what I was about to do, my routine paperwork fetish began, checking, rechecking, making sure every piece of documentation was packed.

It was time, but suddenly my daughter looked up at me as her eyes instantly began to well, tears now streaming down her face. *How could I do this and just leave her behind?* I thought.

From the beginning, we had done everything together, gone everywhere together; it had always been just her and I. The only thing I could do was grab her, holding on for as long as she needed, crying right along with her. That moment was the most difficult moment of my life, and suddenly I felt so bad, yet she had supported me, even encouraged me to embark on this fascinating journey.

Was I making a mistake? I thought. They say things happen for a reason, and everything leading up to that point had fallen into place so smoothly, with the exception of the visa, yet that had also gone well. Making my way toward the customs gate, the doubts began to multiply as I watched her walk toward the exit door. She turned, blowing one last kiss, then waved goodbye before we parted ways.

What was I thinking, leaving her to fend for herself while I chase halfway around the world to pursue some wild new adventure? Yet I knew she would be fine. Her father and I had just moved her and most of my household belongings into a house she would share with four other girls for the next three years. She had every luxury known to man, including a car.

It was time to board the plane for what would seem the longest journey in history. O'Hare International in Chicago was the first leg of my journey, with twenty minutes to connect with my flight to San Francisco. However, after arriving late due to weather, my connecting time was cut to ten minutes.

As luck would have it, my gate was at the opposite end of the terminal. Suddenly, the question of what I was going to do when I missed the flight, followed by the brief voice of logic, screamed as it penetrated my thoughts. *You're 45 years of age for Christ sakes. What the hell did you think you were doing when you came up with this lame plan? Here you are, out of shape, running like a crazed lunatic, pushing people out of the way, coughing up a lung no less, to catch a plane that will probably be pulling away just as you get there.*

There was no doubt in my mind that investing in new sneakers before leaving home was possibly the smartest decision I had made. It was not turning out to be my idea of fun anymore, and maybe it was time to re-think the strategy to all this madness, use the return portion of the ticket and go home.

Approaching the departure gate, panic ensued after seeing a small line of passengers at the ticket counter and a waiting area nearby full of passengers. Oh, come on, I thought, I'm in a hurry, desperate to catch a plane, and I didn't have time to go through incidentals such as line-ups.

Lucky me, a last-minute plane change was followed by an hour-long flight delay, giving all passengers plenty of time to check in for new seating arrangement.

My pre-assigned window seat became a thing of the past, with my new seating arrangements being next to the emergency door over the wing. It quickly became apparent that all responsibilities pertaining to that door suddenly belonged to me and a young man sitting next to me. One could only hope the plane didn't crash.

With a four-hour flight ahead and no window seat, I knew anxiety would set in to put me on edge, so I had to find something to occupy my time. Ah, soothing music should help, so I instantaneously snatched up the headset and began flipping through channels to find something.

Digging through my pack, barely stuffed under the seat, I scrounged up a pen and some writing paper to pass the time. Who could I write? What would I write? It didn't matter, I thought, who cares, just write something, anything, to anyone. Before long three letters were moving simultaneously, and my anxiety was now manageable.

Descending into San Francisco, the time changes began. Despite the hour and an half delay at O'Hare, the flight continuing on to Shanghai was on time.

The temptation to bail was as overwhelming and powerful as the allure to continue. The thought of a twelve-hour flight ahead was doing nothing for me. You can do this, I thought, come on, twelve-hours should be a breeze, just take a deep breath and keep going.

As the plane departed San Francisco, I looked out the window, suddenly aware I was in it for the long haul and there was no turning back. Instinctively, the pen and paper emerged and the headset went on.

At some point hours later, I glanced out the window while writing, staring momentarily. It was still daylight, and at that moment the sky looked so peaceful. My mind began to drift with the clouds as my pen began to formulate words on the paper from my perspective.

> *Beyond the clouds, the sun never sleeps,*
> *Yet from above the clouds appear as*
> *Ice caps on a frozen bed of teal blue*
> *Tundra, stretching as far as the eye can see,*
> *Hanging suspended, motionless, at peace*
> *With the view each captivates.*
> *In the distance, a sturdy, rigid glacier*
> *Could not hold a truer, more lifelike form*
> *Paling in the background to hide*

Their splendor from view.
A portrait of a perfect mountain
Range running along an ocean's
Edge, peaking with valleys, stretching
To infinity, waiting for the command of
The wind to change its direction.
Until that time, they stand lingering in
Magnificent beauty to extend the imagination
And all it holds to bring forth, in a perfect
Reflection from the sun's perspective.

The unexpected beauty of the sky was temporary, soon changing to bring with it the unforgiving turbulence that almost always accompanies it. Over the intercom, from the cockpit, the pilot requested all passengers and flight crew to take their seats and buckle up, an indication that heavy turbulence was just around the corner.

Minutes later, the plane began bouncing and creaking so bad that I felt the wings were going to snap off at the door jams at any given moment so I could witness luggage descend from the belly and disappear in the ocean thirty-seven thousand feet below. Christ, I really hate flying!

Forty minutes ahead of schedule, Shanghai was now in sight as I peered through a thick haze blanketing the city. My connecting flight to Wuhan in central China was pre-booked for the following day. However, with such an early arrival and smooth transition through customs, two hours was plenty of time.

Before locating an information booth, I needed to use the toilet. My first introduction to China's facilities was also my first mistake. Squatting over a toilet bowl flush to the floor with a hole in the center while standing on two slightly raised platforms was certainly intriguing. It didn't take long to discover toilet paper is not supplied in China, so if you didn't carry toilet paper or packets of tissue on you at all times, it is either drip dry or you're out of luck.

As I stood upright to flush, waiting for the circulation to return in my feet, a hurricane mini bowl came to mind. However, after flushing, it is advisable to get the hell out of the way or your shoes will become part of the rinse cycle.

Instead of sticking around for the night, spending money I didn't have on hotels and taxis, I decided to catch the connecting flight at nine p.m., with one slight problem. All domestic flights from Shanghai departed from an airport sixty miles away. You have got to be kidding me! Speaking no Chinese, the probability of pronouncing, even attempting, to pronounce their written vocabulary was slim to none, and another good reason to catch the flight as soon as possible.

Before going anywhere, I wanted to call my new boss, Hank, and inform him of my arrival and let him know I was on my way. While hunting down a telephone, an English-speaking Asian woman intercepted me. After explaining my situation, she immediately took control of my decision making, and there was no longer time to make a phone call.

She took me up three flights of stairs to China Air's information counter, then down the elevator to a bank machine on the first floor. Finally, she grabbed my hand, dragging me across the terminal at record-breaking speed to a taxi parked outside. Everything was happening so fast, I wasn't sure what I was doing.

After speaking briefly with the driver, she informed me the driver could take me the distance to make the connection with time to spare for forty yuan.

"OK," I replied.

In an instant, she pushed me into the back seat, saying something to the driver before he whisked me off and bolted onto the freeway. Pedal to the medal and sixty miles to cover in half an hour, I looked down for a seatbelt. Although the driver was equipped with one, I was not, and was suddenly embarking on the first of many terrifying rides I would experience while in China.

There were multiple lanes of traffic with drivers all weaving in and out like some sort of psychopath late for his next shrink session. Lines on the road didn't seem to mean anything and must have been invisible to my driver and every other driver on the road as everyone straddled the lines, cutting each other off, even used the shoulder as an extra lane or passing lane. Suddenly my life began to flash before my eyes. I hadn't been in China two hours and my life was about to be terminated during a high-speed taxi ride.

Every driver followed so close I was sure the bumper of the car in front would become a permanent fixture for my teeth. It wasn't long before I realized there were very few restrictions on rules or speed limits, and horns were used as a safe driving tool and in constant usage, even when there was nothing to honk at. In thirty-five minutes flat the ride was over, and none too soon.

With only time enough to change my ticket and snag a seat, barely catching the next flight out, the call would once again have to wait until my arrival in Wuhan. After traveling twenty-five or so hours, I had landed safe and sound in Wuhan and was immediately approached by a representative from a cab company.

It was imperative that I find a telephone, so I improvised, folding my three middle fingers and using my thumb and baby finger as a phone up to my mouth and ear. Ah, the international language of sign, I thought as he handed me his cell phone. Hank's number was on a slip of paper in my pocket, so I pulled it out and immediately handed the phone back to the man to make the call after realizing the buttons were in Chinese.

Seconds later, the representative spoke with Hank briefly before handing me the phone. Hank had been expecting me to call him from Shanghai, and I was under the impression that he had made arrangements for me to stay in one of the nearby hotels. After explaining that no definite arrangements had been set up before departing for China, I had to assume that my stay in Shanghai would be at my expense. With no Chinese background, and arriving earlier than expected, I wasn't about to attempt it.

Hank didn't seem all that upset by my intrepid decision and asked me to hand the phone back to the representative so he could give him directions to his house.

Following their conversation, I was once again whisked away into a taxi. One could only hope the ride this time would be a little less nerve-racking. However, once again it would end up being wishful thinking on my part.

Upon entering the cab, I began to notice many of the similarities from my ride in Shanghai, including a lack of passenger seatbelts. There was a constant blaring of horns, driving at high rates of speed down the freeway while staggering lines, riding the shoulder, slamming the brakes. It seemed to be a normal occurrence no matter where I went in China.

As the driver entered a traffic circle, he wove in and out, honking his horn at vehicles collecting from every direction. No one seemed to have the right of way here, not even pedestrians or cyclists. To grasp and comprehend fully, the experience was a definite must.

Observing what I could as we flew past everything in sight, I watched as a pedestrian, who would normally have the right of way, tried to cross the street after the lights changed. Volumes of traffic continued to speed past, almost running the man over, yet he continued.

All of a sudden, a man riding a bike crossed in front of the taxi's path and three more lanes of fast-moving traffic, only to continue the wrong way through the center of two lanes of oncoming traffic. It was nothing short of insanity as the driver glanced back as if to say, "What's your problem?" after I made a sudden wincing noise from the back seat.

Suddenly entertained by the idea that stress can cause hair to fall out, a momentary epiphany led me to wonder if perhaps in situations such as these it may be more beneficial to pull it out myself and get it over with.

About twenty minutes into the ride, the cab driver was constantly on his cell phone. He appeared to be lost, although I knew the representative at the airport gave him directions. When he stopped the car in a moving lane, he turned, showing me his cell phone, and I could only assume his phone was dead or he was looking to me for directions.

Either way, it wasn't my problem. I had no idea where Hank lived, so I shrugged my shoulders, turning out the back window to see how long it would take before someone would accidentally pile-drive us from behind.

After fidgeting with the phone and banging it several times on the dash, it rang. He answered it, talked for a few seconds, then drove a few more blocks where Hank was waiting for us at the entrance of a securely guarded apartment complex.

Fully expecting to enter a small eight-by-ten flat, I was surprised to find Hank lived in a three-story condo apartment with four bedrooms and three western-style toilet facilities with quite a large living space.

Hank's bedroom was located on the third floor, and mine was on the second with a separate bathroom with tub and shower.

We sat talking until midnight, China time, becoming better acquainted. Suddenly realizing I had been up for almost thirty hours, I decided it was time to call it a day. For the next six months I'd settle into my new home, my new surroundings, teach English and learn more about this new, unfamiliar culture and perhaps be fortunate enough to make a few new friends along the way.

If you look, you will see,
But if you open your eyes
You will see much.

Chapter 2
Bonding with Culture Shock

The following morning, Hank and I were up early. Not a cooking fanatic, he decided on breakfast at McDonald's, perhaps to make me feel more at home. Although I wasn't a huge fan of the fast food chain at home, there was no doubt the Chinese version would be somewhat different. With no intention of offending his generosity or being rude, I accepted.

Hank took me on the scenic route around East Lake, two minutes away by taxi. Along one side of the lakefront are several entrances leading into Wuhan University, famous all over the world, encompassing three very large sections throughout the city.

In comparison, McDonald's was much more expensive than other local Chinese eating establishments. Hash browns and Egg McMuffins were similar to home. With the exception of the sauce, however, much to my surprise, it was quite tasty.

The school was within walking distance, so after breakfast we went to the school for a few hours to observe a few classes and become better acquainted with the teachers and staff.

Greg, a teacher from Canada who taught at another language school on the outskirts of the city, was filling in until my arrival.

Mac, who was Russian, spoke very good English and taught English at the school part time.

Class sizes were small, between ten to fifteen students ranging in age from four years to thirteen. Yet the ages didn't necessarily correspond with the level of a class. Regardless of whether a student was five, eight or ten years of age, they were placed into a matching level of ability. After sitting in on a couple of classes, the teaching techniques appeared to be very basic and pretty straightforward.

Legally, foreign teachers are limited to twenty teaching hours a week. A typical teaching week for me was to consist of two fifty minute evening classes four days a week, six classes on Saturdays and Sundays, with Mondays off. Being an early riser, this gave me plenty of time to explore, even catch up on some sleep. It was the perfect schedule.

Before leaving the school, Hank made arrangements with the bookkeeper to advance me 500 yuan for groceries. Lindsay, a university student who worked in the office part time, was given the task of taking me shopping.

On our way to the store, we stopped on the corner of a sidewalk were a gypsy woman was banging a tambourine while a small child about two years of age contorted her body, performing the most amazing display of maneuvers I had every seen.

Like many other spectators, I stood in awe, watching this tiny child twist her tiny body backward into a complete circle, resting her chin on a support between her feet.

Lindsay motioned me to continue, and as we walked, I turned back to catch another glimpse of this remarkable entertainment taking place on the corner.

Exploring the aisles of a Chinese grocery store was entertaining, to say the least. Lindsay spoke little English, so relating what I wanted was very difficult. While shopping, she ran into a friend who had recently returned from Australia and spoke English. Once she translated for me, Lindsay had a much better understanding of what I wanted.

Spicy, hot foods didn't agree with me, but because the Chinese diet was mainly hot and spicy, my choices were very limited and, for the most part, labels with pictures I could identify or compare with those at home seemed the best option I had.

We were to join Hank and the others from the school for dinner at a restaurant nearby, passing the child again on our way. We stopped briefly to watch as the child balanced her head and chin while holding her body in a perfect circle. She was so incredible that I asked Lindsay if I could take a picture. After a grimacing look, she bluntly replied, "No! You don't want to take a picture of this."

I dropped it, only to learn later that Lindsay had watched a special news program about panhandlers who exploit small children in this fashion. Children are taken at a very young age, preferably babies, to perform for money. In some instances the child's bones are broken, reshaped and most times re-broken and reshaped to heal in such a way they can perform extraordinary acts. Although very profitable for the panhandlers, it is pure torture to a child.

We continued walking. Two beautiful young women stood at the front entrance of a lavish Chinese restaurant greeting patrons dressed in traditional long elegant red satin dresses that caught my eye.

"Are we going in here?" I asked as we approached.

"Yes."

There we stood, blue jeans, sneakers and bags of groceries like bums on a Sunday stroll looking for handouts.

"Wow, this place is posh," I muttered.

"Posh?" she asked. "What is posh?"

"Never mind," I replied.

The interior was exquisite as we were escorted to the elevator, furnished with plush red cushioned carpeting, crystal chandeliers, and decorated entirely in lavish reds, golds and whites.

On the third floor we were led to a private room where Hank and the entire school staff were waiting. I was seated next to Hank at a large round glass table that could easily accommodate ten to twelve people. The table was covered with beautiful bright red and white linen topped with a giant swivel lazy Susan to accommodate numerous serving dishes.

Chopsticks and tiny fruit-size bowls were placed in front of us for our food. As the swivel turned, everyone would take food with the chopsticks.

Food was plentiful, and I made of point of at least trying most of it, including a very spicy dish Hank overlooked in telling me was spicy. In an instant I was red as a beet, downing water as I began gagging and choking.

Laughing with the others, Hank asked, "Why did you eat that? Don't eat any more of that."

"Nice time to tell me that now."

Under the misconception that actual Chinese food was similar to the Chinese food at home, it didn't take long to discover it wasn't even close. Many locals ate out regularly because it was just as cheap, if not cheaper. The old saying, "When in Rome…" became my steady diet.

The following day Hank departed for Taiwan to see his wife and three children for the next three weeks, and I would have the run of the house. He had made arrangements with Lindsay to move into the spare room while he was gone to keep me company, and because my Chinese was pathetic. Although not terribly keen on roommates, I chose to remain optimistic.

Lindsay wasn't a morning person, but I didn't mind, as I enjoyed going for early walks to observe, walk or just sit at the lake and write. My daily routine involved waking at six, and I was on the move by six-thirty.

East Lake, a five-minute walk away, was one of the biggest in China, and a great way to start the day. Everywhere I turned, something was going on with so much information to process that it became virtually impossible to comprehend.

The entire park ran along the river. Near the entrance was a large recreational section where several full-size pool tables sat covered up in the open.

It seemed to be a daily ritual for the elderly to pick a spot along the path, patting themselves about the arms and legs, perhaps to get the circulation moving.

Beyond the pool tables a small gathering of elderly people were gracefully engaging in a Tai Chi routine. A calm, relaxing sensation came over me as I observed many along the path partaking in some form of meditation.

Scattered randomly all about the park, students were reading aloud while walking, many standing, others squatting, while there were those who just sat in the grass under the shade of a tree.

Near the university, farther along the lake, was a dock displaying the most extraordinary-looking boats. Most appeared to be old-style fishing boats, one of which no amount of cord yanking would get it going, and several others needing the water bailed out with buckets.

At the large U-shaped dock, a couple dozen men sat with their twenty-foot adjustable fishing poles extending into the lake. The poles contained no reel, just a short piece of line with a wooden bobber that hung from the end of the pole that was emerged into the water. It was an amazing spectacle to witness, yet similar to fishing as a kid, using fishing line attached to a tree branch with just enough line dangling from a hook to submerge in the water.

As I walked along the streets, many older women carried heavy bamboo baskets on their heads, filled with an assortment of items. Others hauled square wicker baskets balanced on rope from a long flexible hollowed out bamboo shoot horizontally cut in half across both shoulders.

Street sweepers were constantly on the move, diligently sweeping with brooms made from nothing more than a bamboo shoot for a handle and branches of a tree. Most pull small wooden garbage carts three feet high with large wheels and long wooden handles. Others have a bike with a box rigged to the back.

Smaller than average-size dump trucks are parked in various locations of the city. Each street sweeper transports their full cart to a truck nearby, where it is then loaded on a lift at the back of the truck before being emptied.

Although I was fortunate enough to have a washer, on many sidewalks it seemed primitive as I watched mothers do laundry in a bucket by hand using a washboard and hand soap. Dryers were non-existent, even for me.

It wasn't unusual either to see an upperclass establishment mixed in with a society of lower class, particularly strange when you were not used to it. Many areas of the city were living in what I would term as severe poverty-stricken conditions. There were odors that would gag a maggot at ten feet away, everything blending as one, almost impossible to begin describing.

In some more high-class establishments, like the one I lived in, security guards protected the grounds. There were several I passed where guards stood at attention in full uniform, not moving, not even their eyes. I was convinced that one was checking me out as I walked by, though.

As I continued to walk, I couldn't help notice the extreme modes of bicycle transportation, ranging from almost ancient to brand new, including many pedal bikes. Yet others were quite unique with motors installed on the frame below the seat. There didn't seem to be any consistency, as police also rode motorcycles and wore helmets resembling those from the Hitler era.

Bicycles generally line the streets in scads. Usage seemed to range from hauling passengers; delivering mail and packages for China Post; lugging full tanks of propane balanced on either side of the back wheel; holding 4x8 sheets of plywood or plate glass windows rigged to a gadget on one side of the bike; toting recycled cardboard piled four feet high on the back; to cases of bananas stacked five high and two wide balanced on either side of the wheel.

After four days of free time following my arrival, I needed to get a good night's sleep. Perhaps jet lag had thrown my sleep patterns out of whack. The night of my arrival, I slept, but each night following brought false hope that my eyes would shut and I would wake well rested to the sun beaming through the window.

It was midnight on the night before I was to begin teaching, then one, two, four o'clock, and suddenly a thunderstorm burst out of the sky, somehow seeming much louder than I remembered, bringing hungry mosquitoes with it.

By ten that morning I was so tired from lack of sleep that I lay on the bed, hoping to get a couple hours of shuteye before going to the school. Lindsay left for the school, expecting me to show up around two. My eyes closed and then opened. One forty-five p.m.

"Oh, shit! This can't be happening. My first day on the job and I sleep in!" With no phone and no way to communicate, like a maniac I bolted to the shower, dressed and stuffed myself into a cab, showing the driver the school address Lindsay had written in my notebook. Sometimes something as simple as an address can turn into a dilemma, as the driver pointed to different sections of the page and began asking questions in Chinese.

All I could do was nod and hope he would take me to the right place. At two forty-five, the cab dropped me off in front of the building. There was a sigh of relief from Lindsay as she hugged me, as if to say, "Don't ever do that again. She had been waiting, worried that I had gotten lost with no means of communication. Two days later I was given my own cell phone with her number at the top of the list.

Classes didn't start until six-thirty p.m., but because it was new to me, I needed to familiarize myself with guidelines and also acquaint myself with the teacher guidebooks for seven different levels.

My first class was a level two, a step up from beginners, and went extremely well. Teaching was going to be a piece of cake, I thought. As I entered my next class, a level six, the children ranged in age from seven to eleven years, and it didn't take long to pinpoint the problem "children."

Bob and Pat and Billy seemed to be the worst, the instigators, and it was a toss up as to who was worse when it came to disrupting the class. Once Bob got on a roll, the attention span of the class went out the window.

Tony, Jack and Rosa were followers, running around the room kicking and tossing each other, screaming, turning the class into an instant shambles and one chaotic nightmare.

The class was out of control, and there was nothing I could do to stop it. Bob's face had a destructive evilness about it as he began throwing bottled water, paper, books and even the girls if they happened to get in his way.

If Bob wasn't spitting or adjusting the air conditioning, he was flicking the lights on and off, with the others imitating his every move. Once the class was wound up, he would return to his desk in the back corner, singing an entire rendition of "Edelweiss" beautifully, in English, before falling asleep in the fetal position and sucking his thumb.

Oh my God! I was not ready for this, I thought. I just wanted jump on the first plane out of town and get the hell out of there. Before throwing in the towel, I decided to step back from the situation, giving it some thought.

It was my first night as a new teacher, and perhaps it was their way of testing my limits. Maybe they were all tired and just having an exceptionally bad day. After all, the classes are late at night. I couldn't rule out the fact that they just didn't want to be there, and there was always a possibility they had ingested too much sugar.

Things were bound to go wrong at first, and it wasn't the first time I was thrown into something were I'd have to rely on my creative skills to bail me out. Perhaps I'd at least give it another chance before making any rash decisions. Sink or swim.

On our way home, Lindsay suggested renting a movie, partly because there were no English television stations, but mostly to lift my spirits and cheer me up.

As we walked, the same welders I had passed on the sidewalk early in the morning were still working diligently long after sunset. Everyone that passed by automatically covered their eyes or turned their heads to avoid having their eyes exposed to the bright rays emanating from the welding torch.

Most welders wore minimum protection while they built iron-barred window covers, not only to serve as security helping to eliminate break-ins, but also to serve as a closed-in balcony that owners could cover with plywood flooring later.

Running parallel, several steps down on the same street, was the DVD rental shop and poverty alley, a section of businesses and small shops serving as a dual-purpose residence in some cases. It resembled a Third World country all on its own. The smell was horrendous, not fit for humans let alone animals, but if you wanted a movie, this was the place to find it.

DVDs rented for one yuan, requiring only a deposit of ten yuan before being written in a logbook. There was no filling out of forms or leaving ID with personal history for the rental.

It was a five-minute walk from the DVD shop to Hank's. As we walked through the alley, families were cooking outside their shops in woks over a stove. Propane or four-inch high charcoal bricks were mostly used for heat to cook.

All along the alleys you could usually spot outside taps on the wall and a communal toilet facility that everyone shares. Many parents along the streets used a small round bucket, barely big enough for a baby to fit in, to bathe themselves and their children.

One evening Lindsay came flying down the stairs, yelling, "Sharon, there is no hot water!"

"Yeah, I know," I said, shrugging my shoulders. "I found out yesterday when I was taking a bath. I don't know what's wrong with it."

She gave me somewhat of a daft look, as if I should have known what the problem was. Hank, probably assuming I knew the water was heated with propane, neglected to mention it before heading out of town.

A reality was beginning to take hold. As North Americans, we assume and take things for granted, including having an abundance of hot water at our disposal at all times, and the option of eating and having access to food consistent with our normal diet, excluding hot spices. Within my first month of settling in, life was not as it seemed, and many things were becoming perfectly clear.

An open mind will lead one far,
Beyond shadows wonder who you are,
Once uncharted places all but seen,
From a distance or just in between.
Each dark crevasse now passed by,
To ponder how or question why,
We walk by day, but yet so blind,
To everything left far behind.
A wall will always have a door,
Leading somewhere never seen before,
You close your eyes, just take a look,
And imagine if you once had took,
A thought that crossed a second glance,
When fear then passed up every chance.
Yet not for those who choose to wait,
To catch a glimpse behind one's fate.

Chapter 3
Discovering Buddha

Before class one afternoon I had a couple hours to kill, so I decided to pick up a few things at the supermarket. My brief walk led me into a short alley, and each new experience began leading to new worlds of discovery. An opening into a large building full of live animals caught my attention. It was an indoor market and a slaughterhouse catering to some of the more elite restaurant establishments.

A young Asian couple sat directly inside the door next to a large sack jam-packed with hundreds of live frogs. The Asian male quickly pulled a frog from the sack, holding the legs and back portion of the frog down with one hand on the concrete floor while cutting off the head off with a semi-sharp knife in the other. Before being thrown into a bucket of water, the frog was skinned in one easy motion, as if wearing a wet suit jacket. The entire slice and dice procedure for each frog took less than twenty seconds.

After five minutes of viewing the bizarre ritual of frog mutilation, I decided to look around. On the floor surrounding my feet were several buckets containing live fish and several types of snakes, apparently a delicacy in China. Merchants seemed to have the infinite task of picking up fish that had bailed from buckets throughout the building.

As I wandered, slabs of meat hung from the ceiling from giant meat hooks, chicken feet and who knows what else were crammed in buckets, all for immediate sale. At the back, live pigeons, chickens, ducks and wild birds were caged, waiting their turn. Flies were hovering over the exposed meat. The smells inside were so overwhelming that I almost hurled, yet I was so intrigued I continued walking.

In the midst of it all, in a more secluded section of the building, was a small room. Groups of Chinese sat around tables, gambling their money away on a fascinating game that looked similar to dominos but is much more complicated.

Both Hank and Lindsay had told me they didn't care for the game because people, especially older and retired people, became addicted to it and ended up losing everything, even their lives.

Beyond the gambling frenzy were more cages of fowl, rabbits, even goats, awaiting their fate. They lined the wall, stacked two and three high. Finally, I'd had my fill of market culture and left.

There were hundreds of convenience stores and shops throughout the city to purchase grocery essentials, as well as numerous grocery stores and markets.

One of the larger shopping mall/grocery stores combined was several blocks from the school. Since my arrival, I still hadn't slept much and, according to Lindsay, this particular mall carried a large selection of herbs that would help, so Lindsay and I decided to check it out.

The store didn't carry the herb Lindsay was looking for, so she called her doctor friend Yean. As they spoke, she searched each bin looking for a specific flower, finally locating and scooping the brownish-orange stems of a lily flower.

The meat department was next on Lindsay's list. To say the Chinese don't throw anything out from an animal is an understatement. Behind a glass display case was every pig part imaginable. It took a few seconds to comprehend and identify the large leaf-shaped parts as pig's ears. Everything was displayed, including the feet, tail, intestines, tongue, parts of the head, nuts, and parts I didn't recognize and almost made me want to stop eating all together.

We had rented a movie on the way home, then settled in to watch it. Less than convinced a small bag of flower parts would do much of anything, I added plenty of the flower stems, brewed a strong cup of tea, and let it steep for a long time.

It was about a quarter through the movie when my eyes began getting heavy, and it was lights out for the rest of the night. Although I had been sleepless for so long, I wasn't convinced the tea had done anything, and the following night I brewed another strong cup. Twenty minutes later, I was out like a light again.

After a few good nights of sleep, I was refreshed and ready to go. Mondays off were suddenly turning into an outing of intrigue and excitement.

There were several tourist spots around the city, so Lindsay and I planned to catch a 608 bus to spend the day in Hanyang at Guiyuan Si Temple on Cuiwei Lu. Across the Chang Jiang River is an ancient Buddhist temple dating from the late Ming Dynasty.

The famous Yellow Crane Temple, near Hanyang, was on the way, perched big as life in the distance out the back window. Time would not permit us to see it on our return trip, so it would be an adventure to save for another day.

Getting to the temple required crossing the Wuhan Chang Jiang Bridge, one of two bridges over the Yangtze River. Hanyang and Wuchang are both linked by this 110m-long, 80m-high bridge. The 1957 completion of the bridge marked one of Communist China's first great engineering achievements.[1]

After getting off the bus, Lindsay realized fence barriers in the center of the road ran the entire length of the street as far as we could see, making it impossible to cross. Instead, she flagged down a taxi, and we arrived at the front entrance of the temple within ten minutes.

The Guiyuan Temple is Wuhan's most famous Buddhist temple, both in religion and architecture.[2] With the exception of television, it was my first time ever seeing a Buddhist temple up close, although it was an example of classic architecture commonly seen in southern China.

Upon entering the temple grounds, we were given three incense sticks. Beyond the entrance is a large open area displaying a rectangular-shaped iron pit filled with white sand on four steel legs.

In front of the pit, the incense sticks are lit, then clasped between your two hands until the flames burn out. The customary ritual includes bowing three times while praying and wishing good luck and happiness to all those around you before placing each stick of incense into the pit.

A huge Buddha statue seemed to occupy the center of each temple. Thick pillows are placed strategically for prayer directly inside the entrance doors, usually facing the main Buddha statue. Visitors kneel on the pillow and partake in a prayer ritual, bowing slowly three times.

Many Chinese, including Lindsay, believe very strongly in the Buddha religion, stopping to pray in each temple they enter. The first couple of temples I did as well; however, I was just as content to watch after that.

Lindsay's friend Yean joined us while we examined a tall freestanding iron structure comparable to a wishing well above ground. Lindsay and Yean tried to explain the finer points of Buddhism to me; however, their English wasn't fluent enough for them to explain or me to understand.

While inspecting the piece closer, a university student stood next to me, pressing a coin firmly against an outer section of the structure before letting it drop to the ground. As I watched him repeat the procedure, he began telling me the theory behind the coin and what he was doing.

It is believed that if you press a coin against the structure, let it go and it sticks, you will have good luck and good fortune, he told me, reaching into his pocket.

"Here, you try," he said, handing me a coin.

After several attempts, I had no luck getting the coin to stick, nor did the student. Instead of allowing me to return his coin, he asked me to throw it into the structure as a gesture of respect.

The original temple building took over six years to finish; consisting of a grand hall, guest hall, meditation hall, and abbot's room, and covered an area of 46,900 square meters. The main attraction is the statues of Buddha's disciples in an array of comical poses. It was an incredible place to see. Inside the temple is rare collection of sutra, a jade Buddha and five hundred gilded gold Buddha disciples encased in glass called Arhats, all of which survived the ravages of the cultural revolution.[3]

Each one was believed to have represented a pre-existing Buddha holding his own unique power; each had in different postures and highly individualized facial expressions illustrating a spectrum of human feelings.[4]

A fascinating and interesting theory accompanied the five hundred statues. After viewing the statues, you choose the one most appealing to you. Naturally, the one most appealing to me was a three-headed Buddha. My age being forty-four, the theory was to count forty-four statues, in order, to the appropriate statue in the series, which in my case represented the Buddhist of fortune and luck.

Once the number of the Buddha is established, a fortune card for that Buddha is obtained from a booth outside for a small fee, and for another small fee the card can be taken to a monk who can then properly translate it into your fortune. It turned out the Buddha I chose was of the highest standing of all the Buddhists encased in the temple.

It was difficult for Lindsay and Yean to understand the translation of the card, as the writings were of an ancient origin and more difficult to translate in English. Nonetheless, the gist of it was, the statue represented good luck and fortune for the remainder of the year. I would also be offered a once-in-a-lifetime opportunity by the end of the year that I was advised not to pass up. Essentially, by accepting the position, I would have much happiness, good fortune and wealth for the remainder of my life to pass on to my family. It seemed all very interesting; however, time would tell.

At the far end of the grounds, mounted on the side of one of the buildings, was a plaque with a small description about the goddess of mercy, dating back before Christ, whose birthday was the same day as mine, August fourth. How bizarre, I thought, as Lindsay pointed out a large stone statue of the goddess on display in an open area behind the temples.

After exhausting our tourist skills, we wandered through Hankou, a much cleaner and nicer area of Wuchang. Wuchang is a modern district with long, wide avenues lined with drab concrete blocks of flats, businesses and restaurants.

A large cluster of people began exiting a compound enclosed by a thick iron gate and a brick wall as we turned the corner. I asked Yean where all the people were coming from.

"A prison school," he replied.

"A prison school?" I questioned. "You have schools for prisoners?"

"No, um, how you call this?" Lindsay jumped in.

I pointed out the word "prison" in my Chinese/English dictionary, and we all broke into hysterical laughter.

"No, no, this word is not right," Yean said.

While walking, Yean suddenly exclaimed, "I know. It's a *criminal* school!"

"A criminal school?" I responded, flabbergasted.

After explaining that a prisoner school and a criminal school were the same, Yean asked for my dictionary, and it turned out a primary school was what they meant, and the joke carried on throughout the day.

In the center of Hankou is pedestrian street, a famous walking street separated by main streets accessible over an enormous spider-shaped overpass. The entire street was lined with many beautiful old buildings dating back to the early 1900s and the Second World War, with shops and places to eat. Throughout the city were some beautiful old government embassy buildings dating back to the early 1900s that left me awestruck.

Not far away from was a street designated entirely to cell phone companies and shops. If you needed to get a cell phone or a deal on one, this was the place to go. For most Chinese, to rent or own a cell phone is very expensive. Nonetheless, it appeared to be an obsession, as everyone had one and they were in constant use.

Nearby was another street designated specifically to art galleries and shops. Inside many shops, artists were busy working on a new painting, quite eager to sell something. Most paintings were canvas paintings, others enlarged photographs. Landscape scenery from all over China seemed to be the most common art, and are some of the most beautiful pieces of work I have ever seen. There were also many unique Chinese calligraphy pieces drawn with fine black ink on rice paper.

Yellow Mountain, or Huang Shan Mountain, is the name of a 72-peak mountain range in Anhui Province.[5] A picture depicting a single tree on top of a mountain caught my attention. The gallery owner explained the tree at the top of the famous mountain is the only one of its kind in China, and the configuration of the branches resembles a hand welcoming all who visit the mountain.

Many of the European-style buildings from the concession era have remained—particularly Russian buildings, along Yanjiang Dadao on the northwestern bank of the Chang Jiang or Yangzi River, with German, French and British structures on Zhongshan Dadao. Government offices now occupy what was once foreign banks, department stores and private residences.[6] At night, Hankou's main street, JanJiang Dadao, is stunning, resembling a mini-Las Vegas strip. A charming park separates the river from the main street. Each of the several entrances to the park had a series of steps, each displaying blue flashing lights. In the park itself were gardens, a sunken amphitheater and massive fish market running from the street to the beach at the edge of the Yangtze River.

To help reduce flooding, retaining walls ran along sections of the beach comprised of three tiers of concrete, two of which were steps. Lindsay and Yean explained the river rose each year, and during the month of August it reached maximum flood levels. Every year the government spends a great deal of money designing the park and planting replacement trees because floods destroy many.

The park was bustling with people walking. As we walked, I saw what looked like a bright flying saucer in the sky; however, upon closer inspection it turned out to be a high-tech model pirate ship kite with the most intricate of design and lights. Many families fly kites lit up like Christmas trees at night.

Further along, part way up the concrete steps on the second level of retaining wall, a dance instructor was performing an aerobic exercise routine with close to one hundred willing participants in attendance. Nearby, some older couples were participating in a dance session similar to jive, neither of which I would ever witness in public or outdoors at home.

With my day of adventure over, it was back to the grind. Things had been going well, but not extremely well. To use the Internet at the school became a continual stream of interruptions and, half the time, was a real chore.

The school was subjecting me to training videos, usually online from head office in Shanghai, and this day was no exception. I was required to watch a video with a guy demonstrating how to teach children aged four. He made it look pretty easy, dancing and prancing around the classroom; however, he may have been gay, and I couldn't see myself imitating his style, especially with the older children I had.

There is always something to be learned from anything you do in life, so I figured I'd experiment using a couple of games from the CD. I discovered right away there was a slight problem with this teaching theory. The children on the CD were extremely good children. Also, "Yummy, yummy, the caterpillar is still hungry, what can he eat?" just wouldn't cut it with students aged seven to twelve, especially the boys. The reality becomes a figment of the imagination for many English teachers.

The day continued to plummet as the two classes back to back would have only been somewhat tolerable with some form of mild tranquilizer. Instead, my entire mission became one of trying to dismantle an entire class of obnoxious little brats from running, flicking lights off and on, adjusting the temperature on the air conditioner, and throwing little girls around the room like rag dolls.

My second class turned out identical to the first with one exception: Spitter Bob, the little "Edelweiss" operatic singer. He was back with vengeance, his follower's right behind him, once again putting the entire class in an uproar in no time flat. He was hocking spit balls across the room in fine form and was particularly keen on aiming for the facial area. It didn't take long before a few of the boys he nailed began leaving for the toilet in groups to rid themselves of the spit balls Bob had just blessed them with. It became so bad a few of the staff members had to intervene, working out about as well as my attempt. Perhaps playing a game might help settle them down, I thought; however, they were so preoccupied and uninterested by that point that I couldn't get it going.

As I glanced around the class, Spitter Bob was sitting at a desk in the corner at the back of the room, sucking his thumb while taking a nap. I thought, whoopie-frickin'-do, this sucked! What the hell did I think I was doing trying to teach English to a bunch of whacked-out little Chinese children? They didn't have any intention of learning, and I was ready to throw in the towel, permanently.

On the way home I was very quiet, and my thought process was quickly going into overdrive. To make matters worse, my throat was becoming scratchy and sore. Lindsay knew I'd had a bad day, so she put her arm around me, reassuring me that these boys were bad for Jake and Mac, and not to worry, things would get better. But how was I going to teach to these kids when I couldn't even get their attention? I had to relax and focus. To relax and unwind, I would either go to East Lake for a walk or to write, or go to the Internet cafe to write. Because classes didn't finish until eight-thirty at night, East Lake was out of the question.

Due to the fact English television was non-existent, I became a frequent visitor of the Internet bar. At two yuan per hour during evening hours, it was well worth the money, and a great way to get rid of any pent-up frustrations, not to mention an hour or two of privacy I couldn't get at the school.

It was becoming apparent to me that my fast accumulating experiences to friends and family suddenly had potential. As well as being the perfect outlet, the makings of a great book was in sight, as well as being a realistic goal.

The possibility of catching the next flight out was still playing havoc, not to mention a game of ping-pong with my mind, but instead I opted for a good night's sleep, hoping the following day would be much better.

Chapter 4
Life is Like a...

In my opinion, the first month was an experimental period, not only to familiarize myself with children, but my continued existence. An English/Chinese dictionary and food translation books were on my person at all times, as pronouncing anything in Mandarin was very difficult. Trying to convince a local Chinese merchant you knew what you where doing was something of a chore. To prevent being ripped off was even more of a chore. If it seemed fair then I would make a purchase; however, dividing everything by six worked best.

Using mornings to explore was usually a good way to locate interesting places and food, sometimes helping to give me the boost I needed for afternoon classes.

Usually, I would frequent a local outdoor market for breakfast. One yuan bought four nice-size steamed vegetable dumplings. They were good enough to live on if I had to. During a small hike to the post office one day, I picked two up, not paying attention. One looks like another before biting into it. Inside, the center was dark brown and absolutely foul, identical to baby poop. To coin a phrase, "You can eat it, but it tastes like shit," immediately emerged.

The Chinese also have a mixture of instant porridge high on that same phrase list of offensive food groups. While it looked very appetizing on the box, like something you would make a point of jumping out of bed in the morning just to eat, it was to remain in the cupboard.

After leaving the post office, I continued on past a quaint little pond swimming with oversized goldfish and lily pads. Nearby, some university students played basketball on a huge court. Being somewhat directionally impaired, I continually checked my bearings, since getting lost could have proved fatal. Following the path led to a charming little rainforest park setting filled with trees ranging from palm trees to hardwood, softwood, ferns, you name it. In the center was an amazing open concrete gazebo completely intertwined with vines and plants throughout each opening.

Scattered about the park were small round concrete tables and chairs occupied by university students diligently studying.

All around were the echoes of foreign birds with the faint sound of a tiny creek running downhill on my right. The tranquility was incredible, and as I listened more closely the sound of a Chinese flute was playing a beautiful tune off in the distance.

The park ended at a road. Facing me was a very old building with a steep incline of at least a hundred steps to the top. I don't think so, I thought, continuing to walk. Curiosity and my nagging intuitive side was getting the better of me. With nothing visible to the eye to even intrigue one's curiosity, what could possibly be up there worth making me turn around? I had to go back and walk to the top.

At the bottom of the steps I paused. The bricks and structure of the building was very old. Several levels of hallways and classes, perhaps dorms, led to the top. "Ninety-eight, ninety-nine, one hundred," I counted the steps to the top. It was breathtaking. The steep climb was worth every effort, and my gut was right on the money.

I stood in awe momentarily, taking it all in. Although part of the Wuhan University, it was unlike any university setting I have ever seen or perhaps ever will see again. Ancient Chinese architectural structures were perched at the top edge. Each building was very extraordinary, some dating back hundreds of years. The outside walls revealed gargoyles and primitive-looking carvings and traditional old style Chinese green roofs.

Looking over the edge was the most amazing view and, surprisingly, a minimal haze for miles across a very large area of Wuhan. The haze that day wasn't particularly bad, so one could see for miles.

Directly behind and twenty or thirty feet below the structures existed two student living quarters revealing a very narrow courtyard. A row of dorm rooms no wider than eight feet apart ran along one side, with a solid brick wall along the other side of the courtyard.

Ropes were strung, extending from one unit to another, crammed with laundry. Dryers seemed to be nonexistent. Everyone's laundry was hung out to dry, including mine. Washers were a luxury for most in China, yet it is not uncommon to see many using a bar of soap, a bucket of water and a tiny washboard. Even though Hank's house came equipped with a washer, Lindsay still hand washed everything in a bucket.

Outside, at the far end of the series of buildings, a mature wooded forest sheltered a concrete terrace setting. Two groups of male students were scattered about the terrace practicing a Hong Chou Wu dance routine, a fascinating traditional Chinese dance with long red streamers and sticks.

After completing the practice session, the students joined into one group, performing the entire dance routine in rhythm to some traditional Chinese music playing on a tape in the background. It was a remarkable event to watch, although watching the performance in a traditional costume setting would have been incredible.

Wuhan University is one of the most famous universities in China, comprising a large portion of the city. Many Chinese and foreigners were drawn to and attend from all around the globe, including many from Russia, Africa and England.

Teaching weekends excluded any form of travel, but instead were chocked-full with six to seven classes each day. Before beginning my second weekend, I had developed a cough and my throat was becoming worse. Lindsay immediately called her doctor friend Yean, asking for advice. Within half an hour I was prescribed a bottle of herbal cough syrup. It was thick as molasses and tasted so good I could have had it daily as a meal supplement.

Three other types of pills were prescribed, including antibiotics and a bottle of licorice pills not bigger than a quarter of my baby fingernail in size to dissolve on my tongue. Not a pleasant medication by any stretch of the imagination.

After teaching the first couple of classes, my voice was fading in and out. Suddenly my voice took on an entirely new characteristic and disappeared completely, leaving my ad-libbing skills the only thing left to hold the attention of each class. Students snickered and laughed, viewing me as though I possessed two heads, and from my perspective I did.

I could only hope that my new teaching technique would work for the remainder of the day, but because my day started off on with a bang, I knew it wouldn't stay on the same continuum.

I would not be disappointed as I entered the second last class of the day, Spitter Bob's class. It just wasn't possible to go an entire weekend without having a class from hell. As usual, the instigators, Bob, Pat and Billy, were tearing up the class as Frank and Tony came charging out of their cages right behind them.

The power suddenly went out just long enough to present one of them the opportunity to pee on the floor. Christ, why this class? I thought. Once the power returned, a huge puddle filled the floor, and I resorted to bringing the staff in. It was a chaotic nightmare as two staff members entered the class screaming, mostly at Bob, who turned out to be the puddle maker.

Shortly after the staff left, everyone let loose again. Another Chinese teacher came to my rescue when I began to blow a gasket on them. She whacked Bob on the head, grabbing him by the arm and then yanked him out of room for the remainder of class.

By the end of last class, Bob's mother had arrived, talking with someone, perhaps her husband, on her cell phone. Bob was like night and day, portraying the perfect good little boy image, saying nothing. If Bob was indeed gone for good, there was a chance that the class may settle down. Still, Pat and Billy were left to contend with. Bob wasn't entirely to blame for episodes of spitting, however, and seemed to have come by it honestly. It's a part of everyday life in China and absolutely disgusting. Chinese men, women and children alike spit no matter where they were, hocking it right up from their toes before letting it fly.

As another week ended, I put Bob, Billy and Pat out of my mind, keyed up for another day of adventure. On Snake Hill, the 413 bus dropped me off near the front entrance of the tower.

The Yellow Crane Tower, first built in 223 AD, dominates much of Wuchang, the riverside and Wulu Lu. This modern Qing-style reproduction of a temple was originally situated about 1 kilometer away, but was destroyed by fire in 1884. Despite the fact that it is not an important historical relic, it served as an inspirational place for poets and artists over the years.[7] Being a poet myself, I would have great difficulty finding inspiration, as the water is now very dirty.

Chinese tourists hovered around the entrance in droves, lining up for photos in every available space, as I stood at the entrance staring in awe. The tower itself is 50 meters high and covered with tiny tiles glazed in gold. Frescos decorate the walls, and the entire construction is hung together with red auspicious columns.[8]

Observing the view of the city from the perimeter, a young Asian man who I will refer to as Jason, approached me and asked if I spoke English. When I told him I did, he began to strike up a conversation, asking me questions, including where I was from. When I told him from Canada, he asked if he could tag along and translate what he could for a while to practice his English. I didn't mind and was glad to have the company.

Jason's English was poor, but he spoke well enough for me to fill in most of the gaps. He worked for an air-conditioning company, but was on a business trip and was passing through on his way home to his six-month pregnant wife in Guangzhou. He had a twelve-hour layover, so decided to do some sightseeing.

We wandered away from the tourists that seemed to all conjugate in and around the tower and the entrance. We ventured beyond and into two smaller towers behind the Yellow Crane Tower to have a look. Displayed on one floor were replicas of the most unbelievable ancient ships dating back to the Han and Ming dynasty. One looked like a floating Chinese temple, so I asked Jason if that particular ship existed and if it was real. He confirmed it had many years ago. Wow, I thought, if they had cruise ships around like those now a day, they'd make a fortune. Wealthy people especially would pay plenty to ride on something that unique.

The grounds were absolutely beautiful. At the far end of the grounds was a huge statue of a famous general from the Song dynasty that I wasn't really familiar with. Jason explained he was a general, a hero who was murdered because some of the people didn't like what he stood for. As I listened, the story was similar to Robin Hood, and Jason laughed when I compared it as such.

Jason was convinced that hanging out with me was helping his English. He was impressed that I listened so well and could understand much of what he meant. I told him that sometimes I could understand much of what he was trying to say and with a little patience could figure it out. In return for my kindness and the pleasure of my company and help with his English for the entire day, he wouldn't allow me to pay for anything.

Near the general's statue was a concession stand of ancient Chinese costumes, and Jason was adamant about renting me a queen's attire to wear so he could take my photo. I went along with it and ended up having a blast.

As the photo session began, some Asian men were dressing in king's apparel. Jason overheard one group say they should have their photo taken with me. One woman began yelling at her husband, and sometimes it is difficult to tell if the Chinese are having a discussion or yelling at each other. Nonetheless, after everyone was dressed up, the fun and the photo session took place.

We made our way back toward the entrance, taking a different footpath. Many trees were transplanted, wrapped with rope around the base partially enclosed in some sort of a tent-like mesh. When I asked Jason what the rope and mesh were for, he told me it was to prevent them from dying from the extreme heat. Unfortunately, some had died and looked much like dead stumps that had never survived the transplant.

As we walked we encountered more beautiful ancient-looking buildings. In the center there was a huge pond with black swans and ducks swimming around, and birds were carved into one section of a long stone wall. It was breathtaking, like heaven, or at least how I might imagine it, and then some.

Buildings surrounded the pond, and overhead and all around the pond hung big red Chinese balls. It was like being on the set of a movie. At that point there wasn't much more to see, so after spending three hours exploring, Jason offered to buy me lunch and we left.

While making our way through narrow alleys, we passed a shop where a merchant began rubbing the handles of a brass pot perched on a small wooden stand. In the bottom of the pot were little gold beads. As the merchant rubbed her hands back and forth vigorously on the handles, the water began dancing, almost jumping out of the pot.

Jason spoke to the shop merchant momentarily, then handed her some money so I could to try. After wetting my hands in the water, I began doing what she did and nothing happened at first. A few seconds later, the water was dancing and jumping around like fireflies, and it was the coolest thing I'd ever seen.

Away from all the hustle and bustle of tourists, we found a wonderful restaurant that served Chinese and American-style food. Because the establishment was somewhat elegant, I decided to try the specialty of the day, frog. Before our meal arrived the waitress brought each of us a glass of water. Expecting the water to be at room temperature or ice cold, I almost spewed it across the floor upon gulping a mouthful of hot water.

A small dish of frog stew arrived, served with rice, vegetable greens similar to spinach, some kind of watery egg custard dish, watermelon, and some sort of bean dish. After witnessing the skinning preparation process of a frog I had been adamant about never eating frog; however,

I had a slight change of heart. After spending more time trying to get the meat off the tiny little bones, I discovered a frog has very little meat. The meal was delicious and after lunch, Jason asked if I liked duck neck.

"Duck neck?" I asked.

"Yes, it is famous all over China."

He took us by taxi across the bridge so he could purchase some. According to Jason, Wuhan was the only place the Chinese could get it. His workers loved it, and to show his appreciation he wanted to buy some to take home to them. I couldn't believe people traveled across China just for duck neck.

Jason had the vendor slice a small piece off for me to taste, and there was not a chance in hell I would ever travel that distance to purchase even one piece. The spices alone would curl even the straightest hair.

The taxi cost him twenty-one yuan one-way to go to a remote area of Hankou, and another thirty-six yuan back over the bridge to Changchun Taoist temple. It hardly seems worth the money to travel that distance for duck necks, but he made it worth his while. The taxi dropped us off at the entrance to the temple. Just inside the entrance gates were two beautiful smaller temples separated by a walkway, very rich with blue, gold and yellow colors.

The largest, best-preserved Taoist temple in Wuhan, it consists of numerous corridors and stone staircases, all of brick and wood, with grand eaves and arches suspended from the ceiling.[9] It was quite different from the previous one I'd visited. We observed as two girls did an exquisite job of recapturing some of its grandeur on an oil canvas. Inside the temple were 10,000 identical miniature gold Buddhas about a foot high. Jason explained the focal Buddha sat upon layers and layers of gold lotus flowers—meaning good luck, with tiny Buddhas poking out from between each leaf.

In the larger temple we had the opportunity to observe an unusual Buddhist ceremony. A dozen or so monks, some dressed in yellow robes, some in black and the rest in orange robes, sat around an oblong table. The monks dressed in black looked to be beginners, and the orange were superior. One was tapping on something using a small stick, maintaining a rhythm while the others read from books from back to front.

To the back of the grounds, high on a hill in amongst the trees, was Mt. Hong Shan pagoda, displaying superb granite gargoyles supporting each of the ten levels to the top, which dated back to approximately 1700 or 1800 AD.

As we climbed the steps to the top, I was amazed with the structure's small dimensions from that time era as we squeezed through a tiny, steep, but very narrow little stairway. I had to duck to avoid hitting my head against the ceiling after watching Jason smash his head twice.

Climbing the steps reminded me of the leaning Tower of Pisa in Italy, only more difficult. The height of the steps at each level was not consistent, some being a foot high. At the top were four different views over the city, and definitely worth the climb. However, the journey down proved to be a little more difficult.

Our adventure was fast drawing to a close, ending in a quaint little out-of-the-way cafe, drinking coffee for two hours, talking about anything and everything. Within eight hours Jason's English had improved immensely, and before leaving for his train he thanked me for allowing him to hang out with me, then I returned the gesture.

He made my day, and as he turned and walked away, I was suddenly reminded of the movie *Forrest Gump*, staring Tom Hanks. Sometimes life was like a box of chocolates. You never knew what you were going get.

Early, long before the crack of dawn,
A sudden bolt of lightning strikes,
Filling every crevasse of my room,
Waking me from the dead of sleep.
Mistaken for the repetitious sound of
French-fries being placed into a deep
Fryer of hot grease was the continuous
Pelting of the rain off the roof outside,
Pounding the concrete pavement below.
A crack of thunder immediately follows,
Temporarily resembling a train running
Tracks overhead, spitefully vibrating the
Plate glass window throughout the house,
Close to the point of shattering them.
Wide awake, forced to listen attentively,
Until torrential downpours eventually move on
Once again, leaving only the pitter-patter
Of lingering rain, harmonious with the songs
Of each bird now rejoicing in its passing.

Chapter 5
Do I Stay or Do I Go?

Almost the end of April, Hank finally arrived home from Taiwan, and within ten minutes of seeing him he was gone again. Being away three weeks, I naturally assumed he had much to catch up on. Besides, it wasn't as though he had to hold my hand or anything. I was rarely ever home either.

An intensive thunderstorm filled the night, increasing the already flourishing mosquito population. By seven a.m. it was still raining, and a little chilly, so I took along a light jacket, but within an hour was peeling it off. To avoid the crowded, noisy, smoke-filled Internet bar, I would arrive before seven a.m. to catch a couple hours of peace and quiet at a reduced price. It is mandatory for students to leave at seven a.m. and all computer terminals shut down. Each day hundreds congregate for hours on end, watching movies, chatting on line, but mostly to play war games while screaming at the monitor for hours on end. One particular morning I hadn't realized it was only six a.m. There was a mob of young people, some with their eyes either pasted to the screens or sound asleep at the terminal. I glanced at the clock suddenly realizing the time, knowing I had an hour to kill before one would be available.

It was a nice day for a morning stroll. Directly across from the apartment complex was a very long, narrow alley with other narrow alleys leading off it. Lined with markets, merchants of all types and small eateries along this alley, and it was barely wide enough for a vehicle, making things interesting when two vehicles tried to pass going in opposite directions.

Walking the alley took about ten minutes. It felt as though I was out of my element in some Godforsaken hole in the middle of nowhere, and the Asian good guys would soon come and duke it out with the Asian bad guys.

Along the alley, anything and everything was available, ranging from food to bedding, household wares and knickknacks, and anyone looking would probably find it. Beyond the alley was a huge iron gate leading to a road and reality, or perhaps something close.

Sheltered by mature trees and bush, I began the journey up a winding concrete mountain road, having no idea where it led. Many others, older people in particular, were making the same journey, yet I wasn't complaining.

Along the way were some trenches dug for laying pipe, so I had a closer look. At least six feet deep and four feet wide, I could tell by the mounds of dirt piled alongside that the trenches had been dug with shovels. One main trench ran diagonally along the walking path, while the other extended down the mountain as far as the eye could see.

A few days after my arrival, I recalled seeing a trench being dug along the main street. Several workers were slugging their guts out, shoveling dirt by hand with shovels from a trench. Being in construction for five years, it was difficult for me to imagine.

About halfway along the path, I stumbled onto a small group of ten or so women who were practicing Yao Gu, a form of Chinese dance in the middle of the path. All the women had a small bongo drum attached to a thin strap around one side of their neck, with the drum dangling under their one arm about waist level. Each woman held a small round stick ten inches long by one inch in diameter in each hand, and had a thin red streamer around each wrist. While banging the drums with sticks, their rhythm and movements were slow and very graceful, comparable to tai chi.

It was somewhat less aggressive than the Hong Cou Wu dance routine I watched the boys partake in at the university. It was unclear why they chose the middle of the path to gather, although for a calming setting and surroundings with lots of tranquility, it was a perfect place.

After observing for several moments, I continued. The path ended at a road, so I followed it for a short distance to an area overlooking a forest below and beyond the road. From behind I heard a man's voice say, "Hello." A Canadian teacher from St. Catherine's, Ontario, not far from my hometown, was attending the University of Wuhan to teach for one week before returning home. After we spoke briefly we parted ways, and I made my way back down the mountain.

After a day off and almost another entire day of leisure, it was back to the business of teaching to establish a new teaching strategy. My first class of six students were older and very bright; in fact, it was a class I actually enjoyed teaching.

After a trial run preparing an assignment that went extremely well, I tried my hand at acting out and drawing my rendition of a word. Although rather pathetic, it was quit amusing, not to mention entertaining, securing a few laughs in my favor.

My second class, a level three, consisted of about sixteen students. To me it seemed boring for each student to read sentences from the book, so I divided the class into three groups and had each group rap each sentence in order, in rhythm. At first, their puzzled expressions said it all, but they found it quite amusing.

One of the Chinese teachers had taught the children a Christmas song from a previous lesson. Part of my lesson plan included a Christmas song that I had never heard off. As I prepared to start, the class took over and began singing. It was the most amazing sound I have ever heard as this large group of little children sang the entire song in unison beautifully. At the end, I applauded, praising them. What a treat to teach!

My evening was complete after a Chinese student teacher had observed my class etiquette. She told me I had more energy than a person of twenty years of age, pointing out my teaching techniques were very unique, and she liked the way I presented myself.

That night there was another thunderstorm, and with temperatures beginning to soar into the mid-thirties Celsius with the arrival of summer, they had become a frequent nightly occurrence, making sleeping almost impossible.

As I left for work the following morning, the rain was still pelting down. I had neglected to buy an umbrella, and the puddles were well over the soles of my sneakers, so I was drenched within twenty seconds of leaving the house. Taxis were scarce and very difficult to flag down with any sign of rain, but within moments, soaked to the bone, I was on my way to work, hoping it wasn't the onset of how my day was going to unfold.

Like every other Sunday, I had an exclusive class, a special class more advanced in English than all the others. They were gearing up to take an exam for acceptance into a middle school. Yeah right, that was debatable! The students were to listen to life-related situations on a cassette, such as going shopping, riding a bus, getting directions, etc., all in English. After listening, they were to then give me the answers to the questions in the book about the cassette. With the exception of one student, no one would answer, or speak at all, for that matter. They had no interest whatsoever in learning. I had students in levels four and five that could comprehend more than this class could. Play the tape, stop the tape, over and over, waiting for them to listen before I finally stopped teaching and stopped talking. To cover the required material each week took longer and longer as I played catch-up each week.

After several classes, I was noticeably frustrated. It was evident the class was clueless. I finally stood up one day, my arms crossed, saying nothing to see if they would notice, yet it had no affect. A few minutes passed before they finally noticed, and I lost it.

"Why are you here?" I bellowed. "Do you want to learn English?"

They just sat looking at me, then the bell rang and class was over. Where the students only there because their parents wanted them there?

After lunch, I had the Spitter Bob's class from hell again, and surprisingly, Bob was still in attendance, not to mention his sidekicks Pat, Billy and the boys. There seemed to be a noticeable difference between Bob and Pat, however. Bob still couldn't resist getting caught up in the moment with the others, yet he was somewhat tolerable. Although Bob was a little shit disturber, never paid attention and thrived on disrupting the class, it was evident from day one he was the smartest in the class. I could fire anything at him at any time and without hesitation he always had the right answer.

Pat and Billy, on the other hand, were another story. They would never answer one question, nor would they speak in English. If they weren't screaming or chasing each other around the room, it was a constant race back and forth to adjust the temperature settings on the air conditioner up and down. They didn't seem to care, and both spent much of the class alternating turns to the corner, directly behind the classroom door. After sending Billy to the corner during one class, I turned to do something on the board. Jack and Tony had a perfect opportunity to race for the door, opened it and use all their body weight to sandwich Billy, crushing him between the door and the wall. When I sent Billy back to his seat, Pat ran to the front of the class, turning the lights off and on while the others ran in and out to the bathroom. Billy took the lids off my markers, then pulled everything out of my goody bucket.

Once again they were out of control, and nothing was going to hold the class together. I came unglued. It was as if they saw horns sprouting from my head and flames shooting from my nostrils, and for a brief instant I saw fear in Billy's eyes. I finally had their attention, and then class was over.

Every Sunday the school offered English Corner, a free one-hour class for students who wanted to practice and learn more English and talk about anything they knew. The problem was many of the children would spend much of the session speaking Chinese.

Mac had been doing it for some time. Jake refused to do the class, and I had no interest. Although learning foreign English teachers were obligated and expected to give up their free lunch time, I still declined.

Before the session, three of the girls came looking for me in my office.

"Aren't you coming in to talk to us today?" they asked. "Do you have more pictures? We want to find out more about Canada and your daughter. Can you come when you're finished?"

How could anyone say no to that? They were the sweetest little girls, and they wanted to learn, so I finished what I was doing then joined them.

As I was leaving the class, the two girls told me they thought I was a good teacher and must also be a good mother too. They blew me away, and it was perhaps just the boost I needed in that moment.

In my quest for change, adventure, challenge, knowledge and perhaps even wisdom, things present themselves from the most unparalleled angles and do so when you're not really looking. Like everyone in North America and our Western society, we can only assume that every living being on this planet has hopes dreams, goals and aspirations in their life. We seem to falter, however, on this preconceived notion that every other society or culture on earth should also view life the same way we do. Yet they don't, and sometimes we can't seem to understand why.

From my perspective, many Chinese have the same dreams and aspirations in life that we do, but seemed a more regimental society with goals focusing more on survival. Chinese parents didn't seem to share the same, "I can't afford it right now, maybe next month, year…" views that Western civilization does. Life there is all about education, honoring your parents and succeeding, even superseding in life. For children to have extra schooling here is a luxury and very expensive. Parents offer their children the opportunity for a better life and the chance at a better future, and if that means using up the last bit of funds in the cookie jar to do it, then so be it.

Throughout China, there are over a billion people with over several million people populating each city. In Wuhan alone there were over nine million people, meaning the competition for jobs was extremely high. It also stands to reason that any high-paying jobs would be very scarce. It is something very difficult to imagine or even comprehend unless it is staring you right in the face. For the most part, North

Americans have many options, opportunities, and the big one: choices. Yet sometimes we can't comprehend what's right in front of us. We can get where we want, any time we want. We mull it over in our heads so long we ending up building barriers and end up with more excuses for why we can't instead of how we can. For the average Asian to reach or accomplish goals equaling the same standard of living we take for granted would require at least four to five times the effort, unless they were lucky enough to be born into money.

In one of my older classes, I asked, "What do you do when you play after school?" Of course, none of them had a clue what that was. They looked at me with the most peculiar expressions, as if I just flew in from Venus or perhaps it was part of the lesson they weren't getting, a new concept in their book they needed to learn. There is no playtime. With the exception of television, computers and perhaps the occasional Game Boy, playtime was not a option for many Chinese children. Although nothing was mentioned in the teacher's handbook about this, those like Bob, Pat and even Billy had their own definition of playtime, choosing to save it all up just for my classes.

Life in China seemed very structured, to the point that every waking minute of the day is taken up with something necessary for them to succeed in life, and it begins at a very young age. It was difficult to understand how children attend a regular school during the day, then sit through evening and weekend classes. The school I taught at had a purpose, to do what they needed to learn the basics and to better prepare children for a good middle school.

During school hours, I watched as staff members ran around like chickens with their heads cut off. It was as though they would be dismissed at the first sign of a mistake. There were many occasions when they weren't so busy and took any chance available to talk with me, especially Lindsay. It gave her and them a chance to practice their English, but also gave me a chance to get to know and understand them better.

After sharing my life's adventures with them, it was difficult for them to comprehend or even imagine being able to do what I had done in my life, traveling to so many other countries. For them, packing up everything to move to China just to teach English for six months was a dream they couldn't even fathom. It is beyond the normal and logical thought process to them. They have all told me they have dreams of traveling to America, and all have the same answer. It would not be or is not possible. Thinking I could play some small part in their life to make it a little better, even if just to make it a little more interesting, I got satisfaction watching them take a chance or do something they otherwise would not normally do in their normal everyday existence.

Sometimes our perspective of things can catch us off-guard, even as I observed my new friend Lindsay. At twenty-two years of age, she still lived with her parents. Yet, like many, she was very structured, family and school oriented, reaching for goals and dreams that seemed so unreachable. Hanging out with me was no doubt creating some serious disruption to her normal routine way of life. It was clear to me she wanted more from life, but I wasn't sure if she even realized it. There was another side of her beginning to shine through, intrigue, curiosity, a thirst for adventure, only she was right in my face now just waiting to get a piece of the action. I didn't mind, as I was a curious as she was.

Chapter 6
What's on the Menu?

Shortly after arriving home from school, Hank called, wanting me to meet him, Lindsay and the accountant for dinner at the Fengyi Hotel in the Elation Western restaurant. It was a ten-minute walk from Hank's. The hotel and restaurant were quite new and quite upperclass. Lindsay and I stopped in to have a look on our way home from the bus stop one day, only to conclude it was much too expensive for our taste.

Every table was lined with red and white linen with a small cooking pot at each place setting, similar to a fondue pot. Each pot was filled with water continually boiling to cook the food. The food was set in a buffet fashion, ranging from cold cuts and various other types of meat to salads fish and seafood dishes, much of which I wouldn't eat. There were soups, every kind of mushroom you could imagine, desserts, and items I had not a clue as to what they even were.

I wasn't entirely sure which items on the buffet tables were spicy and which ones were not. While I gathered enough food to fill two bread plates, Lindsay took care of preparing a small bowl with several items mixed together to make a sauce for dipping my food. After returning to the table, Hank cracked an egg open, separated the yolk and the white, then dropped the yolk into the sauce for me to mix.

"It's very delicious," he said.

"Uhu," I replied, quite familiar with the expression.

The style of eating this type of dinner was a little different than I had experienced previously, so I was unfamiliar to the procedures using the pots and had to ask which items went into the pot. After everything except the desserts were thrown in, the lid goes on and everyone waits until the water boils.

During the main course, the waiter arrived and set a small plate at each place setting containing a baby turtle. Staring at it momentarily, I thought, No way! Saying nothing, hoping no one would notice if I didn't dig in, didn't work. My expression must have said it all. Hank confirmed it was a turtle on my plate, adding that it was very delicious. He continued, informing me Wuhan was one of very few areas in China where turtle was available or could actually be ordered from the menu. Lucky for me I had lucked out, picking the only place in China to purchase either a delicious duck neck or baby turtle delicacy!

Watching Hank and Lindsay devour their turtle was a painful experience. I almost lost any appetite I had left. Everything, including the head, feet, shell and guts, were still intact. Next to my turtle was a plate with a variety of different desserts, chocolate cake, cheesecake and chocolate balls. With the two plates side by side, I was almost tempted to quickly fill up on cake just to ensure I had no more room left for turtle. I thought it impolite to not at least try such a scrumptious-looking delicacy. Yum-yum. I began to separate the shell from the turtle's body, eating the section attaching the shell to the body, the entire rubbery edible portion, sucking the remnants from the shell. It was so gross, and I wasn't sure how much more I could endure before spewing it all over the table. Maybe I could grab a piece of dessert, using it as a turtle chaser, and wolf it down if only to add flavor. With everyone so engrossed in enjoying turtle, I didn't think anyone would even notice.

In the end, I had earned the right to a piece of chocolate cake; hell, why stop at one? It takes at least two or three pieces to neutralize the taste of a turtle. Although I did eat it, it was definitely not something I would ever order again, and before leaving I politely informed Hank I never wanted him to order it again.

The end of May and another Monday had arrived. I was to meet up with Lindsay in Hankou for the day and have lunch. With a few hours to kill, I headed to the lake. Some kayak's kept the momentum as they paddled by, right on schedule. Stopping to observe before continuing, the land across East Lake was actually visible, and the haze across the lake wasn't quite as bad as usual.

Passing a small gas station, like many other mornings, I noticed that running along the end of it was an open iron gate into some sort of complex. A sign at the entrance read "Feng Huang Cun," Cun meaning village. At first glance it appeared to be a small cul-de-sac, ending down a short road revealing a gorgeous flower garden arrangement at the end of it, so I had the urge to take a look.

As I approached the garden, it was nothing special, but as I got closer, there was the most amazing Chinese garden pond at the edge of a large courtyard, just off to the right of the garden that couldn't be seen from the road. In the center of the courtyard was a large structure where some individuals were fishing with extended twenty-foot fishing poles. A few feet from the garden was a tiny bridge crossing a narrow section of the pond into the most incredible Chinese gazebo set on a small raised island of grass at the edge of the pond fed by the lake.

Stretching north and south across and a few inches above the pond was the most incredible floating bridge walkway in the shape of a maze with a tiny railing, zigzagging across the water. Emerging from the water through two sections in the center of the maze were two very unique petrified tree stumps. Extending east to west from the center of the bridge was a tiny concrete raised walkway to another incredible Chinese gazebo.

On the east side of the maze bridge, a row of several staggered tree stump stepping stones jetting out slightly above the water linked the bridge to the courtyard. On the west side, tiny round concrete stepping stones a couple of inches above the water linked the bridge to small landmass where the gazebo was perched. This tranquil setting wasn't part of any tourist itinerary, but perhaps should have been, as sometimes the little things have the ability to capture more of our imagination, maybe even give a new sense of perspective to something we may or may not have been anticipating.

About eleven I made the hour-long bus ride to the heart of Hankou to meet Lindsay for lunch. Because Lindsay had been sleeping when I called, it was going to be at least a hour before we'd meet up, so I thought I'd wander around Pedestrian Street a block away. Although not impossible, getting lost on one long street would be somewhat difficult.

After meeting up with Lindsay in front of a McDonald's near the bus stop, I showed her one of the postcards I had bought, revealing an incredible scene at the top of a mountain in Wadang Shan. Some of the scenic landscapes on the postcards existed somewhere nearby Wuhan, and I began to get antsy, needing a change, something out of the city.

"Lindsay, how far away is this place?" I asked.

"I think maybe two hours by bus. Why, you want to go there?" she asked.

"Sure, two hours by bus isn't far."

"OK," she said. "I think maybe next Sunday. I will ask my friend."

Lindsay had never seen much outside of Hankou, or Wuhan for that matter, and began getting excited at the prospect of going. As the day went on, her excitement and perhaps even her curiosity began to grow. She had the initiative and drive, and I was the perfect candidate to give her what little push she needed to help her venture out, taking each baby step a little further each time.

Booking a tour, jumping on a bus with a group of tourists, following that group, not having to worry about arranging anything would be easy, but depending on the tour group, could end up more or less expensive, depending. For the moment, Lindsay was convinced that was the way to go. However, from an adventurous standpoint, what fun would there be in that?

Each week, bit by bit, Lindsay was edging out of her shell, continually getting in my face to get in on the events of my next day off. There I was, the tourist wanting to explore every facet of the world with every option and opportunity to do so on a whim. There was Lindsay, so eager to relay everything she knew, whatever tidbit she could offer. With each venture we entered into she tried everything in her power to make sure I understood, yet became frustrated when she couldn't make things clear for me. I found it the most intriguing characteristic about her, forcing me to view everything from an entirely different point of view. She acted so grown up, then I came along, the adult, unintentionally imposing childlike tendencies upon her. Quite an oxymoron, I'd say, but by the end of the day I had convinced her to go the following Monday without a tour.

After spending part of the afternoon wandering through a huge six-story shopping center and various other streets throughout Hankou, we decided to catch a bus across town to Jiefang Gongyuan Park, across the street where Lindsay attended university. Lindsay had never been to the park because none of her friends ever wanted to go. In fact, I was convinced that since my arrival she had seen more of Wuhan hanging out with me than she had during her twenty-two years living there. From the road it resembled any other park, but this park was just a bit different upon entering the grounds. It was becoming obvious that unless one makes a conscious effort to find what's behind door number one, so to speak, some smaller areas of the city were not listed as points of interest in the tour book.

A very short walk led us to the BuYue Tower beyond a fenced-in area of the park. Getting to it required a short walk over a cute little stone bridge that crossed a small river. From the bridge, the tall, striking pagoda suddenly appeared. To enter the grounds, it was necessary to pay another small fee of three yuan. Our curiosity got the better of us, so we paid to have a look around. Inside the gates, towering over our head, were hundreds of mini concrete pagodas, replicas of every existing pagoda from all over China. They were so amazing, yet there was no doubt the genuine pagodas were much more authentic and spectacular to see. Each one contained a plaque with information regarding the pagoda and its replicated origin in China. Passing one odd structure bearing a resemblance to a seven-foot tree mixed in amongst the others, I stopped to stare. Lindsay joined me, and I had to ask, "Is that a tree?" After examining it briefly, she didn't know either. Eventually, around the opposite side of the huge mound of dirt we discovered a plaque and the mini pagoda perched on top behind the trees. Although we had a limited amount of time to cover the entire park grounds, we did have the most amazing view of the entire park from the top of the BuYue Tower.

As we made our way out of the park, through an amusement park sheltered by evergreen trees, we stumbled upon a beautiful quaint little pond blanketed in water lilies three to four times the size I had ever seen. In July and August they come out in bloom, filling the entire pond with color. Near the exit of the park, located next to an old rundown building that looked like an abandoned amusement park, a court was packed with boys busy playing basketball. Running parallel to the court stood an astonishing spectacle. Intact and in mint condition was a complete team of white stone horses.

It was getting late when we left the park. Lindsay called her parents, and we caught a bus to meet them for dinner at a restaurant somewhere in Hankou. Lindsay was getting familiar with the kind of food I could eat, and began searching through my food translation book, helping me choose what I could or couldn't eat, and it appeared there was quite a lot. However, all was not as it seemed. As the last of our food arrived to the table, so then did a platter of food accompanied by one plastic glove for each of us. The contents of the platter looked an awful lot like—Holy pig's feet, Batman! You've got to be kidding me! No way! What had I gotten myself into now? I thought. Better yet, how do I get myself out of it? There was no way devouring pig feet was going to take place. However, before I ate anything, it was routine to observe everyone else.

First, everyone put a glove on the hand they would be using to pick up the pig's foot, before grabbing it to chow down. It wouldn't take a less intelligent individual long to notice the toes and thick outer layer of skin still attached. As I sat watching Lindsay and her parents devour this delicacy, I wanted to hurl. The sheer thought of sinking my teeth below the skin was less then appealing, not to mention unappetizing. It wasn't long before Lindsay and her mother motioned me to follow their lead. Crap! The whole turtle episode was one thing, yet after analyzing the entire situation, I concluded it was probably rude not to at least try it, no matter how disgusting it looked or tasted. Giving it my best shot, my teeth made it past the thick layer of skin when suddenly a gag reflex began to take over. Not a chance! No way, no how! The best I could do was to politely refuse to eat it and apologize for not being able to eat it before confirming I wasn't going to.

Asians consider these types of foods to be a delicacy, and Lindsay continued trying to convince me it was delicious, yet I still beg to differ. Therefore, turtles and pig feet will never become a regular part of my diet. Traditional Chinese food is very cheap, yet for those who are not inclined to experiment, there were still many things available to eat, including the backup peanut butter and jam sandwich. A number of larger stores stock Western food for foreigners; however, it is much more expensive.

For three days, as I made my way to work, I passed a long line of people waiting to purchase something. Square wicker baskets the size of milk crates were stacked in the promenade outside the supermarket near the school. Getting a closer look, I observed the empty baskets were lined with clear plastic bags containing a reddish substance caked in them. Upon closer inspection, the substance was some type of red gunk that could perhaps be compared to something that had been rotting in the center of the earth for many years and had just been dug from beneath some ancient tomb. Like the empty containers they came in, inside the other baskets were two types of eggs, green eggs and those coated with the reddish-orange substance, which was seemingly the most popular. Curious, I had to solve the mystery. I later asked Hank what the big deal was and why the eggs were covered in a thick reddish orange muck. He told me the substance was used to pack and preserve the eggs so they wouldn't go bad. Although the substance will keep them fresh for up to a year, Hank presumed the year was almost up and the supermarket was having a sale to get rid of the eggs.

When Hank returned from Taiwan, Lindsay returned home, so I no longer had someone to eat with. It was time for me to search for a place that might serve food I could eat, so I began searching. After I wandered through the narrow alley across from the apartment complex, passing many eateries, I stumbled upon a small, depressed-looking establishment where an Asian man was cooking a stir-fry. The vegetables on display looked fairly fresh, so I pulled out my Chinese food book, to show the cook's wife the phrase pertaining to no hot/spicy food. She made a motion with her hand around the sauces, smiling, as if to say she understood what I wanted. Persistent, she persuaded me to choose several vegetables I recognized, then she escorted me to one of four tables inside her establishment. While waiting, I observed others and watched Chinese television on a small twelve-inch screen located above the fridge near the exit.

It was difficult not to stare as I watched customers shovel food into their mouths as if it was going to be their last meal. In the time it took to breathe in, three scooping motions of rice with the chopsticks was devoured with each loud smacking sound. I hadn't really noticed it up until then, or maybe I had and hadn't paid attention.

My stir-fry had arrived on a dinner plate, accompanied by a bottomless bowl of rice. While eating, I was suddenly aware that I too was shoveling foot to the same extreme, imitating the locals. I began to consider the possibility that after being immersed in a culture long enough you were bound to fall into some of the same habits, a prototype, perhaps a new breed of white Asian. Regardless, the food was delicious and without a doubt the best meal I had eaten since my arrival. For four to six yuan a meal, it became my home away from home for dinner every night, and the couple always treated me like royalty.

At ten a.m. one day, while sitting in the Internet bar, my cell phone rang. Frantically, I searched through my pack to find it to discover it was Yvonne calling.

"Sharon, you must come to the school right away," she urged.

"What, now?" I asked.

"Yes, now. Some instructors from our head office in Shanghai are doing a course, and you must attend," she replied.

Any normal company preparing for a meeting or event of this nature requiring your presence would inform you well in advance, or at least the day before. To say the Chinese could do with organizational skills would be an understatement. There was nothing like last-minute surprises to start the day off right.

I couldn't help wonder why they waited until the last minute to spring something like that on me. Nonetheless, I flew out of the Internet cafe, tore down the street, caught the first available bus and rushed to school. Within half an hour I arrived at the school and had missed an hour. To my surprise, there were no instructors from Shanghai at the school, but instead it was a training session via the Internet, recorded live from the head office in Shanghai. Teachers and staff were huddled around a fifteen-inch computer screen, which was very difficult to see, let alone hear. It was hard to believe I rushed to the school for this, yet made every effort to try and pick up a few tips for the remaining hour before returning home.

On my way out the door to go home, Yvonne stopped me. Everyone was going for lunch at somewhat of an elaborate restaurant across the street. The first item on the menu was a huge sizzling hot bowl of liquid containing small red critters. Out came the plastic gloves. Rolling my eyes, I turned to Yvonne.

"What's on the menu today?"

"Lobster," she replied.

"Lobster? That looks nothing like lobster. Are they babies?"

"They are lobsters from the river."

"Lobsters from the river? Yummy! That's a new one. Since when do lobsters come from a river?"

"Try them, they are a little hot, but delicious."

"How many times have I heard that since my arrival?" I replied hesitantly.

I watched as everyone put the gloves on, then followed suit. Not sure what to do with the critters, I finally asked Yvonne. She broke the claws off before snapping the tail away from the body.

"You only eat what is in the tail," she said, "but first you have to get the shell and everything off it."

After assisting me with the first one, I had things under control and took it from there. The meat inside added up to less than a mouth full, but overall they were very tasty, and lunch was delicious.

After lunch I had just enough time to go home, get showered and changed and return to school. After being subjected to watch some new techniques, I thought I'd try a few of them out on my two evening classes. What the hell was I thinking? I was dying all alone at the front of the class. What kind of nightmare am I living? I thought. No matter what I tried, nothing seemed to motivate the little brats, and it was to the point where I didn't much care. It suddenly occurred to me that if or when parents wanted to know why their children hadn't learned anything, I'd have someone translate, "Your child doesn't want to learn!" At that moment I walked, away mumbling to myself, "Stick that in your pipe and smoke it, you little brats!"

My day had reached its peak when I was blessed with Spitter Bob and friends to complete my day. Fortunately for me, Bob and Billy weren't there. However, Pat, Tony, Rosa and Jack were all together on one side of the room.

Pat and Jack sat banging on the wall, waiting for someone from the class on the other side to bang back. Tony had this sudden notion to walk across the room and pound the crap out of Rosa, a tiny little thing all of maybe fifty or sixty pounds, hardly big enough to defend herself. As she sat on the floor in tears, Tony returned to his seat, when I intercepted, grabbing him by the arm, dragging him back across the room to apologize to Rosa. He, like many other boys, took pleasure in hitting, kicking and punching little girls, and usually never gave it a second thought.

For the most part, it was becoming less difficult to ignore those who didn't want to learn and teach those who did. Nonetheless, somehow that night I had changed the course of that particular class by introducing some games and activities I had learned. By implementing my own style and approach, not only had I begun to spark their interest and attention, but hopefully their desire to learn as well. Perhaps I had the ability to turn things around; however, only time would tell.

Chapter 7
A Taoist Adventure

After discovering from Lindsay's friends the mountain we wanted to explore was out of the question, I searched a couple of other places, but they would have taken four hours either by bus or train. I came to the realization that a journey of that magnitude was a very big step for Lindsay, so they would have to wait. Lindsay's pursuit for more adventure led her to investigate other places of interest, and she was determined on planning somewhere special. I didn't mind, because everything was new and different and all quite fascinating.

The following Sunday morning I asked Lindsay what we were going to do for our day off.

"I think maybe we can go to XianYing," she replied. "We take the train, is about one hour. You want to go?"

"Let's do it," I replied.

Monday morning, the train departed for XianYing at 9:20 a.m., which meant we had to catch a bus to the train station and meet up with each other before purchasing our tickets. The 564 buses stopped directly in front of the train station, where the driver pointed across the street to the train station and motioned me to get off. As I stepped off the bus and stood waiting to cross the street, I thought, Oh my God! How the hell am I going to find Lindsay in this mess? The station was massive and insanely overloaded with Chinese people coming and going in every direction.

Before crossing the street, I stood there, just watching, pondering what to do next, when suddenly I heard, "Sharon, Sharon!" from behind. Lindsay's bus had arrived. She spotted me and was walking toward me. Wow, such a load off my mind. What were the odds?

"Do you know where we need to go to get tickets? I asked.

"No, maybe I ask someone," she replied. "Give me your hand," she commands.

Before pushing our way through the mob of people to the ticket counter at the far end of the terminal, Lindsay grabbed my hand with a grip so tight I couldn't get free even if I wanted to. The lineup to purchase tickets was staggering. Two men ahead of us were also trying to purchase tickets for the same train, when suddenly Lindsay's facial expression changed in midstream.

"There are no seats," she said.

"No seats, what do you mean no seats?

"This man, he says there are no more seats for that train."

"So we can't get a ticket?"

"No, we must stand," she replied.

Lindsay purchased our tickets for what may end up the longest hour-long train ride in history. If the trains were anything like the buses, then if nothing else it would prove to be interesting.

Train departures and platforms were at the opposite end of the building. Lindsay still had a grip on my hand, and for good reason. If one got lost in the mess, forget ever finding each other or your train, because I had no idea where we were even going. We pushed our way to a gate, passing through with our tickets before having our bags checked through an x-ray machine to proceed. People were pushing and shoving to get to the same place, but apparently had to be there first. Lindsay had no idea where we were going, as this was all quite new to her as well. After finding the platform, we boarded the train with yet more people crammed in, pushing and shoving to find their place, whether it be standing or sitting.

The train had a running schedule of about 13 hours, and anyone who had a seat was fortunate. We were out of luck. Once on the train, we simply sat in a seat until the occupant of the seat arrived. We had boarded the train over half an hour early, and after twenty minutes or so, a woman walked through the aisle yelling something in Chinese as she made her way through to the next car. Lindsay made another strange facial expression as she listened.

"What is it?" I asked.

"She says that we can pay twenty yuan for a seat in the dining car."

"Let's go," I replied with little hesitation.

We followed the woman through several cars to the dining car. People were jammed in like sardines everywhere we turned, and I would gladly pay the extra money. The woman escorted us to a bench seat table. The tables had linen, and the windows had lovely lace curtains. Lindsay had brought along some snacks for us to have for breakfast, spreading them out on the table. Ah, now this is the life, I thought, riding in luxury for the same price as a coach seat anyway.

We arrived at XianYing. As we exited the terminal gates, Lindsay spotted a map of the town outlining the points of interest. Nearby were the Hua Zhon Di Yi Quan Hot Springs, Yaiy Bamboo Forest, Yaiy Taoist Temple, and underground caves full of stalagmites and stalactites.

Lindsay drew the map in her book before making our way to a nearby street. At a small local outdoor restaurant establishment, Lindsay asked someone how to get to the caves and the temple. It was quite a ways out of town. One of the local taxi drivers offered to take us for three hundred yuan. The most peculiar-looking modes of transportation, motorcycle taxis were coming and going. The front end consisted of a motorcycle enclosed with a canvas canopy. Behind the driver was a wooden compartment and seat for two passengers, like a horse-drawn wagon, only on three wheels. I couldn't help thinking they resembled Flintstone vehicles that could be reduced to a pile of rubble in no time with one big wind or hailstorm. Intrigued, I suggested to Lindsay we hire one to take us around.

"It's too far!" she blurted. "I not ride in one of them!"

She began calling the numbers she had written down from the train station only to find her cell phone wouldn't work. It was obvious to me she was becoming frustrated, and her facial expressions were giving that away. After all, she had spent so much time preparing and planning this little excursion and suddenly everything was falling apart right before her eyes. I decided to back off and let her make the next move.

"Three hundred yuan!" she exclaimed. "That taxi driver is crazy. I think we walk along this street and we will find something else," she announced.

Along the street was a small establishment with telephones you could use for a fee. She called a travel service to find out how to get to some of the places we had come to see. Within five or ten minutes she had all the information she wanted and the smile had returned to her face.

"We catch the bus," she said. "The number two bus goes there."

After walking for about five minutes, we intercepted the main street, and a number two bus was parked in full view directly in front of us. Bus fare was collected by a woman whose job was to walk and entice people onto the bus, then walk back and forth collecting money from them as the bus continued en route.

Lindsay began chatting it up with a few locals, collecting information regarding the sites we wanted to see that day. After about half an hour, we got off the bus but still needed transportation to reach the caves located in the mountains on the outer edge of town. Parked everywhere up and down the street were several more motorcycle taxis, including one that was enclosed like a mini car and some that looked so old and dilapidated they wouldn't make their way up the street, let alone a mountain. A motorcycle taxi driver parked along the curb yelled to Lindsay. She walked over to him, and they spoke briefly in Chinese before translating to me.

"It cost eight yuan to take this taxi to the caves and temple," she said, looking less than enthused about our choice of transportation.

"Come on, Lindsay, it's an adventure," I said.

"You want to ride in this taxi?" she asked.

"Sure, why not, it's only eight yuan."

She gave in, and we got into the taxi.

The caves were quite a distance out of town, and as we left the city limits the scenery began to change. Miles of green lush mountains were boasting with trees and huge ferns. There were people up to their knees in the grass fields of vegetables, harvesting crops, wearing peaked hats to shade themselves from the already scorching hot sun. It was iffy whether the taxi would make it up some of the hills, but it gave us an opportunity to observe some yaks and cows closeup along the roadside. Chickens of various assortments ran loose everywhere, dodging out in front of us to cross the roads. It was absolutely beautiful. The further away we got, the more poverty became prevalent, more real, and something one would rarely get to see unless they ventured off the beaten track.

We finally arrived at the caves, out in the middle of nowhere, to less than a huge crowd of people. In fact, no one except us and a small group of ten tourists on their way by van would join us once they arrived. Our guide only spoke Chinese, so Lindsay translated what she could. Inside the caves it was extremely cold, more so the deeper into the caves we went. It was only my second time exploring caves of this type. Not only were these caves massive, dripping with water and moisture at every turn, they had some very impressive and unique rock formations, some having a sign posted in English and Chinese. Leaving one section of the cave to enter another, an eerie sound of bats could be detected from above us. The roar of small waterfalls echoed through the walls of the caves in a couple of sections and running water could be heard everywhere. Near the exit was a bow and arrow target practice area. For about ten cents, the rest of the group opted out while Lindsay and I each had a go hitting the targets with no problem at fifty feet away.

Just beyond the archery area was what the Chinese referred to as the ghost wishing well. Each person throws a coin, trying to hit the well. Lindsay was the only one who had any success with the toss. Once the coin hits the well, the ghost begins to churn the bucket in a full circle.

Theory has it that once the full turn is completed, you make a wish and the ghost of the well will grant it. OK, let the wishing begin!

At the exit of the caves, the sun was beaming in, and the next leg of the journey was the steep climb up the mountain to a Buddhist temple at the top that was over a thousand years old. From the summit to the base of the steps was a stone fence, the top being a dragon's head with the dragon's body extending down the hill to the bottom.

The Buddhist rituals seemed to include large amounts of prayer and fortune telling. In the main building, the monks had cylinders containing long sticks. You pull a stick from the cylinder, matching it up with the appropriate fortune card. For another twenty yuan, you can visit with a monk who can then read your fortune, expanding on it further. The entire group lined up to have their fortune read, including Lindsay. I, on the other hand, chose not to. Instead, I wandered around the awe-inspiring grounds.

Our tour came to an end, but instead of exiting the way we came in, Lindsay and I decided to take the back way out, a path we found down the side of the mountain leading to the highway. At first glance, the walk down didn't look that steep; however, on a couple of occasions I almost lost Lindsay as she began to slide on her heels and buttocks trying to keep from falling. Being a little more experienced and somewhat of a tomboy in my day, I took the lead to intercept in case she did fall. The entire way down the mountain I kept thinking, How are we going to get out of this place and back to town? There was no bus service, no taxis, nothing unless you had pre-booked a tour.

At the road, in each direction, nothing looked familiar, and we were both confused as to which direction we should take. We were lost. It's funny how you think you have all your bearings and directions in order at times. We picked a direction and began walking. After about fifteen minutes we ended up in a small community at the exit of the caves and entrance of the Taoist temple, and not where we needed to be. Our tour guide, tending to some chickens, looked puzzled to see us there. Lindsay and he spoke briefly before asking her to turn around. The back of her pants where completely soiled in dirt from sliding down the mountain. After they finished talking, Lindsay translated our options.

We could either climb back up the mountain the way we came down or backtrack and continue on the same road in the opposite direction.

In the ninety-nine degree sweltering heat, we began walking, when a man riding a motorcycle attempted to converse with us as he passed. Lindsay turned her head away from him, ignoring him. Slowly, he rode alongside us then stopped, making a second attempt to talk to us.

"What did he say?" I asked.

"He wants to give us a ride," she replied.

"Maybe he could give us a ride to the main road," I suggested.

"No," she said sternly, "Three people is too dangerous."

I was sure he was only trying to help, but he rode on. He must have known the walk ahead of us would be a long one. When we finally arrived at the main road, about half an hour later, now two men sat on parked motorcycles, waiting for us. They both began talking to us, and Lindsay continued to walk, ignoring them as if they weren't even there.

"Talk to them, Lindsay, maybe they can help. Look around. Do you see any buses, taxis, anything? There is nothing! Do you have any idea how we are going to get out of here? At least talk to them and see what they can do to get us out of here," I said.

Lindsay hesitated momentarily, then began to engage in conversation with the two men. When they finished talking, Lindsay turned to me with a solution to our problem.

"They will give us a ride back to town. They also say if we want to go to the stone forest and bamboo forest they will take us for forty yuan each and give us a ride back to the hot springs in town. What do you think?" she asked.

"Let's do it," I blurted.

To go back to town and take a tour would cost us that or more. They had made us an offer we couldn't refuse. Getting on a motorcycle with total strangers, riding in any form of transportation for that matter, in a foreign country was something I'd never consider in a million years, yet I could think of no reasons not to trust them. We had no other options, as the two locals genuinely tried to help us.

My helmet consisted of an ugly dilapidated yellow construction hardhat, and it was the only one in use during our adventure. Their driving was impeccable, and they were nothing less than courteous and careful as they took us everywhere. Now this was the way to tour China, I thought. The countryside, filled with lush green mountains overflowing with rich green foliage, trees and massive ferns was absolutely breathtaking as we made our way to an area referred to as the stone forest. As we pulled into the parking area there were three small vans parked outside the entrance. Our chauffeurs waited with their bikes while we ventured in. There was no one there to collect money to get in, so the price was right.

A tour was just beginning, and since the path was so narrow, we more or less had to join the group and follow the tour. Several of the people from the cave tour were among the group and began talking to Lindsay while we walked. The points of interest along the way were all translated in Chinese, so I just followed along, fascinated by the stone formations, waiting for that spectacular view I had seen in the book. Of the impression we were entering the famous limestone pillars of Shilin, I became exited and had remembered seeing pictures of the famous stone forest. Unfortunately, as our tour ended, I suddenly came to the realization it was not. Later, I would learn several areas throughout China were referred to as stone forests, and the one I was thinking about in particular was located in southwestern China in Yunnan Province. Although the bamboo stone forest was interesting, it was not all that impressive.

Our chauffeurs were waiting for us at the entrance when we returned. After saying goodbye to our new friends, they got on their bikes, then parted ways. We continued on up the mountain, stopping at another section of the bamboo forest. The sound of cowbells clanging was echoing in the distance as we made our way up some steep steps to the top of the hill. With the exception of several cows grazing in a pasture and a few poisonous snakes hiding in the grass, there was nothing but miles of forest abundant with bamboo trees.

We continued up the mountain to the Bamboo Forest Hotel. Located on a cliff overlooking a deep ravine, large winged birds, perhaps hawks, soared beyond the cliffs overhead, their cries echoing. Once a luxury resort miles away from civilization, the now dilapidated hotel sits perched on the mountain, abandoned, closed up tighter than a drum.

After exploring, we made our way back down the mountain toward town, dodging stacks of cut bamboo trees about every two or three miles that had been dumped off the back of a truck and scattered all over the road. One man for each load worked diligently, stacking each tree into a neat pile off to the side of the road. From my perspective, it would have been more logical to just dump the load off to the side of the road and pile it there.

As we passed several men bricking a house, I couldn't help but think not only were the bamboo scaffolds secured with rope ancient, the method of brick laying was as well. Perhaps the story of the Three Little Pigs was derived from this place, I thought. Our drivers didn't seem all that concerned that in each small town and community we rode through we were dodging every farm animal imaginable: baby ducks, dogs, cats and pigs were roaming loose in every direction. It was amazing to see the difference between how the country and city people lived.

The journey ended at the edge of town near the entrance of the Hua Zhong Di Yi Quan Hot Springs, where Lindsay and I gladly paid both our drivers our forty yuan each before we parted ways. For me it was worth every penny for the sheer enjoyment of having the wind blow through our hair on a hot, humid day as we rode through the wide-open countryside.

"Now that's what I call an adventure," I said to Lindsay.

Although I wasn't quite sure either of us where entirely sure what had just taken place, we laughed. I could tell by her beaming face she agreed, and knew it would also be a day she or I would not soon forget.

Ah, now a trip to the hot springs! What a perfect end to a perfect day. Both exhausted and after eating junk food snacks the entire day, we were starving. The hotel offered a discounted rate if we decided to eat before going for a swim. The prices on the menu were very reasonable, so Lindsay ordered, then we were escorted to a private dining room with a perfect view of the river from the second floor.

Items on the menu included bamboo shoots with pork. I had assumed bamboo would be very chewy and quite gross, but to my surprise, the more I ate, the more I wanted, and it was very tasty. After dinner we decided to let our meal settle and wait awhile before plunging into the hot water. Lindsay also needed a bathing suit, purchasing one of two hanging on display in the lobby that immediately caught her attention.

The pool was continually fed with hot water through three tall spouts from somewhere along the river beneath the ground, or perhaps from a natural spring fed by the mountain. Wherever it came from, it was hot, and with the exception of three or four others, we basically had the entire pool to ourselves for the next two hours before returning to a civilized version of reality. One thing was for sure—we were going to sleep like a baby once we hit the pillows.

After leaving the hot springs, we stumbled upon a community exercise dance program in session across the street. While we stood watching, one couple from the tour had recognized us, trying to get Lindsay's attention. What were the odds? While Lindsay caught them up on the events of the day, I wandered over to the edge of the river to watch two boys jump off a funky old wooden Chinese boat and chase each other around the dirty brown water. Although less then enticing or appealing to me, the temperature was so hot, so muggy, the sweat seemed to ooze from ever pour, even as the sun set.

As we made our way back toward the train station, we crossed paths with two more from the tour, and after a short chat we were on our way once again. Running into two different groups three times in one day had to be ten thousand to one.

At the station, once again, no seats were available for our return trip. However, Lindsay didn't care, as she pushed her way through the cars, dragging me until she found two empty ones available in the upper deck. The face of a ticket collector never appeared once on our return journey. There was one downfall to sitting in the upper deck. After coming in from sweltering hot temperatures, the continuous blast from the air-conditioned car had me feeling like I was locked in a meat locker. The day was so strange, yet so perfect. Perhaps there was something to the wishing well legend after all.

Chapter 8
An Ancient Way of Life

For a change of pace, I had planned on venturing off on my own to explore the Chu Market and Cutian Platform Pagoda visible from the lake, and the botanical gardens on East Lake. For weeks I had dragged Lindsay with me everywhere and thought she might like to have a day to herself to rest and hang out with her friends. However, before leaving work Sunday, she tracked me down to find out what I was doing on my day off. After telling her my plans, it was apparent she wanted to come along and hang out with me. Asking immediately confirmed my suspicions, and she was so excited I thought she was going to hug me.

Because East Lake was only a few minutes' walk away, we had made arrangements to meet at Hank's house around noon and go from there. Lindsay's bus ended up stuck in a traffic jam on the way from Hankou. It was a good thing we didn't have to go far, as by the time we got going, it was after one o'clock.

Small islands on East Lake were plentiful and all accessible by vehicle. A short twenty-minute drive led across a long, shallow bridge road toward the entrance gates. Passing a large body of water filled with giant water lilies was a section of the Plant Research Institute and Botanical Gardens. The remaining area encompassed a Moshau arboretum, Wuhan Botanical Gardens, Cutian Platform Pagoda, Chu Market and Daziran Hotel of Wuhan.

Floating on the lake, across from the Daziran Hotel was a beautiful Chinese architectural-style restaurant. As the bus passed the restaurant, Lindsay seemed eager about the prospect of eating there.

"Would you like to have lunch there?" I asked.

Her face lit up like a Christmas tree.

"OK," she said. "You want to try?"

"Sure, if you want to, let's check it out."

"What is 'check it out'? I don't understand these words."

Laughing, I replied, "Never mind."

The last stop was the entrance to the grounds and quite obviously a tourist attraction. We should have stopped to eat somewhere along the way before getting on the bus; nonetheless, we didn't. The restaurant was a four- or five-minute walk. Once inside, Lindsay briefly glanced through the menu. Instantly, I recognized her change in expression. I knew by looking at her it was too expensive, as is anything tied to a tourist trap. Knowing she would not say no if I had wanted to eat there, I also knew she wouldn't let me pay, and she only made one-sixth of what I did. She was a very proud individual, and each time I had offered to pay in the past it seemed she always felt obligated to pay me back, rarely accepting my generosity to pay her portion of anything.

"Lindsay, these prices are very expensive."

"Yes."

"We don't have to eat here. We can see if there is something up the road or inside the grounds if you want.

"OK," she replied, and with that, we grabbed our things and walked out.

There weren't really much in the way of places to eat, and I was starving. Although I had eaten breakfast, I decided to wait for Lindsay before eating lunch. In the end, we resorted to eating at the snack bar near the entrance, our snack bar lunch consisting of a large container of

Chinese noodles, with a peel-back aluminum lid. Just add a packet of spice and sauce, add hot water, set the lid back on and voila, instant lunch for six yuan, three times the normal price. In comparison, my bottomless bowls of rice accompanied by a heaping stir-fry dinner for four yuan was a huge bargain.

The entry fee was forty yuan. However, once inside the grounds, a separate fee was charged to enter each section of the grounds. To reach the Cutian Platform Pagoda at the summit of the mountain, there was an additional cost of twenty-five yuan each way to ride the chair lift.

"The price we just paid doesn't cover the lift up?" I asked.

"No, you pay each thing," Lindsay replied.

A vehicle for transporting tourists drove past and pulled up alongside the main entrance building, and I asked Lindsay to ask the driver what it would cost to take us up. She returned, mumbling with a scrunched face, shaking her head.

"What did she say?" I asked.

"They are crazy. They want, um, one hundred and forty yuan to ride this car."

"What! That's retarded."

"I told her she was crazy," Lindsay exclaimed.

We did have one last option, the steep hiking trail ascending to the summit. As I looked up to the summit, my eyes almost bugged out of my head. It had been a long time since I climbed a mountain, but there was no doubt in my mind I still had that ability in me.

The mosquitoes regarded as us as a mid day snack, but the view alone was well worth the hike. What an amazing view, spectacular in every direction for miles, or at least as far as the smog would allow. Looking down, I could have stared into oblivion for hours. The Chu Market and small fortress-like structures, now off in the distance, were clear and in full view. Everything was so green and lush, so quiet and peaceful, as we continued to make our way through the jungle-like surroundings. It was heaven, or at least what my interpretation might be.

In a small courtyard setting at the top of the mountain was a very strange, ancient-looking statue of Zhu Rong dating back to the eleventh century, around the period of 221 B.C. and the Zhou Dynasty. Lindsay referred to him as "Watcher of the Stars," and he was believed to have read the stars and the future they held in life.

Inside the pagoda the Chu history was kept alive with the ancient history and music. Performers played a traditional musical Chu instrument while dressed in customary attire from that time period. The instruments resembled cowbells, ranging in size from tiny to grand, suspended from large frames, each having two or three different tones. Other instruments were stringed somewhat similar to a steel guitar. Still others played flutes with the most intriguing design that left you to ponder its origin long after you left. The synchronization of music from the instruments resulted in the most incredible tones I had ever heard, bringing me to tears, although I wasn't really sure why. The performance ended with "Old Lang Syne," the most incredible sound I had ever heard, and well worth the climb and an admission of five yuan.

Some Chu history was revealed on a wall plaque and stated: In the period of Zhou Chen Wang, about 1030-1014 B.C., the Chu state lasted about 800 years. On the base of initiating central China culture and its original culture, the Chu people created a brilliant culture of local and national characteristics by absorbing the cream of Western, Eastern, Southern and Northern culture, which made a great contribution to the establishment of multi-national combination of ancient Chinese culture.

It was a long, steep walk back down, and by the time we got to the bottom the park was closing. The entire afternoon took up one section of the park and would require a second, perhaps third, visit to explore other facets of the park. With so much walking and hiking, it suddenly occurred to me that treating myself to a foot massage might be just the thing I need for my sore, tired, aching feet. In China, foot massage establishments seem to be on every corner, every block for that matter, and I had heard it was very soothing and relaxing. It was definitely something I'd never tried but had always wanted to do.

Each night on my way home from work, I passed several foot massage establishments, but I was never sure which ones were good.

Elly usually walked home with me, so one evening I asked for her advice. Out of three in the area, she chose the cleanest one and the one most reasonable. It was thirty yuan for an hour and ten minutes. Before continuing home, I asked Elly to write down everything I needed to know or ask in Chinese, and I would venture back after dinner.

Upon arrival, I was escorted to a small room and seated in a large heated lounge chair with pillows and footstools. Before the massage therapist arrives, someone brought me a hot cup of green tea to sip on. After a few minutes of sipping, my massage therapist entered the room carrying a large wicker bushel basket lined with a clear plastic bag half full of some sort of hot Chinese medicine. The liquid consisted of an orangey-brown mud mixture to soak your feet in and was very soothing. I could hardly wait for my hour and ten minute session to begin.

So many people had told me how much better in comparison a foot massage was to a body massage. All geared up, I couldn't wait for this wonderful, relaxing event to get started. An entire room to myself, and not one person could speak English. If any sort of translation was to take place, it would have to be relayed through expressions or sign language.

With my feet still soaking in the lovely mud/water mixture, the male massage therapist motioned me to stand up and turn, facing the lounge chair and sit on the foot stool in front of him. Suddenly, he began to massage my shoulders, neck, arms and back. My interpretation of relaxation instantly turned into a rigorous procedure involved knuckles, slapping, clucking noises of the hands and pounding. Oh, and let's not forget chopping. Good grief! What had I got myself into now? It was turning into a grueling discovery of what torture must have felt like to the peasants who wouldn't follow orders in ancient times. Oh God, make it stop! I thought, looking down at my watch only to discover I still had another hour to go. Hopefully while getting my foot massage, the enduring pain elsewhere would cease.

Ah, finally, he stopped, gesturing me to sit back in the lounge chair while he went to replenish my tea. Upon his return he sat on the small footstool facing me. First he took my left foot out of the bucket, dried it off and put some sort of cream all over my foot. It was evident he was trying hard to tell me something about my big toe and middle toe, but I couldn't understand a word, so just smiled, and he continued.

Compared to what would follow, the upper body massage was just a warmup exercise, perhaps a routine exercise to get his hands limbered up. What I was about to endure would have made a lifeless doll spring to life, sprout wings, maybe even teeth for that matter, just to get even and be gone.

He began using his hands and thumbs first, and then began slapping my toes back and forth with the palms and backs of his hands. It was so bizarre I almost burst out laughing. Suddenly everything changed as he pushed his knuckles up and down, back and forth on the bottom of my foot. Tears began to well. As I sat there with my eyes bugging out of my head, grinning from car to ear, pretending it was the most pleasurable experience I had ever been involved in.

To try and take my mind off the excruciating pain, I began to concentrate on a Chinese television program behind the therapist before he resorted to placing pressure on the under sides of my toes. By that time, the sweat began oozing from every pour in my body. As I reached over to the table next to me for my tea, the only thoughts going through my head were: This is going to be the longest hour of my life, and when is he going to change to the other foot so we can get this over with?

While sipping my tea, all I wanted to do was cry because it hurt so bad. I nonchalantly looked down at my watch only to find that twenty minutes had passed. It had crossed my mind that maybe if my feet were hurting that badly, I must have been in need of a treatment. That was surpassed by another thought: No pain, no gain should never be in the same sentence as a Chinese foot massage.

The term "foot massage" took on a whole new meaning when he began jabbing his knuckles into various sections of my heel, almost springing me from my chair. Again he pushed on the spot, perhaps looking for a reaction or to ensure he had located that tender spot. He nodded, then scrunched his face and eyes to confirm his findings. To indicate what that part of the heel pertained to, he put his two hands together, resting his head on his hands, and I understood that it had something to do with sleep.

The slapping of the toes was repeated several times before changing the technique by punching the base of my foot with his knuckles, alternating once more, rigorously turning my feet in half circles. Making a fist, he used his knuckles for pounding, making the most bizarre clacking noise. In between bouts of excruciating pain, it was quite entertaining, and I almost broke into laughter. The slapping was nothing short of exhilarating, leading me to believe the therapist had aspirations of becoming a drummer one day. The finishing touches involved massaging and pounding my ankles and calves before continuing the entire outlandish nightmare on my other foot. There may be some truth to the relaxation element of this practice; however, I did not discover it that day.

A couple days later, Hank had a business trip to attend in a small village in the country an hour from Wuhan by taxi, and he invited me to go along. On the way we passed many fields with crops of vegetables and fields submerged under water, with Asians working the crops in their bare feet. As we drove, a yak standing on the shoulder of the road grazing suddenly caught my attention. Further along was a two-man road crew rolling asphalt on a section of road. The primitive piece of equipment they used was a roller, with rollers approximately three feet long by eight to ten inches wide, with a rope attached to the middle of it. One man stood on the roller (I presumed for weight) while the other stood on the grass to one side of the pavement, pulling the roller.

In town, we arrived at the building Hank was meeting his friend Thomas. Thomas worked for the Chinese International Foreign Education sector for the entire region. Part of his job was to help with the setup of English in the schools. Many smaller country schools, I discovered, did not teach English, and if they did it was usually a Chinese who only taught them the basics. Hank was interested in this particular school because of its location, and he wanted to take it over to set-up a school like the one he already had. The facilities were already there; however, it needed a facelift.

Before the meeting, we were taken on a tour of several fair-size classrooms and a small library with books piled and sprawled everywhere. It was so disorganized that to locate anything specific may have proved somewhat of a chore. The classrooms were very structured, with older-style desks; almost replicas of ones I vaguely remember from grade one. The chairs were tiny little wooden stools with no backs. There was no air conditioning, only rickety old ceiling fans. Some of the windows were completely bricked over, with the glass missing. It was like going back in time, and I hadn't seen anything that primitive since the series *Little House on the Prairie*.

I was introduced to the staff as his foreign English teacher, something they were having a great deal of difficulty comprehending, not quite sure why I was invited to sit in on the hour-long meeting, as I couldn't understand a word. However, at several points throughout the meeting, it wouldn't have taken a genius long to figure out the meeting wasn't going well. At various intervals during the meeting the principal began laughing, and the silence and body language alone was beginning to paint a dreary picture. There were six in the room, including the three of us, the director, sitting at his desk, the headmaster next to me, and another staff member sat on the couch.

There was something very strange about the headmaster, and something odd about the meeting in particular. As I sat watching, listening, I was becoming uneasy, but couldn't put my finger on why. It's funny sometimes the things that suddenly go through your mind when you know you're in an awkward situation you have no control over. It felt as though I had already witnessed the same sequence of events before, like deja vu, or a clip from a movie that I had already seen.

The headmaster was a thin, rigid woman with spiked hair. Joining the meeting late, I immediately picked up on her instant distrust and disapproval of Hank, suddenly drawing images of her as an authoritative figure working under Hitler's rule. She seemed to take over the entire conversation not long after she entered the room.

As I watched the director, I couldn't help notice his hair and the way he presented himself, suddenly picturing a shady little weasel not to be trusted. All I could envision was a cocky little Nazi man walking about with one hand clasped behind his back as he took a drag of a cigarette affixed to a long fancy filter on the end, while hiding behind the tough, commanding woman.

After we had left, I informed Hank I got the impression things didn't go well and asked what happened. Hank confirmed my suspicions. They weren't interested in upgrading or having him take over the school.

"What happens to the staff if you take over the school," I asked.

"They would work for me," he replied.

Neither the headmaster and director gave us the impression they were big on change. Thomas interrupted, pointing out that many of the rural Chinese schools had no idea about foreign English teachers and how arrangements worked for them, and because they didn't like change, it made doing business much more difficult.

We left the school, taking a private taxi van to another rural school on the other side of town. The trip left something to be desired, not to mention the roads. As the driver continued down a ninety-degree incline in the road, we hit a large exposed drainage pipe in our path, almost pole vaulting me head first through the roof. Quickly, Hank and I both began to bust a gut as we grabbed the handrail above the door to hang on.

The school was located on a low-lying landmass between two bodies of water, but from the outside it wasn't quite as primitive-looking as the first. Because of its location and elevation, there was probably a very good chance that any heavy rains or monsoons would flood the entire area, causing much of it to end up under water.

It was past noon, so we left to meet up with two of Thomas's staff members at a local restaurant for lunch before returning to the school. Al, the youngest of his associates, also worked for the same foreign education sector of the government, and his English was excellent. He had the most incredible eyes and smile I had ever seen, and I found myself very attracted to him. Throughout the meal I caught myself staring at him, only to find him also staring at me, smiling. Perhaps he felt the same way, and I could hope perhaps an opportunity would present itself again at another time. We dropped Thomas off on our way out of town and continued on to the school before classes started.

My teaching skills were broadening as I tested the waters in areas of singing, exercising, even doing pushups and sit-ups to demonstrate various lessons. A new student Chinese teacher decided to sit in on my class that night. As usual, the class began to go astray, so I gathered them in a group in the center of the room to teach them the words and actions to the "Hokey Pokey."

"You put your right hand in, you take your right hand out, you put your right hand in and you shake it all about…" I suddenly realized I had no clue as to how the rest went, so I began to ad-lib, and they didn't know the difference anyway. It was a way for them to have a little fun and let off some excess energy before returning to the lesson. In their eyes I was strange, I'm sure, yet no longer the ogre they originally cast me out to be. A more entertaining side of me began to develop as I persevered with each class.

After class, the student teacher pulled me aside to tell me she thought my way of teaching very amusing and fun. I laughed. She ended by telling me all of her English teachers were very stern, rigid, had no sense of humor, and she wished they could have been more like me. Spared the company of Spitter Bob and friends, for time being anyway, it was finally a good week of teaching. However, there were always exceptions.

Yvonne had a special class, a group of students apparently much smarter and more advanced than any other class, and I was given the exclusive opportunity to make sure they passed the course. From my perspective, not one of them knew anything, had any interest in learning or listening, and I really had my doubts as to whether three-quarters of them could speak English as well as some of my other lower-level classes.

After having a heart to heart with Yvonne, their Chinese teacher, she informed me their English was much better than I thought, and they needed to pass the course before they could take an entrance exam to get into a middle school. I told her that from what I was seeing, they wouldn't get into a middle school, or any other school for that matter, and perhaps she should talk to them.

One could only hope my image was changing in the eyes of the students. However, jumping around like a teenager at my age, doing sit-ups and strenuous exercises, may have been pushing my luck just slightly, but only time would tell.

Chapter 9
A Foreigner's Worst Nightmare

With temperatures beginning to hit sweltering highs, a homeless person sauntered past, dressed for weather in Antarctica, looking and smelling worse then anything I could ever have imagined. As I stood at the bus stop, I watched him kneel down after pulling a set of chopsticks from inside his coat, and he began eating a small pile of food remnants off the sidewalk. The sheer image and idea of it was turning my stomach to the point of almost hurling.

For lunch that day, I felt like having some hot dried noodles. Less than a block away from the school was a long, narrow alley of food vendors selling noodle dishes. Picking one, I showed the vendor what I wanted from my Chinese food book. While waiting, I observed several people having a few laughs as they spoke with the vendor. Smiling, the vendor gave me my noodles. I handed him a ten-yuan note, and he handed me my change. As I walked away, I turned to see them all watching me, laughing. Something didn't seem right, so as I continued walking, I briefly glanced down at the change before putting it in my pocket. Curious, I turned back, only to see all of them still laughing.

Upon returning to the school, I pulled the change out of my pocket to examine it. Jake was in the office, and I told him I wasn't sure if I'd just been ripped off. It didn't really dawn on me until I walked away to ask him if he knew the difference.

"Jake, is this note worth five yuan or fifty cents?" I asked.

"About fifty cents, why?"

"I just gave a vendor ten yuan for hot dried noodles, and this was the change he gave me." I showed him the fifty-cent note and change.

"Hot dried noodles?"

"Yes. Here is what I bought." I showed him the noodles.

"That bastard just ripped me off, then had the balls to laugh in my face while doing it."

We both had classes for the remainder of the afternoon, so I couldn't return that day to sort it out.

"Don't worry," Jake reassured me, "these guys are pulling this shit all the time, and they think it's funny. We'll go back there tomorrow and straighten him out. I've had dealings with them before, and these people are always pulling stupid shit like this. Don't worry."

In China, a note for fifty cents is almost identical to ones worth five yuan, the difference being the size and color. Having seen only one or two since my arrival, I couldn't be sure, giving what I though was an honest vendor benefit of the doubt.

The following day, Jake and I returned to the vendor. As we walked toward the vendor, he and a few from the previous day were there again, and began laughing again. Jake began speaking to the vendor in Chinese, but the vendor and his buddies just started laughing.

"What is he saying?" I asked.

"He's saying he gave you the correct change."

"Bullshit, Jake. Look at them, they're all pissing themselves laughing. He knows he ripped me off, and so do they!"

"I know he's lying, don't worry. I'm going to fix this right now."

The discussion between Jake and the vendor became a full-blown heated argument back and forth as Jake began screaming and yelling in Chinese. The vendor was denying he had made a mistake, yet he and everyone were still laughing. Jake pointed out that if he did in fact give me five yuan change, then in reality he would have ripped himself off, and he told the Chinese vendor he knew they weren't that stupid. He told the vendor he owed me money, commanding him to give me back the proper change. The laughter increased in the background as they continued, and the shit began to fly. Wow!

All of a sudden, the shouting ended, and silence took its place. The smirks vanished, as if someone had just wiped them off their faces without them even knowing it. Once more, Jake presented the vendor the fifty-cent note, exchanging it for the five yuan he should have given me in the first place. After the exchange was made, Jake grabbed me by the arm, gave me my proper change back, and led me out of the alley, telling me not to look back.

A few moments later I asked him what just happened and why they stopped laughing. He informed the vendor he was going to call the police, and he didn't care if he had to pay the hundred yuan it would cost to get them involved just to make a point and get my five yuan back.

According to Jake, the police were like God in China, holding more authority than most others, even bank officials. It is disgraceful for a vendor to have the police involved, especially when it comes to ripping off a tourist.

After thanking Jake for his efforts, he advised me to be very careful with what I say or do. "When it comes to money and the Chinese, out to make a quick buck off naive tourists, you must also be very careful," he warned. Having resided in China and attending university for three years did not necessarily give Jake immunity to problems. In fact, he managed to encounter a few surprises and difficulties of his own.

Whether a foreigner or living in our own country, we were all vulnerable to some extent. But imagine being the foreigner, like Jake and one of his friends, living in a foreign country and suddenly losing your passport, all your identification and everything of value.

Jake had been sitting at a computer at an Internet cafe. His bag was on the desk next to him when someone taped him on the shoulder. He turned around to look, but no one was there. When he turned back, his bag was gone. With no identification to prove who he was, his situation suddenly took a drastic turn. Without proof of who he was, he basically no longer existed. It's just that simple, just that quick. Jake not only had a sizeable sum of money in a Chinese bank account, but also a copy of his passport. As a foreigner, it is wise to open a bank account. Not unlike any other financial institution in the world, it is required you give them all the credentials to make that happen, as Jake did before putting all his hard-earned money into the account. However, by giving them your passport information, you basically hand over your life.

After arriving at the bank, Jake wanted to take all of the money out of his account. After explaining that his ID, passport and everything in his bag had been stolen, the bank suddenly had no record of him, his account or any money belonging to him at that bank. Within a very short time, he was becoming non-existent, ending up his worst nightmare. How would he prove his existence when he had nothing?

He couldn't believe what he was hearing or what was happening, ending up in a heated argument with several Chinese bank officials, getting nowhere. After they all denied he had an account, Jake informed them he was going to call the police in to sort it out. They told him to go ahead and, knowing it was his only choice, he did. He also knew they weren't going to take kindly to what was happening. After the police arrived and had a discussion with the bank officials, mysteriously, the bank account was found and all his money and passport information along with it.

Within the first couple of weeks meeting Jake, he told me he was from England and was English. His accent was so obscure I finally had to ask him why his sounded otherwise. His parents' heritage was British, Jordanian, Turkish and Russian. His mother was English and his father was Jordanian, who met while working for the same government agency in Africa. They fell madly in love, eventually getting married. Both their parents were strongly against it, but their love kept them together.

When Jake was younger, his parents wanted him to get to know and understand the heritages he came from. He was to live with different relatives and attend schools in many different countries, including England, Jordan, Turkey, Russia and China, where he learned the languages and lived while doing his schooling. When his dental education from Moscow Medical University was completed, he moved on to attend the university in central China. Jake was a well-rounded and well-cultured individual who probably had more of an advantage than most who visit foreign countries. Jake hated being sent to so many countries to learn, but in the long run it became a great benefit to him.

When it came to tourist traps, however, he was no different than any other foreigner, but only after a turn of events unfolded did he realize it. Sometimes, no matter how careful we are, there will always be that element of surprise or unexpected difficulties we end up sharing with each other, to make sure our new friends are aware of what can happen when it is least expected.

While cruising on his bike one day, Jake saw an old man lying on the road. Spectators were standing around, doing nothing to help the man, who was dirty and wet. Being a student studying to be a doctor, he couldn't just continue past, doing nothing to help the man, so he stopped and put his bike down to see if he could help. The man was in very bad shape and looked as though he'd been hit by a motor vehicle. Jake asked the spectators what happened, but no one was saying anything, just shaking their heads. Jake tried to ask the old man what happened, but he couldn't understand his local language. Jake yelled to the spectators to call the police and an ambulance, because the man needed emergency medical care. No one would help him, so he assumed they didn't want to get involved and he made the call himself.

When the ambulance arrived, Jake told them what happened. They put the man in the ambulance and left for the nearest hospital. When Jake tried to get his bike, two guys holding his bike insisted Jake hit the man, urging Jake to give them money to keep quiet about it. Jake told them they were crazy and he pulled his bike from their hands.

A few hours later the police called Jake. They questioned him, asking him if he struck down the man with his bike. Jake told them no, that he was just passing through and saw the man lying in the middle of the road not moving. None of the spectators were helping him, and he told the officer he was a medical student studying at the university and couldn't just ignore the guy. He got off his bike to try and help the man, but after discovering the man's condition was very serious, requiring emergency medical treatment, he called for an ambulance when no one else would. The officers advised him he had interfered with police business and should have left the man alone.

As a medical doctor, Jake told them, he had taken an oath to help people in trouble. He didn't care whose fault it was or who did it, knowing the man's health was more important, but more so, once the man was in safe hands there was nothing more he could do there. Jake pleaded with the officers to check out his story with some of the people watching if they didn't believe him. They all saw what happened; why would they lie?

The officers asked him to wait while they checked out his story. When they returned, the officers informed him the witnesses said Jake hit the guy with his bike and then *they* called the ambulance to take him to the hospital. He asked to see them. It was the same two guys he met at the scene who wanted money. Jake couldn't believe what was happening and went ballistic. Having witnessed him in action, I knew firsthand he didn't take deception well.

He argued with the officers, trying to convince them the two men were lying. Again, he explained to the officers he did not hit the man, who was already in the road when he arrived, but the police told Jake he would have to go to the police station with them.

Jake was stunned. He knew as well as all the witnesses he was innocent, but his bike was confiscated, and he was taken to the police station for questioning. At the police station he told the same story over and over, trying to convince the officers he was not guilty, but he was now getting worried. He asked the officers if there was any way he could prove his innocence, and they told him two ways. One, to find a witness that could confirm his story. The other was his bike. If indeed he did hit the man, his bike would not be balanced and would fall over when driven. Urging the police to do what they had to do to check the bike out to prove his innocence, he added that the doctors in the hospital would confirm what really happened to the man.

The officers took Jake outside to where they would test the bike. An officer was motioned to get on the bike and drive it. Jake, along with several other officers, all watched as the unqualified officer got on his bike, hit the throttle full tilt and crashed it into the ground. Jake could not believe his eyes. What the hell is this? he thought. He began screaming that the officer didn't know how to ride a bike and had just smashed it up. An officer informed Jake his bike was unbalanced because he hit the man, and *that* was why the bike fell over.

Jake continued arguing that the officer was inexperienced and couldn't ride a bike, and they knew it. He crashed it while they watched him do it. Jake was baffled as to how he was going to prove his innocence, offering to ride his bike for them in an effort to prove he was telling the truth. Giving Jake the benefit of the doubt, the officers let him go, advising him that his only option was to get a lawyer and find a witness. Jake agreed.

After leaving the police station, Jake called a lawyer, then went to see him. The lawyer told him to put an ad in the local paper to see if anyone had witnessed what really happened. The second thing was to visit the man in the hospital who he had allegedly hit and talk to him about what actually happened.

He called the newspapers first, but no one would write or print the ad. They didn't want to get involved because he was a foreigner. Finally, after talking to a woman from one of the local papers, she agreed to run the ad.

In the meantime, he decided to pay the man in the hospital a little visit to ask him what really happened. The man told him he was suing Jake for hitting him with his bike. Jake lost it, calling the man a liar, then telling him he was crazy. The man wouldn't back down and demanded five thousand yuan to drop the lawsuit. Jake was furious, knowing now he had been set up. He screamed at the man, calling him a bastard, and ended the conversation by telling the man he would pay him nothing.

Jake had many Chinese friends, and he called all of them to see if maybe they could help him. After several days they all called, apologizing, saying it was very difficult to help him because he was a foreigner.

A few weeks went by, and Jake still had to prove his innocence or he would undoubtedly be going to jail. With no bike and no witnesses, he was running out of ideas. He hadn't heard anything from the newspaper, so he went to see the journalist who ran the ad to see if there had been any calls. She told him she had one call, but then she had received two calls from the police and the university, asking her to pull the ad and not to publish anything further. When Jake inquired why they pulled the ad, he was told they didn't want the ad in the newspaper, so they asked her to pull it.

Flabbergasted, Jake concluded that everyone was covering everyone else's ass. No one would talk and no one would get involved. Before leaving the newspaper firm, he asked the woman if she could at least give him the name and number of the one witness she did get.

The witness turned out to be a foreigner who was passing by and saw the whole thing. He told Jake while he was helping the man on the road, two guys picked the bike up and dropped the bike in such a way that it would look like he did strike the man with his bike.

Jake returned to the hospital to inform the injured man he had a witness who could verify his story, but the man still wanted Jake to pay him, now two thousand yuan, and he would drop the charges. Once again Jake informed the man he was a liar and would give him nothing. As far as Jake was concerned, the scam was finished.

With one last plea and one last attempt to get his bike back, Jake returned to the police with new information and the one witness who could make things right and convince the police he had been set up. For his efforts, he was told that a foreign witness was not credible, and now he needed *two* local witnesses.

Jake also knew they knew it, but for some reason they trashed his bike to make it look like he was guilty and were refusing to acknowledge anything. The police offered him his bike back after one hundred and forty days, yet to get it was going to cost him an additional two thousand yuan. Jake bellowed, informing them he would not pay that much money to get his bike back. A brand new bike would cost three thousand yuan, so he asked why he would pay two thousand for a bike after one of their officers had smashed it up.

In the end, he told the police to keep his bike as a present, and he would buy another one. Jake walked out with no bike and no more hassles, then a policeman called him and asked him to speak with the boss of the garage. They wanted to know how much they could get for the bike. It was a nice question, Jake thought. This time the bike was worth only three hundred yuan. It was like buying something where there are no rules. Finally, for five hundred yuan he got his bike back, but only because he spoke Chinese and had put enough pieces together to get him off the charges.

Had Jake been any other foreigner, with little or no Chinese background, his situation would have turned out quite different. In fact, very badly. Setups of this nature happen quite frequently in China. At least three participants were involved in this particular set up, with one seriously injured all for the sake of making a few bucks.

For a foreigner to end up in a similar situation would not be unrealistic, and the outcome may have been much different, especially when it involves communicating in a foreign language. Jake knew how things worked, and I was fortunate to have him constantly watching my back.

Why do you throw such angry words, Pepen?
I do not know, as sometimes haste will come,
Although best not to bottle it up,
Pour instead in a forgiveness cup.

Why do you look so troubled, Pepen?
I do not know, as worries thrive,
Although unsettled thoughts move to and fro,
Unclouded are those free to flow.

Why do you weep such rueful tears, Pepen?
I do not know, as sadness works that way,
Although translucent moments may begin,
Salt droplets cleanse from deep within.

Pepen, what is that look you now portrait?
I do not know, as it simply shall unfold,
Although heavy burden, conscience sighs,
New hope brings with it compromise.

Chapter 10
Banking, Chinese-Style!

Pay day! Six thousand yuan cash, all in hundreds, counted out for all to see.

Before leaving home, I was advised that if I had a Visa card I should pay any excess money on the card, and it would be less hassle and easier to save. Lindsay went with me to the Bank of China to translate for me. The teller informed Lindsay that my gold card Visa was not an international card and could not be used for saving money. I relayed to Lindsay that I was not saving money on the card, but was making a payment on the balance owing. Still, they insisted the card was not an international card and money could not be saved on it.

"Lindsay," I said, frustrated, "tell them it is a gold card and automatically recognized and accepted all over the world, so therefore is as an international card."

She made one last attempt on my behalf, but it wasn't going to happen, at least in Wuhan. What was normally such a simple procedure suddenly turned into an aggravating inconvenience. How would I get money from point A to point B? The option of carrying that kind of cash around didn't appeal to me. There was no choice but to open a savings account and deposit the money.

Back at the school, fuming mad, Jake laughed and said, "You know, I tried this also, but the banks will not allow you to do anything with a Visa. It is too complicated."

"That's retarded," I said. "This is the biggest country in the world and they don't have an up-to-date banking system?"

"No."

"How do I get my money home then?" I asked.

"Western Union," he replied.

"OK, so I'll get the bank to change the money over and send it, right?"

"It doesn't work that way," he said with a laugh. "To do it at the bank is very complicated. The only way to get foreign currency is to buy it through the black market."

"What? Are you insane? You're kidding me, right?"

"No, trust me. It is very simple. Mac and I do it all the time, so I will help you. I deal with the same guy all the time, and he will meet with us here at the school."

"This is for real?"

"Yes," he replied, hesitating before he continued. "Oh, one more thing, you can also only send seven thousand yuan through Western Union at one time."

It was so ridiculous and so hard to fathom, I could only shake my head. China is an enormous country with a banking system so far behind they can't even do a simple Visa transaction. It was unbelievable. What kind of country doesn't change money or do Visa transactions or, even more important, how do the banks stay in business? What a screwed-up system.

Jake took the liberty of making all the arrangements with his black market contact to ensure the transaction could take place the following day. We were to meet with his contact in front of my bank during lunch to exchange my entire Chinese life savings for Canadian funds.

When Jake and I arrived at the bank, the man was waiting. The three of us entered the lobby of the bank, where we sat on a couch near the window. Our transaction then began to take place. Looking to Jake for clues after sitting down, he told me to exchange my envelope of Chinese cash for the Canadian cash with the black market man at the same time. Each of us counted the stack of hundreds we had just received to ensure the money was all in order. The experience was so uncomfortable, I felt like a drug dealer doing business in public.

After completing the transaction, Jake asked for the money and my bank book, then went to the teller window, where he asked the teller to deposit the cash into my account to show as Canadian funds. With one money transaction completed, I still had another to go, and there was only one Western Union, located in Hankou, that didn't have a limit on how much money could be sent at one time.

Jake was unavailable to accompany me to Hankou to wire the money, so the following Saturday, Mac, the Russian English teacher, volunteered. Twelve-thirty the following Saturday, after classes, we made a stop at the bank to pick up the Canadian funds before catching a bus across town to Hankou.

Because it was Saturday, the branch I usually dealt with didn't have the money and didn't carry foreign currency on the weekends; however, they could order it and have it available the following Monday. I suddenly had an overwhelming feeling it was going to be one of those days. With Mac leaving for Russia in a few days, time was of the essence. Mac asked the teller if any of the banks in Hankou had the money. The main branch was in Hankou, and Mac asked the teller to call them and see if they had any Canadian funds available. After trying several times, there was no answer. Our only option was to take our chances at the hour-long journey.

We were in business. The bank had the money, and off we ventured to the Western Union, about a twenty-minute walk away. When we got there, Mac began asking for someone in specific, a woman he knew and dealt with on a regular basis. After speaking with her briefly, he asked me to give her the money. Then there was a frustrating blow: she couldn't send the money unless it was in American funds.

"You have got to be kidding me!" I bellowed.

"I'm so sorry, I didn't know. It's OK, we'll get it changed, don't worry," Mac apologized.

101

"I'm not sure, Mac, this day just seems to get better and better."

"We have all afternoon to make this happen. I'm not going anywhere until it's done," Mac said with a reassuring laugh.

All I could do was smile, shake my head and thank him for being so patient.

There were two banks nearby, so after exiting the Western Union, Mac and I entered the first one, presenting the Canadian money for exchange at the till, but was told that only one of the banks could change it over, the one I had just gotten the money from.

As we began the twenty-minute hike back, out of nowhere, the skies opened up, packing high winds and torrential downpours. Oh man, I thought, perfect, just perfect. My umbrella was absolutely useless, and it took both hands to grip it just to hang on. Our only alternative was to seek shelter for the next ten to fifteen minutes in a nearby store and wait it out.

After entering the bank, Mac began to speak with the same clerk who originally gave me the money. Clearly, I could tell by his facial and body expressions we had run into another glitch. Because it was Saturday and the stock exchange companies were closed, there was no one in the bank available to convert the exchange rate, making it impossible to change the funds into U.S. dollars.

"Can't they just use the rate from yesterday?" I asked Mac.

He laughed and shook his head. "No, because they don't have the rate for today."

"That's retarded!" I retorted, throwing my hands in the air. "I don't believe this! The rate for today will be the same as yesterday. We exchange money all the time on Saturday at home."

Mac was beginning to share my frustration, but he still had one more card up his sleeve. He asked me to wait inside the bank, telling me he would be right back. Outside the bank were several black market contact men that Mac had pointed out when we first arrived at the bank to withdraw the funds. Several minutes later he returned, arriving with two men.

In the center of the bank were several sofas. The four of us sat facing the tellers and began doing business. After Mac spoke with them, he told me they would exchange one thousand dollars for seven hundred and twenty U.S. dollars. Determining the conversion amount of foreign currency was never one of my strong suits. Earlier that week I had looked up the exchange rate on the Internet, and a thousand Canadian dollars was approximately seven hundred and fifty or sixty U.S., so I had some idea at least how much it was then. It wasn't far off, but far enough.

Mac made an attempt to find out from the teller what the exchange rate was the previous Friday, but that still required access to the computers, not accessible on Saturdays. Why didn't that surprise me? My only other alternative and absolute last resort was to send the cash by FedEx, and I considered even that to be iffy. Mac began to translate while I began bartering for a better price, starting at seven hundred and forty American dollars. The best they would offer was seven hundred and thirty, and at that point I really didn't have much choice. The transaction took place in clear sight of the tellers, and I handed one of the men my money.

The man proceeded to approach the teller wicket, took out his bankbook and presented it to the teller. Mac walked up to the counter and stood beside the man, watching, listening and began to laugh. Right in front of us, an illegal transaction of money began to take place.

"Look, the teller just watched the entire transaction take place, yet the bank will do this transaction knowing that these guys are from the black market, yet for you, they will not."

Once the man exchanged the money, he handed me the money in front of the teller and waited as I counted it all out to make sure it was all there. The bank officials could do nothing. They couldn't prove we weren't friends or business associates, and could prove nothing. What a way to do banking!

After wrapping things up at the bank, we made our way back to the Western Union, hitting two more torrential downpours with more driving winds. Finally, the transfer was completed, yet in the end I really had no idea how much money would actually arrive at the other end and, frankly, at that point I didn't care.

It was getting on in the afternoon. Neither of us had eaten anything, so Mac asked if I would be interested in McDonald's, his treat. Normally I would have said no to McDonald's, but I was so hungry, tired and frustrated, I didn't care anymore. Once we had eaten, our endless dilemmas of the day at an end, for the moment everything seemed trivial as we began to make our way home.

The weather was still rainy, windy and rough. It was rush hour and neither of us where interested in sitting through the grueling sardine ride back through crawling traffic. Instead, Mac suggested we take the ferry across the river if they were still running, and catch a taxi on the other side. Unaware there even was a passenger ferry, I was all for it, jumping at the opportunity.

During the crossing, Mac pointed out a docked passenger ship from Shanghai. What an extraordinary-looking piece of work. It looked as though it was an older boat or perhaps just weatherbeaten. The bottom section of the ship was similar to a regular passenger liner, but the architecture of the top was built as a traditional ancient Chinese-style building, including the red roof. From a distance it was the most amazing-looking floating structure I had ever seen.

The ride back was very relaxing and gave me a chance to collect myself before going home to an empty house. Hank had left that morning for Taiwan for two weeks and was to return the last two weeks of summer camp.

It was almost a perfect week of teaching; however, there were always exceptions: I had two classes of older students that weren't worth my time or my effort. On Thursday, at the last class of the day, the anxiety begins long before ever entering the classroom. Out came the Game Boys, comic books and whatever else they had tucked away in their bags. The girls were doing their usual unproductive projects and talking amongst themselves, but learning English was not part of that curriculum.

Not one would participate in anything I had put together or planned. There was no way they were going to even attempt to try or actually find out if what I had planned was any fun. One by one they sat shaking their heads no, then continued doing what I had interrupted. My entire preparation was out the window, and I was dying. There is no getting or holding the attention of the little ingrates, so what the hell is the point to all of this? I thought. I'm out of there!

After walking out of class, I was intercepted by Elly as I passed her desk. The look on my face must have said it all, so she asked what was wrong.

"You know what, Elly. I prepared and arranged an entire lesson for this class to make it fun. They won't even try, and it's just a waste of my time and your money. Find someone else to teach them! They obviously aren't here because they want to be, and they certainly aren't interested in learning English!"

Elly walked back to the classroom with me, and suddenly there was silence, not a word. She asked me to point out the students who were giving me trouble. In my opinion, none of them wanted to learn. The quiet, reserved Elly I knew blew a gasket on them, all of them, and they made a pathetic attempt to participate when she left. To say they were less than happy with me after she left would have been an understatement, but I didn't care.

After class I continued the conversation with Elly regarding the same class. I pointing out that if they were only here for a holiday, then the school should find them another teacher, a Chinese who could speak English. I refused to waste my time on an entire class of children who obviously didn't want to be there, let alone learn.

The following day in my second class began with Tim, an instigator, surrounded by his buddies while he played with his Game Boy. Just as the principal walked past the window, I thought I'd put it to an end before it got started. I left the room and called her in. She immediately began screaming at all of them, then confiscated all of the games. If they wanted them back, they had to collect them at the office on their way out to go home.

It didn't matter what nationality children are, the silent treatment is the same. If looks could kill, I would have been dead two or three times over. I spent the first fifteen minutes teaching half a class of students who were so ticked at me they turned their head the other direction, ignoring me when I spoke to them. It was good for a laugh.

Adding insult to injury, the remainder of the class wanted to play a game of Tic-Tac-Toe, good for testing their skills and intelligence. After splitting the class in half to make two teams, I then drew a blank nine square grid on the board. The rules behind the game were quite simple. A representative from each team did "paper, scissors, rock" to see who got the draw. I would asked the winner a question about a previous unit, and they had to answer by guessing the action of a word, spelling the word, or identifying the picture to receive an X or O in a square.

I was well aware the problem students couldn't answer many of the questions, while the girls could. The boys had no problem winning the toss for a chance at the square, but couldn't answer questions, spell or identify anything I had just taught them. The girls, on the other hand, were kicking their cocky little behinds. Jim and Tim, who never participated or answered any questions, became so angry they refused to play the game anymore. I leaned down to both boys with in a firm tone.

"You couldn't answer one single question, and you have learned nothing, so you lost. Why do you come? I have taught all of this in the last three classes. If you stopped talking during class and pay attention, then maybe you would learn something. I suggest you go home and study what we've been doing in class, because I'm not wasting any more time on either of you!"

Ah, that felt good, whether they understood or not.

Jake and I went out for lunch together later, and as we walked he talked to me, knowing I was wound right up. Even after a couple of years, he said he had the same problems I was having. To try and lift my spirits a little, he told me if I ever had an opportunity to observe a primary and middle school in session I would find a huge difference in comparison to where we taught. The children sit in the classroom very disciplined, not speaking unless spoken to; however, the teachers did not teach the way we did, and very few got involved with the children when teaching them. From his observations of some of those schools, the atmosphere was more like prison or military camp. The teacher usually sat at their desk for the entire class, reading, with little or no class participation or interaction. The students spent the entire class doing assignments. For the most part, many of the children who attended our school were spoiled and came from well-off government families who lived and were housed on a street nearby.

The previous Christmas, Jake had asked one of the students he taught what he wanted for Christmas. The little boy's response floored him. The only thing he wished for was for all Chinese teachers to be dead. It wasn't exactly an answer many would be prepared to hear from a small child.

Schooling is a much different way of life for children in China, yet in that respect, one has to wonder. If getting them to participate or become involved in games to help them learn and at the same time give them a brief moment of laughter, perhaps I could overlook *some* of the misconduct from time to time. Sometimes I was lucky enough to offset a disastrous class with a class that is an absolute pleasure, only to be accompanied again by another unforeseen disaster right after.

During one class, while demonstrating the word "throw," I used a small ball a little harder than a sponge ball. I hurled the ball across the room to the back wall and then again. The second time my hand slipped. The ball nailed a little girl square in the side of the head. My eyeballs grew as big as saucers, and the entire class and one parent outside the room began to laugh hysterically. I immediately ran back to see if she was all right, giving her a hug to say I was sorry. I felt really bad, but she was a trouper, laughing, holding the side of her head, telling me she was OK. The entire class was rolling by this time.

The following Monday morning, I walked into my second class and rolled my eyes. Jim and Tim were in their usual spots in the back, playing with the Game Boy. Great! Apparently there was no rest or grace period for the wicked!

As class got under way, Jim's hand began going up for every question. What was this? I thought. Was I seeing things? Had he taken my advice and studied? Apparently he didn't like to be made a fool of and was doing whatever it took to change his image. Tim, on the other hand, could care less. As class continued, Jim was so eager to answer every question and pronounce every word that I didn't want to discourage him. That would be like kicking him into the hole he was trying to dig himself out of.

As the game of Tic-Tac-Toe progressed, Jim moved to the front of the class to participate. This was impressive I thought and progress was progress, no matter what form it came in. To further encourage Jim's new learning curve, I pulled him aside after class, praising him on his efforts to learn, congratulating him by giving two thumbs up for a job well done. With a confused expression, he replied, "Thank you, Teacher, you're welcome." Perhaps there was hope after all.

Two days later, I gave the same class an oral test, and Jim came through with no errors. Tim, like Spitter Bob, had a short attention span, but a natural ability to do well regardless. A couple of students did poorly, answering only two questions correctly, and I had to give them a failing mark. After handing the tests in to the staff after class, I was informed that we could not fail any students. Marks had to be 80 percent and higher, therefore the failing marks were changed. The reason was because the parents paid a lot of money for their children to attend our school.

Although I did not agree with this logic, I was not there to question the rules, only to follow them. Having said that, I had advised them that somewhere down the road the child usually suffers because of it. Knowing they would continue to attend my classes, I still had the power to try and turn things around and, hopefully, before I left I could do what I could to make a difference.

The days begin to get hotter as a thick haze
Blankets the stillness of the lake, yet today
The water seems to have a similar haze about it.

As you breathe in, the rendering odors seem to permeate
Your senses, when suddenly, a motorboat rushes past,
Breaking the stillness, blending in with the continual
Passing of motorists gripped to their horns.
For today, at least, the sound of crashing metal
Was absent and you wonder why.

Still, there seems to be peacefulness about it,
Until a faint stroke, stroke as you glance up,
Catching a glimpse of kayaks propelling by in unison,
Almost as though they were never in sight at all.

Behind, the sound of birds chirping, although somewhat
Of an unfamiliar tune, when abruptly a steel pipe is
Dropped on the concrete nearby, and they scatter to
Escape the commotion; however, this disruption only
Seems to resonate their songs, at least for an instant.

In comparison to the overpowering pandemonium of
Costly construction equipment; or the deafening,
Head-clutching vibration of jackhammers or the
Constant repetitious echo of hammers or power tools.
Perhaps it is a blessing, for today, here
In this world, such luxuries do not exist.

Chapter 11
Summer Surprises

Summer had officially arrived, bringing with it the sweltering, muggy, stifling heat that sucked the life right out of you. By seven a.m. you prayed for a breeze, as your wardrobe started to fit like nylons, forbidding your clothes to leave your skin. By midday the hot temperatures left you feeling drained, sticky and dripping wet. Any shaded areas or seating available along the streets were carpeted with locals lying down to seek one ounce of brief refuge. During the summer months the temperature reaches forty degrees Celsius, and by then it doesn't matter what type of thermometer you look at.

As the weather changed, so too did the smells as I walked along the lake. One day I couldn't help but notice the aroma coming from the lake. Some fish were floating belly up near the shoreline and out toward the middle of the lake, but it wasn't the normal dead fish smell. The dead fish were frying from the intense heat and smelled identical to fish being cooked on the stove.

There were probably thousands of outdoor street markets and merchants throughout the city selling fresh fruits, meats and vegetable products that basked in the sun all day. Not unlike the fish, food sitting in heat could only mean one thing. Even under a canopy shelter at those temperatures, food will cook or go rancid. Some of the fruits and vegetables could probably survive, but by the end of the day, everything will have lost its freshness to end up dilapidated and wilted looking.

As for the meat, after having a firsthand look at how meat is slaughtered or prepared, seeing the open markets with no refrigeration, the lack of hygienic measures and swarming flies, I would just as soon give it a miss and become a vegetarian.

The stench of garbage could not escape the dredges of heat, multiplying in intensity two or three times throughout the day. Lingering smells you came to recognize in passing suddenly clutched your senses and wouldn't let go until a much more potent one replaced it. That too became a reality the further I continued to walk.

Many people in Wuhan had air conditioners in their homes, but they were so expensive to run people would only turn them on when temperatures hit thirty-five degrees Celsius. What an unbelievable way to live.

Some of the newer buses were equipped with air-conditioning. Chinese will bypass a bus with no air to wait for one that does, piling over top of one another, packing the buses, trying to find some relief at least for the ride home. The drawback for such luxury was that the rate was almost double the standard fare. It didn't take long to figure out that when that many people were crammed in a bus, air or not, it makes no difference. With that much body heat, whatever cool air was circulating quickly ceased to exist. Crammed in like sardines, one could only assume there was no such thing as load capacity. It was rare to board a bus in either direction and not end up buried. If you were unfortunate enough to get shoved to the back or somewhere between the two exit doors, more than likely, you won't get off at your stop.

Being the first, even second, in line to board a bus never made any difference. Somehow, among the chaos, I would always end up last on. It was as if the planet was going to explode at any second, and boarding the bus was the only alternative to save yourself. This aggressive behavior not only happened on the buses, it was a ritual within the entire public service sector.

Ninety percent of the drivers jam the brakes to the floor, weaving in and out of traffic at high rates of speed, tossing people everywhere. It wasn't unusual to hear a constant high-pitch squeal that at times was so bad it would deafen those with perfect hearing. For break shoes and pads to last a week would be nothing short of a miracle, yet at the same time it amazed me how drivers avoided creaming the vehicles in front or beside them.

There was always that rare occasion when you jumped on the bus and actually had a seat to choose from, and if you were really lucky the bus came equipped with a stereo or television system, or both. On one occasion I had that rare opportunity. A beautiful Chinese arrangement of flutes and stringed instruments flowed from the stereo overhead, accompanied by an Asian woman singing a soothing piece, as I briefly drifted off to a place of peace and serenity in the comfort of a seat.

When it came to the elderly riding the bus, I couldn't help but notice how they were treated. When a Chinese occupy a seat it is regarded as gold and they won't give it up to anyone, not even the elderly carrying bags or parcels.

One day a feeble elderly woman boarded a crowded bus lugging a load of bags. Curious, I waited to see if anyone would give up a seat for her. As she bounced around like a flimsy rag doll, I was surprised to find it just wasn't going to happen. Finally, I tapped her on the shoulder, stood up and offered her my seat, but made sure no one but her got it. While the vultures stared me down, I shook my head, smiling, knowing the woman was grateful. Then she made a gesture of thanks. It felt good, and I felt good for doing it.

Every now and then performances were held in the walking square near work. What an amazing display of talent, I thought, as I stopped to watch several teams of seven and eight-year old children competing in a ballroom dance marathon. In the sweltering heat, dressed to the nines, the boys looked so handsome in their black dress pants and a white long sleeved shirt and black dress shoes. The girls, with their hair all done up in buns and bows, were dressed in beautiful frilly dresses, all looking so sophisticated. They looked so pretty and graceful as they moved around the square, never missing a beat. To see an Asian, or any child for that matter, dancing in that fashion was a rare treat and something I had never seen.

When the dancing was over, I continued along the square toward the bus stop. A father balancing his young child between his two forearms caught my attention. Upon closer observation, the father was using his forearms as a seat to enable the child to do his business in one of several square planter boxes that had trees planted in the center, while the father held him. Chinese children do not wear diapers. They wear outfits specially designed for children who are potty training with the entire crotch gapping open from front to back. When a baby or young child needs to relieve themselves, the parents simply rest them over their arms wherever until they were finished.

July first was officially summer holidays, and with it came sudden changes. It had been brought to my attention that a week-long school trip to Bejing was being planned for the second week of August. Twice a year, in May and August, staff, parents and students travel together for a week to different parts of China. As I was the only foreign English teacher left to teach, it was compulsory for me to attend.

The trip would involve many hours traveling by train. My eyebrows did flips upon hearing the news, and I suddenly pondered how much hair I would have left by the end of a week. If the children traveling on the trip included any of the horrid little brats I'd had the pleasure of teaching, I could hardly wait.

Because Jake and Mac were leaving for the summer, Hank informed me I would be the only foreign English teacher at the school, and hours would increase. Instead of teaching twenty hours a week as stipulated in my contract, Hank asked me if I would try working twenty-four hours per week. It would only be for a short period of time, however, and would also mean an extra eighty yuan per hour for any hours above twenty. Agreeing to give it a try for one week, I made it clear that should it became too much, he would have to cut them back. Not really sure he was aware of the problems, I also informed him that if the children were a little more disciplined and wanted to learn, I wouldn't mind. The fact that they were draining every ounce of energy I had trying to make classes fun was really beginning to wear me down.

Shortly after my conversation with Hank, Jake told me the reason my hours were being increased. Most of the month of August was a holiday, and there were no classes at all; therefore, from my standpoint, no pay.

Sometimes, when it comes to the Chinese, everything seems to be a big secret. Instead of giving the entire picture, they will only reveal bits and pieces, filling you in on left out pieces at the last minute. It occurred to me my contract had been set up otherwise. Even if there were no classes, I would be paid regardless, yet my situation wasn't quite that cut and dry.

There was still the uncertain matter of my work visa. At the end of the month my visa would expire, so it needed to be dealt with. Shortly after my arrival, I had given Hank all the documentation he had requested to have the work visa completed. However, he missed the deadline. I approached Jake regarding my options and learned this same approach is used with many foreigners teaching in China.

"In order to extend the visa and rectify the problem," Jake explained, "you have to leave the country for a couple of days."

"Leave the country? What do you mean leave the country?" I questioned. "And go where?"

"Hong Kong."

"What the hell are you talking about?" I asked. "Hong Kong is part of China, so how would that qualify as leaving the country?"

"Technically, Hong Kong is not part of China and is considered a separate country from the rest of China."

"You're joking, right?"

"No!" He laughed. "I can't explain this, but it's OK. It happens to many teachers.

"I can't speak Chinese, so if the plan is to send me alone, don't expect to see me back any time soon."

"Don't worry." He laughed again. "It's not like the rest of China. Everyone in Hong Kong speaks English."

After our conversation, Jake decided to enlighten me with an experience he had concerning a work visa. While attending the university, he found a part-time job teaching English, his present teaching position. One night, shortly after being hired, he observed some visitors who were wandering the facilities taking pictures. Assuming they were parents who wanted to get a better idea of the school set up, he thought nothing more of it.

In China, and any other country for that matter, not only is it against regulations to teach without a visa, as a foreigner attending university in China, it is against the law to teach at all.

The following evening, the photographer, an informant, returned with the China police, asking Jake if he taught at the school. He told them yes and was then asked to show his working visa, of which he had none. Eleven o'clock at night, Jake was arrested and taken to police headquarters for questioning, were he was harassed and interrogated by police. For the next few hours, Jake was drilled about the rules of working in China as a foreigner, and the consequences for disobeying those rules. Jake informed them it wasn't his fault, that he was innocent, asking them if something could be done to resolve the situation. They asked him to pay them five thousand yuan and he could go. After telling them he had just started working and didn't have that kind of money, they told him to return to the station the following morning and pay them five hundred yuan. He agreed.

The following morning Jake returned. The officers on duty were much more pleasant. When Jake asked why he was put through all the harassment and hassle for five hundred yuan, the officers reiterated the same story from the previous night. In the end, Jake had to pay the five hundred yuan, and the school had to shell out the remaining forty-five hundred.

As summer began to get underway, hours and rules were changing faster than I could change my shorts. Liela began dictating my hours, even when I was to arrive at school each day. The contract was set up specifically with twenty hours of teaching, plus class preparation, yet Liela was bluntly informing me my hours of teaching were forty hours a week because I was now considered a full-time teacher. I told her it was not about to happen, and she would have to take it up with Hank.

Later that day, Liela handed me my class schedule, revealing that my hours had just shot up from the twenty-four Hank and I had previously agreed on to twenty-eight, not including the free session of English Corner for those who wanted to learn English. Mac had been teaching it and preferred not to anymore, and Jake refused from the beginning because it was free.

English Corner was scheduled for two o'clock, but my classes finished at eleven thirty, meaning I had to wait around and do nothing until then. In the meantime, Liela prepared my schedule for the following two days of classes, Friday and Saturday. Friday I was scheduled to teach six classes, and the two on Saturday had changed to four. Beyond pissed off by that point, I set out for a walk to cool off. Lindsay entered the room to tell me lunch would be arriving shortly, and before I knew it, I was yelling at Lindsay, taking my frustrations out on her. When I finished, she confirmed the fact that full-time teachers all work forty hours a week.

"No!" I bellowed. "Maybe the Chinese teachers work forty hours a week, but I am contracted to teach twenty, period!"

Realizing it was not her problem, I asked her not to worry about it, apologizing for my outburst, and told her I would discuss it further with Hank.

Hank's office was on the main floor, one level below, and when I discovered he wasn't in I had to return to my office. As I walked past the principal's office, Lindsay and a few other staff members were gathered, no doubt discussing the events of the day. Shortly thereafter, Hank arrived and had been filled in by the time he intercepted me on my way back from the toilet.

"I understand you want to talk to me."

"Yes," I replied.

Once confirmed, he asked me to come down to his office after lunch. Never actually having the guts to stand up for myself, I was about to embark on my first confrontation with Hank and his staff. Although it was something quite new and gutsy for me, I didn't really care, because they began breaching the contract more and more by the minute. Really, I had nothing to lose, and also had the option of jumping on a plane and going home if things weren't sorted out. Before entering his office, I had everything I wanted to discuss, all my facts and figures, written on paper.

"First," I noted, "I have three classes on Thursday morning, then I am expected to hang around until two o'clock to teach English Corner, which I'm to understand I don't get paid for. Also, did we or did we not just have a discussion about my hours not three days ago? The arrangement you set up with me was for twenty-four hours per week."

Hank snickered slightly, then apologized, informing me it was his fault.

"Hank, that's not the point," I pointed out. "You and I discussed and settled all this. Suddenly, I'm getting rules and orders thrown at me after the fact, contradicting everything, and that tends to piss me off."

The principal and office staff prepared the schedules for the classes, but he forgot to tell them about our arrangement and promised to straighten out the misunderstanding. He was curious to know if there was anything else.

"Yes," I continued, "according to your staff, I am now suddenly expected to work a forty-hour week. My contract stipulates twenty. This morning, Liela handed me my hours, and in less than four days of our conversation I'm up to twenty-eight hours a week."

Hank agreed that full-time teachers work forty hours per week.

"Perhaps your Chinese teachers are obligated to work forty hours per week; however, I am not. Once my class preparation and twenty hours of teaching are completed, I'm finished. I don't do office work and wasn't hired to do so. I am not and will not hang out for the sake of hanging out," I firmly responded.

As a full-time foreign teacher, he wanted to give me first opportunity to work more hours and make more money, because in August there would be no classes and a nine-day school trip.

I could appreciate that he wanted to give me the opportunity to make more classes and more money. However, I wasn't familiar with how things work in China, and I let him know that if I was to know these things, he had to talk to me and tell me. I don't read minds, and he couldn't just assume that I would just do things. He laughed again and said he knew and apologized for getting busy and forgetting.

Within half an hour of ending the meeting and squaring things away, Hank called me into the principal's office, where we discussed and sorted out my schedule. Not thirty seconds passed when Hank began translating changes on behalf of the principal. The following Monday classes were scheduled for the afternoon. Under the assumption that classes were going to be running through Monday evening, I was confused to find that classes would be taking place from two o'clock onward. I rolled my eyes, directing my reply at Hank.

"This is what I'm talking about. Why didn't you tell me this before scheduling my hours?"

When things began to build up and snowball, my positive outlook and cheerful disposition were sliding by the minute. If the situation had taken a different turn, I was quite prepared to pack my bags, catch a plane and say the hell with it. The fact was, however, that would have been too easy, and I'm not a quitter. I'm not sure I will ever figure the Chinese out, but taking the plunge into confrontation did feel good, and I felt much better.

Two days following, I received my schedule for Saturday's classes. I still had four classes, and nothing had changed, so I stroked off the last one with a pen. Liela stood watching me do it, then went on another rampage. She demanded to know why I crossed the class off my schedule and told me not to before erasing it.

"No!" I bellowed. "I have three classes today, not four!"

She tore off in a huff, returning soon after, protesting they had no English teacher for that class. I didn't care. I had three classes that day, not four. If she had a problem with it she could take it up with Hank and the principal. Liela left again, returning in a flustered panic to tell me Jake and Mac were already teaching classes during that time and no other English teachers were available. She began pleading with me. Finally, I caved and told her I would teach the class, but it wasn't one I was particularly fond of. In the end, she did find a foreign Chinese teacher to take over the class. Essentially, my dilemmas had settle down for the time being. All the same, I wasn't sure if they were pushing my buttons or just testing my limitations.

What do you see beyond the streets
Of concrete, broken bricks and dirt?
As I watch from the tiny eight-by-eight restaurant
Across the alley, the woman scolds him, laughing,
And he kicks her, screaming. The tear-filled
Screams echo, filling the long, narrow street.

Is this life you lead? All you have, but a square
Concrete room, where in the morning your clothing
Is washed in a small bucket, later for you to bathe in.
I watch as he screams, maybe four years old, standing in
The middle of the alley, wearing nothing but his tiny sandals
And dirty shorts, again all eyes upon him, to laugh, ridicule.

Was it fruit that he wanted, perhaps just something
To eat as he began to edge his way closer, grabbing
A peach from one of the wicker baskets.
Suddenly, he screams. She grabs him, discipline
Begins, and he slaps her arm. All eyes are upon him
Now, laughing as he stands with his hands behind
His back screaming, whimpering.

Alas, his brother takes him by the hand, disappearing
Down the long, narrow alley, for I can only watch, wonder,
With little understanding of this life that you live.

Lotus flowers at the Summer Palace in Chengde

Meng Jiagnu Temple garden near Shanhaiguan

Fish park in Hankou

Chu Market, East Lake, Wuhan

Jie Fang Park, Wuhan

Yaiy Taoist Temple

Gazebo in park near Wuhan University

Fishing boat in East Lake, Wuhan

Yu Fo Si Buddhist Temple, Shanghai

Summer Palace grounds, Chengde

Pu Tuozang Cheng Temple, Chengde

Old Shanghai, Chang Huang

Jie Fang Park pagodas

Section of Wuhan University

Park in Wuhan

Chapter 12
A Step Back in Time

My teaching skills were improving, and I had added the Chinese translation of "out" and "quiet" somewhat effective, yet received the most peculiar looks. I still had a few uncontrollable classes of troublemakers, and it was always apparent the moment you entered the room.

Fortunately for me, Spitter Bob's class had been downsized. Bob and Billy were now gone, reducing my stress level significantly. Although Pat was still controlling the class, shutting off lights, throwing things and ticking off the girls. Although Hank and Jack appeared as though they wanted to learn, they always followed Pat's lead. While I chose to ignore Pat's moments in the spotlight, the girls had had enough and chose not to put up with him, locking him out of the classroom.

Pat and Rosa weren't participating at all and still couldn't speak any English. Still, getting them involved would prove to be optimistic but would also be tricky. I could only hope the time I had left would be enough to turn things around and they would learn something. I began playing a game to get the entire class involved. To my surprise, Jack and Frank joined in without hesitation. It didn't take long before Pat and Rosa joined in as well, briefly at first, but it was a start. Perhaps there was hope after all, I thought.

During one of those classes, I escorted one problem child into the hall for ten minutes as punishment. Hank had arrived shortly thereafter, talking to the boy, laughing, while observing my class through the window. It didn't appear the boy found Hank all that amusing, so I decided to bring the boy back in. Before letting him in, I asked him if he was going to be good. He nodded then, returned to his seat, behaving for the remainder of the class.

June 21 had arrived, one day before the annual Chinese Dragon Boat Festival. The staff members were preparing to celebrate this age-old tradition, which according to them falls on the fifth day of the fifth month of the Chinese calendar. According to the Chinese lunar calendar, the fifth month was just beginning, and the Chinese people prepare to celebrate this on June 22 each year. Having participated in a dragon boat race at home the previous year, the legend behind this event held one of special interest for me.

Elly had brought in some traditional zongzi for me to try, a pyramid-shaped dumpling made of glutinous rice wrapped in either bamboo or reed leaves to give it a special flavor. As the staff watched me eat, they told me zongzi varied throughout China, and also explained the festival had been symbolized by eating zongzi and racing dragon boats for thousands of years. The variety I had sampled was very tasty, very sweet, yet was somewhat gummy in texture.

The Tuen Ng Festival is held in honor of Qu Yuan. He drowned himself in the Mi Lo River some 2,000 years ago in protest against corrupt rulers. Chinese legend recounts that the town folk, intent on saving his body, beat drums to scare away fish. They also threw bamboo leaves stuffed with rice into the water to keep the fish from eating Qu's corpse. Today, the festival centers around the dragon boat races. The boats are over 10 meters long and are specially decorated with dragon heads and tails. They're also quite narrow, affording just enough space for two paddlers to sit abreast. The craft are manned by a crew of between 20 to 22 oarsmen that paddle to the beat of a heavy drum played by a drummer at the bow, while a steersman guides from astern.[10]

With the arrival of August, time and summer seemed to be passing quickly, so I returned to Hànkou, curious as to how much the Yangtze (Chang Jiang) River had risen since my first visit with Lindsay. At that time, the beach was exposed some distance from the shoreline, and the river was at its lowest. Water now covered two levels of retaining wall, submerging beach and immature trees along the park. Young children swam in the filthy brown water, jumping off some floating barges a few hundred feet from shore. Locals sat on submerged concrete benches or waded through murky water past their waist to find relief from the scorching heat.

The Chang Jiang, China's longest river, is 6300 kilometers long, and the third longest in the world. Originating in snow-covered Tanggula Shan in southwestern Qinghui, it cuts its way through Tibet and seven Chinese provinces before emptying into the East China Sea north of Shanghai. Between the towns of Fengjie, in Sichuan and Yichang, in Hubei, lie three great gorges.[12]

One evening, Elly and her son dropped by for a visit, and I asked about the flooding of the Yangtze River. They explained that much of the problems occurred during the reign of Chairman Mao Zedong in the 1950s, when he cut down trees to use as a source of fuel, resulting in deforestation and erosion. It is a fact that forest coverage slows down and absorbs the flow of water, and soil erosion is caused in part by forest reduction and cutting down trees. The flood of 1954, one of the biggest of the past century, caused serious damage to millions of hectors of land that devastated the entire area, killing many.

Over the past 2,000 years, the Yangtze has experienced 215 catastrophic floods. China's deforestation problem extends from the Qinghai-Tibet Plateau to the Yangtze River basin, once heavily forested. Forests have the ability to absorb and hold huge quantities of rainfall, therefore allowing water to seep slowly into the ground. Deforestation increased the amount of water being channeled into rivers during high rains.

Between the towns of Fengjie, in Sichuan, and Yichang, in Hubei, lie the three great gorges. Phase one began in 1194 and ended in 1997, with the first diversion of the Yangtze River. Phase two began in 1998. Phase three is scheduled to end in 2009.

Over the past 30 years, the dikes along the Yangtze River have been reinforced several times. China has spent millions of dollars for reforestation projects, many tied to preserving water flows in river systems that feed hydropower projects or combat soil erosion.

A concern is that heavy silt in the river will form thick deposits near the upstream end of the dam, clogging the major river channels of the city of Chongqing. Water pollution in the dammed Yangtze is expected to double as the dam traps pollutants from mines, factories and human settlements that in the past were flushed out to sea by the fast-moving Yangtze currents. There is a fear the reservoir created by the Three Gorges Dam will become a massive cesspool. Certain areas of the river are unfit for human use, and many people are facing resettlement.

Jake left at the end of July to visit Mac in Russia, then headed to Greece to meet with his parents to watch some of the Olympic games before returning to England. With both of them gone, there would no doubt be a few more dreaded classes than usual.

Now the first week of August, regular classes where quickly replaced with summer camp getting underway, and I was hopeful a new group of children replacing some of the old.

Around nine a.m., the first day of summer camp, there was a sudden sense of urgency as Liela flew into my office in a panic to inform me that I had to go with Lindsay across town to the immigration office in Hankou to look after my visa before it expired. Because Hank was still in Taiwan, he had made arrangements for Lindsay and Mr. Lou, a friend of his, to look after it.

Before the three of us finally jumped into a taxi for the half-hour ride to Hankou, Lindsay was still flying around the building like a chicken with her head cut off. Under the assumption we were on our way to apply for a work visa, it would soon become apparent things once again were not as they seemed.

En route, Mr. Lou and Lindsay were engaged in conversation, when Lindsay suddenly looked at me, confused and panicked, almost to the point of hyperventilating.

"We met at the hot springs when you and I were traveling around China," she unexpectedly blurted.

"What?" I replied, somewhat stunned.

"Our stories have to be the same in case the police ask questions," she explained in a serious tone.

Was I going to end up being interrogated? I thought. Lindsay was worried about what she was going to tell authorities regarding how she knew me, so I told her to tell them she was a university student returning to school in the fall, and we me while traveling.

With one dilemma out of the way, I asked her if I could use Hank's address at the house, but were quickly informed I could not. It was suddenly clear why Hank's friend was there to accompany us. He was there to supply information regarding my base address while traveling in China and staying in Wuhan. The scenario was becoming more and more obscure by the minute, and none of us had a clue what we were doing. All I knew was that our stories had to correspond with each other completely, and the possibility of me returning home was quickly becoming reality.

At the immigration office, Lindsay approached a police officer behind the desk to inquire as to what I needed to do. The officer gave her a form to have me fill out, which the two of us did together. Hank's friend made himself scarce, staying out of the loop unless we needed him for something. Once the form was completed, Lindsay submitted it to the officer, along with my passport and two recent pictures of me. It took less than five seconds for the officer to return the paperwork to Lindsay. She stood there, portraying the same look I had seen many times before, and I knew something was wrong.

"What is it?" I asked.

"There is a problem."

"What do you mean a problem? What kind of problem?"

"One moment, wait here," she said, bolting off in a panic to find Mr. Lou.

A few moments later both of them returned, almost expressionless, motioning me to follow them. As the three of us make our way to the second level through two heavy metal doors, Mr. Lou was on his cell phone, talking to someone.

When we reached the top of the stairs, we were met by a man and escorted to an office exhibiting executive characteristics. The two men spoke for the next five minutes while I sat with Lindsay, oblivious to what was taking place. When the conversation ended, the three of us left the building and got in a cab to make the thirty-minute ride back across town. When I finally asked what was going on, Lindsay told me the customs office wanted a signed rental agreement.

"You're kidding me, right? Why do I need a rent contract? I live with Hank!"

"You can't use Hank, and they won't extend the visa until they have a signed contract," she replied.

For the next few hours, Lindsay began putting a contract together. When she finished the contract, she asked me to sign it. The first thing that grabbed my attention was that the entire document was drafted in Chinese.

"Lindsay, I'm sure the contract is wonderful; however, it is entirely in Chinese. I don't speak or read Chinese, and I doubt whether the authorities would believe it as true."

This burst of realism sent her into a frenzy unlike any I had seen. Al, one of the Chinese/English teachers, had been within earshot and jumped in, offering to help. The two of them began the task of translating the entire document into English. Curious as to why there was such a rush was getting the better of me.

"Lindsay, why are you in such a panic? We can go back to the office first thing tomorrow morning."

"No, today is the last day. After today you can't get a visa."

Wow, now things were beginning to make sense, and they really had this last-minute thing down to a fine science.

"So you're telling me I may be returning home in a the next day or two?"

"Don't worry, we will get the visa."

At two-thirty that afternoon, once more chaos struck as Liela charged into my class to tell me I had to leave right away for the passport office. For the second time that day, the three of us fly across town by taxi in a mad rush to sort out my dilemma. Observing, saying nothing, I could only shake my head as I watched Lindsay sort through all the paperwork half a dozen times. As she began to fidget and babble, I realized it was also wearing off on me. Just then, something occurred to me. If the officer took guilty looks into account that day, Lindsay would have it wrapped up in a neat little package and had been pulled aside for interrogation without much difficulty.

Within less than a minute of Lindsay submitting the paperwork to the immigration official, I thought I was denied once again when Lindsay left me standing there to find Mr. Lou. Within a few minutes she returned, handing something to the officer. As the officer handed Lindsay the pick-up order, I knew we were in business.

Lindsay turned to me and smiled. "Everything is OK. Your passport will be ready to pick up on the ninth." Another dilemma was behind me, I thought, knowing my passport was now being taken care of and I could stay for a little while longer.

It was getting late when Lindsay called the school to let the principal know we were going to call it a day and take a cab home, but she had other plans and asked us to return to the school. Lindsay, Al and I all had birthdays within a couple days of each other, and a birthday dinner was planned at a local restaurant. I was grateful to have been included in the festivities.

Chapter 13
Action, Rolling!

While preparing for classes the following morning, Liela paraded into my office to inform me the local television station was coming to do a story.

"Cool, what are they doing a story about?" I asked.

"The children. They are going to film you teaching American-style eating."

"What? The entire class?"

"Ah, maybe, it's not for sure."

"Liela, don't you dare do this to me. All these place settings are usually only used by rich people, not average people. I don't even know what half this stuff is. How do you expect me to teach the children?"

Liela smiled. "It will be fine. Don't worry," she said.

"Liela, why do you always do this to me at the last minute?"

As I entered the classroom, the camera crew followed me in. Great, this was good, I thought, no work visa and my face was going to be plastered all over China. A documentary about teaching Chinese children Western eating etiquette using eight levels of utensils, half of

135

which I'd never heard of or used. With high hopes, the camera crew would move on after ten or fifteen minutes. I began counting the minutes, only to find I was running out of ideas, and they had not intention of leaving at all. I was dying, all by myself, on camera no less.

After drilling the names of sixteen or so pieces of cutlery into their heads, it was time to come up with something new, but I needed some help. Suddenly, I had an idea. It involved a student volunteering to play the role of a customer in a restaurant, while I played out the role of their server. Not one student wanted to volunteer, or participate at all for that matter. Oh, this sucked, I thought. There had to be one in the class who would help me out. Perhaps the camera crew was making them nervous, I thought. I approached Lacey, sitting at the back. She attended English Corner every week and spoke English quite well.

"Lacey, will you help me out? If anyone can do this, you can. Please, I'm dying here."

"Sure," she said.

Lacey was used to being in front of big audiences and cameras, and she was magnificent. She broke the ice for the remainder of the class as we entertained our audience with an old-fashioned mock Barbie Doll tea party. Who would have thought? If nothing else, demonstrating pretend cutlery made from Styrofoam would be good for a few laughs, film at eleven.

After two back-to-back classes teaching and learning the finer points of using knives, forks and spoons, we took everyone to the American Burger Restaurant close by. For lunch, they had a choice between chicken or pork chops and, my favorite, a tasty apple salad. The students weren't permitted to use chopsticks, only knives and forks. I had been given the responsibility of wandering amongst them, showing, helping each of them how to use each utensil properly. While helping one little girl cut her meat, the fork suddenly crumpled in my hand. The entire place broke into laughter.

The truth was, when the meat got cold, it became very tough, and as a result of that, the children were having a lot of difficulty cutting it. My meal had arrived, and I went to the far side of the room to join the others, only to find the principal and other staff teachers eating Chinese food. I believe in leading by example, and although it was their choice what they ate for lunch, I strongly disagreed. Nonetheless, our outing was a lot of fun and a great success, even for the camera crew.

It was so hot that week I decided to have all my hair cut off. The humidity was so bad I could no longer do anything with it, and I was beginning to look like a sheep dog. Yvonne spoke perfect English, so volunteered to go along, not only to translate, but because she also needed a trim.

Chinese hair salons are quite different from those in North America. The moment we walked in, we were ushered to a sink in the back room to have our head washed. If no sinks were available, you sit in a chair out front, where someone massages your head with shampoo prior to having it washed out. A wet or a dry shampoo, I soon discovered, is no ordinary wash. Not unlike any other shampoo parlor, it begins with the washing of your hair, then the woman, using her fingers and hands, massages every part of your neck, shoulders and head, until you are so relaxed it becomes difficult to stay awake. For the next twenty minutes you lay back in the crevasse of a sink, relax in a comfortable adjustable lounge chair, and are pampered with the most invigorating head massage you could ever imagine. At one point, Yvonne glanced over to see my eyes closed.

"Sharon, you are sleeping, aren't you?"

My eyes shut, smiling, I replied, "No, I'm only resting my eyes."

"Really?" she laughed.

I couldn't help think, as the massaged continued, if I had a choice between a foot and head massage, the head massage would win hands down. I didn't want to leave the chair. However, eventually all good things come to an end, and it was time for my haircut. Yvonne asked me how I wanted the hairdresser to cut my hair. At first, I wasn't sure, then said, "Just tell him to cut it all off, leaving about an inch on top.

Stunned, Yvonne's eyes grew wide. "You're serious, aren't you?" she asked.

"Yes."

"You are very brave," she replied, snickering.

"It's too hot, and besides, it will grow back."

By the time my haircut was finished, I had exactly what I wanted, one inch on top, spiked, with a little less at the back and on the sides. The entire session took an hour and a half, and was worth every penny. As we stood at the counter, waiting to pay, Yvonne glared at me, shook her head and laughed, but I didn't care. I liked it.

A couple of days passed, and I was suddenly one year older. My forty-fifth birthday had arrived. The day began with a beautiful Hallmark card online from my daughter, and birthday wishes from my parents. My lesson plans were already prepared when Liela once again showed up to make some last-minute changes.

"We are taking the children to McDonald's for lunch today, so can you prepare something to tell them about fast food restaurants? Maybe for fifteen minutes will be good."

"Fifteen minutes?" I stammered. "You have got to be kidding me, Liela," I said. "What can I possibly teach these children about fast food? It's a boring subject unless you're eating it."

"I know, I know, you can just tell them something and it will be fine," she continued.

"Why do you keep throwing these last-minute plans on me? I can't talk about fast food for fifteen minutes, there's nothing to tell. They won't understand anyway."

I wasn't sure exactly how I was going to tell them. How much could anyone say about fast food before boring the audience senseless? No less than a minute later, Liela had another request.

"Sharon," she asked, smiling, "can you also teach the younger children about colors?"

"What? These children should already know about colors, they're in level four."

"The principal thinks some of the students are very young and don't know the colors, so if you review, it will be good. We are having a birthday party today for you at McDonald's, and we want the children to know about colors."

"A birthday party?" I asked. "Why? The principal took Lindsay, Al and I out for our birthday the other night."

"Yes, but we are going to decorate and set up colored balloons for the children and you today."

"All right, whatever you like," I replied.

While I was preparing my new lesson, Lindsay came into the office to ask what size shirt I wear and how to spell my full English name. They were planning to give me a school golf shirt and have all the children sign the back of it.

The number of students enrolled in summer camp totaled approximately thirty-five. McDonald's wanted the children arriving for lunch before noon so they could leave as quickly as possible. MacDonald's, I thought, was for the children, so I didn't understand the logic.

As we approached the entrance, a giant sandwich board stood large as life on the sidewalk with the announcement of my birthday and my full name plastered across it. Everyone was led to the upper level to a section at the back, already set up for the party. A multitude of multicolored balloons were strung from the ceiling. An board had the school golf shirt laid out on it, ready for signatures. The tables were pre-set for the children, and the food had begun to arrive. My first thought was, Wow, they really wanted the children out of there fast. Not five minutes later, the same camera crew who filmed my cutlery lesson appeared at the top of the stairs.

"Liela, what's going on?" I asked. "Why are they here?"

"They are here to film your birthday party."

"You're kidding. This is a joke, right?"

"No," she replied with a quirky little smirk, "this is not a joke."

As I rolled my eyes, shaking my head, I was led to a specific table, were I was given a party hat. Two younger girls then joined me so I wouldn't feel lonely.

The children had all eaten, and I was still waiting for my food to arrive, starving. However, after all the children had finished eating, the camera crew was set up and ready to roll. To roll what still wasn't quite clear. The older children occupied one table, the younger children another. With the cameras rolling, everyone sang "Happy Birthday." Steven, a younger boy, was given a microphone and sang me a solo.

Whoa, I was not prepared, as tears began to stream down my face and I could do nothing about it.

If that wasn't enough to make me feel special, the camera crew continued filming as two of my favorite students, Lacey and Heather, best friends since childhood, also sang a song. Initially, the two girls sang while standing in front of me, but the camera crew wanted them to sit on either side of me and repeat it. They sang beautifully, and their voices brought tears to my eyes. What was so amazing was how much everyone, including the children, had put together to make it a special event in such a short time.

Everyone, including the staff, had eaten, but I still hadn't. It didn't take long before someone brought me a huge piece of chicken, followed by my meal shortly thereafter. While I ate, a staff member of McDonald's set up a cardboard statue ring game for the children and gave them all turns to throw the rings to hook it on the statue. Many of the students threw too hard, and I was in the direct line of fire. Rings would whiz past my head or almost drill me in the face, and I would catch the strays as I ate.

"Happy Birthday" had been written in large letters on the back of my new golf shirt mounted to a sandwich board so it wouldn't fall while students signed their names on it. One by one, the students began to sign their names on the back with a black marker, then it was Heather and Lacey's turn. When they finished, she approached me and bent down to wish me happy birthday, then gave me a big hug. In my entire life I had never been one to cry, yet suddenly found myself reduced to tears several times in one day by a terrific group of children. It was awesome, the most extraordinary day of my entire life.

It was now my turn to thank everyone and show them my gratitude for making my day such a special one. Needless to say, I would have to do it on camera for all of China to witness. No problem, I thought. I could do this. Of course, thinking this was usually my first mistake. No more than three or four words left my mouth before I choked and broke down once more. Suddenly speechless, tears streaming down my face, I had to turn away from the camera.

"Oh crap!" I muttered, momentarily turning away to compose

myself before continuing. After everything wrapped up, Al approached me.

"Sharon, I was wondering if you could lead the children in a song?" he asked.

"Me, sing on camera? Are you nuts? Not a chance!"

"Please, just one song," he urged once more.

"Al, I don't know what to sing."

"Why don't you lead them in the song 'The More We Get Together.' Please," he begged.

In unison, one student got under each of my arms and swayed back and forth, while the remainder of the children did the same. While I sang, the only vision that came forth was a new version of Mary frickin' Poppins, or Frauline Maria from the *Sound of Music*, leading the children in song for the Chinese to view and enjoy, perhaps even partake, if they so desired. What a wonderful documentary, I thought, certainly well worth seeing.

It turned out the McDonald's establishment had no intentions of rushing the children out—in fact, much of the afternoon's curriculum was planned. The students were all supplied with ceramic hamburgers and Disney figurine characters, complete with paint sets. The next couple of hours were spent watching the students discover their artistic skills and, at the very least, it was nothing short of entertaining. However, there was nothing for adults, including the camera crew, to do except observe.

Three of us, Elly, Lindsay and I, figured we should have also have the opportunity to experiment with our artistic skills. After all, if creating a masterpiece was good enough for the students, it should also be good enough for us as well, so we all asked for a ceramic character of our own.

As the figurines were completed, some of the students began handing them to me one by one. They were all being completed as birthday presents for me. I stood off to the side as the camera crew grouped everyone together in three rows for one last shot. With everyone began yelling in Chinese, I had no clue what was going on, so continued to observe. Finally, the cameraman motioned me to get into the shot. Before the cameraman filmed the group he made a peace sign with two fingers, and all the students did the same. Still not sure what they were doing, I would later learn they were all wishing me one final happy birthday, Chinese style.

It was mid-afternoon when everyone returned to the school. Hank had also returned from Taiwan. While the staff signed my shirt, Hank presented me with one last birthday present.

"Can I open it?" I asked.

"Sure."

It was a beautiful Gucci wallet.

"Whoa! It's beautiful, thank you."

"You're welcome," he said, smiling. "So, will this work to get you to stay in China longer?"

"Nice try," I said, laughing. "I'd like to, but I can't."

How would he know I needed a wallet ,I wondered, when it suddenly dawned on me. One day, while out with Lindsay, I had mentioned I needed a new one. She obviously remembered and told Hank. I don't think I made much money that day to even put in it, but I didn't care. It was one of the best days of my life, one I would not forget anytime soon.

Over the next few days, all the summer school students seemed to eradicate the horrid classes and rotten little children I'd been teaching up to that point. Surprisingly, the previous couple months seemed like an irrelevant piece of history.

Summer camp began winding down with one final outing planned by bus for the children on the last day. The purpose of the trip was not only to see the setup, but also have the children compare and exchange their singing talents for the upcoming competition. We were scheduled to visit one of the subsidiary schools across the river at the far end of Hankou before having a picnic lunch at a nearby fish park. The principal had brought some tapes and a cassette player along so the children could sing. One by one, in groups or in pairs, they were asked to sing. Several of the students would be auditioning for a competition being held at our school in a couple of weeks, so were also practicing. The subsidiary school was new, barely a year old.

Kevin, the Canadian I had met the day I arrived in Wuhan, was an English teacher at the school. While the children were doing their thing, we had some time to briefly become better acquainted.

When we left it was almost noon, but the fish park was very close by. A few staff members had visited the grocery store before we boarded the bus, so we had a hodge-podge mixture of items for our picnic lunch. The park had a beautiful pond filled with an assortment of the most amazing array of goldfish I'd ever seen. The colors were so plentiful and bright they lit up the water beneath several black swans swimming amongst them.

After the children received their lunch, they began to tear off pieces of their buns, throwing them into the water to feed the swans and the fish. It was a mad scramble for both swans and fish, fighting each other to secure that one piece of morsel. The swans, being larger, usually won out.

Keeping a group of children that size together was something of a challenge. The principal had been with me but had walked on ahead, leaving me by myself. While exploring, several of the students who were with me decided to run in different directions when they spotted something of interest to them. Lindsay caught up with me, yelling to keep the children together. Calmly, I reminded her I didn't speak Chinese, and making them understand me was difficult to do.

One section of the park was below ground level, containing some large, very ugly, and very strange fish. One of the species was a prehistoric-looking fish that only lived in the Yangtze River.

It was a wonderful outing, and the kids loved it. By the time we returned to the school it was 2:30 and the kids were exhausted. I naturally assumed the children would rest for the remainder of the afternoon, but there was one more snack and a half-hour rest before getting back at it to cram in more learning. There were not to be any classes that day at all, but because there was an extra hour or so to play with, it was back to the grind. Personally, I didn't know how they did it, and I felt sorry for them.

Essentially, Chinese children start their school day at seven a.m. and don't finish until eight p.m. When they go home they study and do homework for a couple more hours, until it is time to go to bed, usually ten o'clock. How much information do the parents think their tiny little brains can actually hold? I thought.

With summer school over, I was going to have some time on my hands. My daughter had been looking forward to meeting up with me in China for a visit, and I was ecstatic I would get to see her during my time off. We had discussed meeting each other in Hong Kong; however, during the summer months the Chinese flood the airline system, and if flights aren't booked far in advance, it is very difficult to get a seat. If she did, it would end up not only being the longest milk run anyone could endure, but also the most expensive, and those seemed to be the only flights available. As it turned out, she could only get one week off. The flight from Canada takes almost an entire day in each direction, leaving five days to visit and adjust to jet lag. In the end, although she was bound and determined to meet up with me, she concluded it would have been a huge waste of money for such a short time. Although really disappointed I didn't get to see her, I was so proud of her for making such a wise and difficult decision.

Not sure what I would do with my time off, I asked Yvonne if she also wanted to go somewhere when I returned from my vacation with the school the last week of August.

"I'd like to, but I don't believe you have the full month off because the full-time teachers will be returning to work after the trip returns."

"What are you talking about? Hank informed me not one month ago that the reason for all the extra hours was because I wouldn't be working in August."

She laughed and said, "No, I think you are expected to return to work around the twenty first of August."

"And do what?" I asked. "There are no classes, so am I just supposed to come in and hang out?"

Lindsay was passing through the office area, so Yvonne called her over. Upon inquiring, Lindsay was also under the impression I would be returning to work after the trip, but advised me to talk to Hank. Christ, I wish these people would talk to each other and get their facts straight! The disorganization could almost make your head spin right off. Leaving everything until the last minute was bad enough, but my personal favorite was when they only relayed part of the information and left the remainder as a surprise for later.

Everything for the seven-day Chinese excursion appeared to be in order, or perhaps there would also be a surprise or two attached with that as well that I wasn't aware of. What I didn't know was where or what exactly the trip itinerary entailed, and who or even how many were going except the principal and her daughter Nicka.

What I did know for sure—the journey to Beidaihi was seventeen hours by train, and everyone had bunks in a sleeper car. I also knew that the principal's daughter was going, and she spoke English, therefore would have at least one person on the trip to talk to.

Chapter 14
The Oriental Express

Although I rarely saw Hank, I was gratefully when he offered to accompany me to the train station, but before heading out we had to first pick up my passport. Prior to leaving the house, Hank filled me in on a few important details of the trip, informing me it was not a working holiday and I was not expected to teach. The only thing he did ask of me was to play some games with the children on the train to keep them occupied and entertained. He wasn't asking a lot, and I agreed.

Neither he nor I had any idea how many children where going, or even what age groups I would be dealing with. I had playing cards, dice and some information on game ideas for all ages that I photocopied from the school manuals. He did know the entire group consisted of about twenty-five people, and of those he believed there were at least two adults and perhaps a couple of children that could speak some English.

Hank was less than amused to learn I had not been informed of the itinerary, so he enlightened me on what he knew. We were heading for the province of Hebei, where our journey would take us to Beidaihe,

Qinhuangdao and Shanhuiguan, along the Bohai Sea, then on to Chengde and Beijing before returning to Wuhan. To help him better explain, I opened my China Lonely Planet bible to bring both of us up-to-date on where we were going and what we were doing. After reviewing the information on each place, it seemed to me a lot to absorb in one week, and would certainly prove interesting, even entertaining, if nothing else.

We left the house for the passport office about an hour and a half before I had to be at the train station. Time wise, we were going to be cutting it close, and I could feel another last-minute ordeal coming on. When we arrived, Hank gave me the money and asked me to pick up the passport while he waited outside. Because no one was at the pickup desk, I took a seat and waited with everyone else. About five or ten minutes passed, and Hank came in all in a panic.

"What are you doing?" he asked, seemingly annoyed.

Pointing to the empty desk, I shrugged and said, "Maybe they're on coffee break."

Hank glanced down at his watch, then began to scramble, looking for someone who could give me the passport. His luck was no better than mine.

Several others were also waiting to be served and probably had been long before I arrived. Time was of the essence, ticking away, and essentially we were all but out of time. Hank was still trying to find someone to retrieve my passport and followed a woman to the passport desk a few minutes later. She handed him something, and he asked for the money back he gave me earlier, told me to wait, then sped out of the building.

When he returned, two officers, including the woman he spoke with earlier, were returning to the desk. Hank made a beeline to be first in line, but was headed off by another man who had obviously been waiting, but in a much bigger hurry. Luckily for Hank, the woman he dealt with earlier motioned him to one side and looked after him. Hank handed me my passport with my new visa. It wouldn't take a genius long to figure out it was a tourist visa, only valid for one month. The probability of getting an extension in Wuhan was slim to none, and there was no doubt in my mind I would end up going to Hong Kong, Shanghai or Beijing to deal with it upon my return. There was no point losing sleep over it.

Outside, frantically, Hank began hailing a cab. After flagging one down, he spoke briefly to the driver, and we climbed in. He must have told the cab driver we were in a hurry and had to be there yesterday, because the driver began driving like a lunatic. Still, I wasn't a hundred percent sure we were going to make it to the train station, or even catch the train for that matter.

Within several minutes of entering the terminal building and having my luggage X-rayed, I was greeted by the principal and several children, then sent on ahead with the others. Originally, Hank wasn't going to escort me into the station because I had my train ticket, but we had run out of time, and he didn't want to take any chances.

Just as I remembered, it was like being sandwiched like peanut butter between Chinese slices of bread as the people pushed and shoved their way through the gates into a waiting area before making a mad dash to race for a seat that was probably already assigned.

Several of us stood in an enclosed waiting area next to the train platforms. The principal's daughter was there waiting with another girl about the same age. Nicka walked toward me and introduced me to her friend Coco, who also spoke English. While waiting, Coco asked, "Can you find your way to the train all right?"

"Yes, I think so," I replied.

"Just follow the group of people who just left and you'll be fine," she ended.

I followed the others through the train into a sleeping car. Everyone was assigned a bunk, so it was only a matter of finding it. At the foot of the beds, along the windows, were tiny tables with drop-down chairs on each side and very little room to move. The space between the windows and beds was also very narrow. Bunk beds were stacked three high, with each divided section furnishing six beds.

It was not quite the sleeping quarters I had imagined, with four beds and a privacy door, but instead it was an open concept with wall dividers. What I had imagined was located in another section of the train, much more comfortable and much more expensive. Nevertheless, all the beds came with a pillow and pillowcase, clean sheets and a blanket. The beds were anything but comfortable, and very crammed. Anyone fortunate enough to have a bottom bunk also had a table and plenty of headroom. The middle bunk had less room, but the top one had about two feet separating the ceiling from the bed. Naturally, I was assigned one of the top bunks.

As the train made its way toward Beidaihe, China's most famous summer seaside resort off the Bohai Gulf, everyone settled in for the long seventeen-hour journey. It was once a small fishing village over a century ago before Western missionaries, diplomats and businesspeople decided to set the area up as the resort it is today.[13]

Making myself comfortable on the pull-down chairs by the window, I watched as the city of Wuhan disappeared in the distance.

Nicka and Coco were a couple tables away, talking to each other, so I made a point of walking over to speak to them. Coco immediately dominated the conversation, questioning me about what games and activities I had prepared for the children.

"I have a few things planned, but I'm not sure where I'm going to entertain any of them. There is very little space to do anything," I replied.

Suddenly she took charge and began giving orders.

"I hope you have many activities planned, because it's going to be a long journey," she retorted.

Just who the hell does she think she is? I thought, glaring at her in place of a condescending comeback.

"Tell me, what have you prepared for the children?" she abruptly demands once again.

"Listen, don't worry about it. I've got it covered, OK?" I snapped.

"What does this mean, you have it covered?" she questioned.

As I walked back to my seat, she muttered something in Chinese to Nicka, and I could already feel the tension building between Coco and me. I instinctively knew there would be more problems before the trip was over.

Coco and the principal began looking for a cassette player so the children could practice their songs for the upcoming competition later that month. Cassette players were not in big demand on a train, and their impatience was growing by the minute. They were so determined to put the children on display for the entire car to observe and exploit their singing talents. What was wrong with these people? Perhaps it was just the Chinese way to drum up business, I thought. In the end, Coco found a small Walkman cassette player. The only volume was through the earphones, barely hearing anything when it was turned up full. The principal sat all the children on two bottom bunks and had them sing. Heather and Lacey, Mitchell and Zoe were among the few on the trip. Some of the others were new to me.

I had heard these children sing. They sang well; in fact, Lacey and Heather sang very well. After listening and watching their tone and body language, it was blatantly obvious they were uninterested. Yet the principal tried her damnedest to get them to sing with enthusiasm. All they wanted to do was play amongst themselves, with their friends. It was clear the plan to make a spectacle of the children was rapidly backfiring. Coco was fixated on continuing her domineering approach with me.

"What are you going to do with the children?" she demanded yet again.

Scanning bunks and benches lined with people, I asked, "Where would you like me to entertain them?"

"There is lots of room," she proclaimed. "You can use the beds."

Their ages ranged from five to eleven, so it would be difficult to hold their attention. I found a game in one of the lesson books I thought I'd start with, but no matter what I came up with I would end up losing their interest anyway. Rolling my eyes, I pulled a deck of cards out of my pack and walked past her, ignoring her. Coco had all the children sit facing each other on two of the beds, where I joined them.

Sometime later, a few of the older children, including Lacey, Heather and Zoe, wandered back to their bunks to play amongst themselves. I had fully expected it to happen, so it wasn't a big surprise. Several younger children stayed behind, and I taught them how to play crazy eights and go fish.

It wasn't long before Coco surfaced, bringing her judgmental attitude along for the ride.

"You need to play some other games. Your games are boring, and the children have lost interest."

"Really! Look, you know what, it's getting late, it's hot in here, they're tired, and they only want to play with each other. Because there is such a difference in age, the games suitable for the younger students are not going to be suitable for the older ones."

"It is not hot in here! The air conditioning is on," she barked.

It was going to be a very long train ride, perhaps a very long trip. Coco didn't like me, and the feeling was mutual. The sudden urge to deck her was strong, but instead I chose to shuffle the cards and began teaching the children another game, ignoring her. She was less than amused; in fact, she was furious. Maybe I hurt her feelings, I thought. Perhaps she was upset we weren't becoming good friends; well, at least not today anyway.

For a brief reprieve I went to the toilet. Under normal circumstances an actual toilet would be provided. In China, however, it's highly unlikely. To straddle a hole was one thing, yet on a Chinese train you'd better grab hold of something secure, because the toilets consist of a hole that opens directly onto the racing open tracks below.

Later that evening, Lacey's father, Jemmitt, the only male on the trip, asked me if I could teach the girls about the Great Lakes and the Canadian national anthem. Wow, nothing like putting me on the spot. It had been years since I sang the national anthem, and I wasn't sure I could remember all the words, yet gave it a whirl anyway.

Lacey had a friend who lived with relatives in Vancouver, and Lacey missed her very much. Once a year they get to see each other, during summer holidays, and earlier that summer they all met in Beijing. During their visit, Lacey's friend taught her the song, so she knew most of it. Attempts to get it correct were a bust after being corrected by Lacey on a couple of occasions. You begin to feel pretty stupid when an eleven-year-old wanting to learn about your country has to correct you.

We immediately switched the song to learning about the five Great Lakes: Huron, Ontario, Michigan, Erie and Superior. Lacey and Heather knew one or two, but to help her remember all of them, I gave her the code word HOMES, using the beginning of each letter to make a word. After spending an hour and a half or so exhausting their memory and singing skills, the girls returned to playing before settling in for the night. After spending some quality time with each age group, I was quite pleased with myself.

The beds were so uncomfortable; I spent the entire night tossing and turning, getting very little sleep. By six a.m. I was up, sitting by the window, watching the scenery fly past. During my twenty-five years of traveling the globe, I assumed I had seen pretty much every type of poverty known to man, but the train passed through some small villages along the way with the most depressed, ramshackle living conditions imaginable. Miles and miles of houses with no windows, doors and no doubt no electricity. Animals of every kind were running loose everywhere, some rooting through garbage piled several feet high. Many dwellings had roofs and walls missing; cesspools of filthy water edged its way up to the doors of the houses, filling entire yards as far as you could see. This was a reality that many people living in smaller towns and villages were faced with on an ongoing basis. I suddenly began to wonder what would happen if one was taken from their present environment and put into ours to survive. It would be similar to uprooting someone from North America who has lived in small town or community and sticking them into the suburbs of a Third World country. It's doubtful they would last long, let alone survive.

The train was scheduled to arrive in Hebei by ten. With a couple of hours to kill to pass the time, I asked some of the children if they wanted to play a game. Mitchell wasn't long grabbing a deck of cards from his grandmother's purse to play the two games I had taught them the previous day. It wasn't long before a few others joined in. Not long after we began to play, I looked up to see Coco, less than amused, daggers piercing from her eyes. I tried not to take much notice. She wasn't going to ruin my week; I wasn't going to allow her to do so.

Time seemed to fly, and in no time we had arrived at Hebei station. Outside the station, swarms of people where everywhere, and if you became separated, to find someone would have been a challenge. In front of the station a man was waiting to take us to our hotel. After leading us through the mob, we boarded a van parked in a parking area. Not exactly sure what to expect for accommodations, or even who I was sharing a room with, my curiosity was leading me to believe that I would be sharing a room with Nicka because she spoke English. Nevertheless, it would be a surprise.

Our hotel was somewhat out of the way and didn't look all that modern. It was apparent the Chinese weren't all that concerned with anything extravagant, but then again, what did I know? Everyone was assigned a room, and shortly after Nicka received the room key, it became quite clear I would be sharing a room with both her and Coco. Great! That was definitely something to look forward to.

Our room didn't look all that bad. I had stayed in much worse. It was like any other hotel with a balcony, a dresser and end tables, two beds, and a TV with the normal Chinese stations only. But most of all it had a bathroom with a toilet, yes! Who could ask for anything more? Standing at the bathroom door, I didn't see any shower or bath facilities, so asked.

"Do we have to go down the hall or to another floor in the building to have a shower or bath?"

Both simultaneously glanced at each other strangely before joining me at the bathroom door.

"What do you mean?" they asked.

"Where do I shower? There is no shower or tub in here."

"It's right there," Coco said, pointing to the wall.

Upon closer inspection, situated between the sink and the toilet was a very small pipe that ran up the wall. Three quarters of the way up the pipe was a very tiny showerhead and two minuscule levers halfway down that were less than obvious. The floor was tiled and sloped to a drain located in the center of the floor. The decision for me to have a shower first was made by Coco. Still puzzled as to how it worked, I took my clothes and everything in and set them on the sink.

153

"Where are the towels?" I asked.

"Didn't you bring one?" Coco questioned.

"No, why would I do that? All the hotels I've ever stayed in supply them."

"We always bring our own," they replied.

"Well, do you think the front desk would supply one if I ask?"

"There are a couple of small towels in the bathroom. You can use one of them," Coco said.

It was apparent they weren't going to oblige me by making the call, so I made due with what was there.

It didn't take long before finding out the toilet seat was cracked in several places, which was an absolute fabulous treat if you didn't to notice before standing up. With a couple small chunks almost ripped out of my butt cheek, it was not an experience I would care to repeat any time soon.

With all my clothes out of the waters' way, or so I thought, I turned on the shower. Needless to say, everything, including the toilet, the sink and floor, were getting wet with water everywhere. Lowering the water pressure didn't even help. The water was not draining—in fact, the drain was clogged solid. Wonderful! Water began rising, finding its way out the door and into the room.

Nicka and Coco decided to shower together, perhaps to save water or evade time alone with me. Nonetheless, I didn't particularly care, and went for a walk before lunch. When I returned, the shower was still running, the door was locked, and the water had found its way into the hall. Whoa! I could hardly wait to see the rest of our room.

Meals were included in our hotel package, so before an afternoon excursion we cleaned up, and everyone gathered for lunch in a large dining hall across from the hotel. The food was plentiful and, to my surprise, actually quite good, but with so much food for that many people, there was also plenty wasted.

For the remainder of the afternoon, an excursion was planned to Emerald Island on the Gold Coast, a popular section of beach on the edge of the Bo Sea. Traveling along bumpy dirt roads, it took about an hour to reach.

At first glance it didn't look to be anything special, just another beach. As the van pulled in to park, it looked as though we had reached an ocean running adjacent to a desert. It was the strangest sight I'd ever seen as the ocean stretched for miles in one direction while surrounded by huge golden sand dunes sprouting random mounds of grass in the other.

Our first activity involved sand tobogganing, which is not unlike snow tobogganing, only on sand. A cable system transported the toboggans from the beach two thirds of the way up the hill. From there, everyone dragged them the rest of the way up the hill. Most of us took a crack at it. However, the walk to the top was very slow and steep through very fine granulated sand. Linda, an adorable, dainty little seven-year-old girl who was traveling with the principal, didn't want to go alone, so asked if she could ride with me on my toboggan. As we made our way to the top, the two of us watched others ahead of us soaring down the hill at great speeds, anxious to have a turn. On the way up, some took their shoes off, but only briefly, as the sand was extremely hot.

From the top was the most spectacular view, with beach and ocean extending for miles on one side and desert on the other. The starting gate, a wooden box slightly longer than the toboggan on a seventy-five degree slope, was similar to a poorly made Olympic setup. Two long pins attached to a rope stuck up through the base of the box to hold the sled in place before shooting down the hill. When the rope was pulled, the pins disappeared beneath the platform, allowing the sled to bolt down the hill, picking up speed, coming to rest a few yards from the ocean. It was such an awesome ride.

The last half of the afternoon was spent swimming in the ocean. I, on the other hand, opted not to, not only because the beach was crowded, but also because visions of babies relieving themselves in public areas were still haunting me.

It was late afternoon when we left. Dinner was scheduled for seven that evening. With well over an hour's drive back to the hotel, the driver stopped at a roadside market on the way so we could purchase some fruit to snack on.

As I walked in for dinner, Jemmitt motioned me to join their table and sit in the empty chair next to him. Coco and Nicka, not far behind, also joined the table. When dinner ended, everyone had left except Zoe's mother, Jemmitt and I. Jemmitt spoke a little English and didn't seem to be in any particular hurry to leave. The three of us sat for another hour talking, drinking beer and picking at the surplus of leftover food on the table.

Day two was scheduled to begin at four a.m. with an excursion to Pigeon's Nest, a famous part of the ocean to watch the sunrise. I could hardly wait. Apparently we would be having an early evening; I spent the remainder in my room, eating my snacks from the market and listening to Nicka and Coco talk in Chinese while watching Chinese television programs before nodding off to sleep.

Chapter 15
Defying Peaks, Pigeon Nests and Dragon Heads

By 5:00 a.m. we were on our way to watch the sunrise at Pigeon's Nest Park, a sea-viewing pavilion between Beidaiha and Nandaihe. The ride took all of five minutes to an already half-packed parking lot and a five-minute walk to the entrance, where masses of people had already arrived. It was rather cloudy and doubtful whether we would see anything.

Inside the pavilion, near Eagle Pavilion, Mao wrote a poem about the sea. At the top of the steep cliff overlooking the sea is a statue of Chairman Mao that has the poem engraved in Chinese calligraphy.

The morning tide was out as our group made the steep climb down the cliff. Chinese tourists already crammed the beach to wander the seaside, taking photos and looking for shells, and for the next hour we did the same. Like most other tourist traps, this was no different, complete with shops and boutiques selling trinkets and souvenirs on top and along the base of the cliffs.

Sunrise was normally ten past six, and everyone gathered patiently. Six ten came and went, six twenty, six thirty, but no sunrise. It was time to pile back in the van and return to the hotel for breakfast before our long ride to Mengjiangnu Temple (Meng Jiangnu Miao), six kilometers east of Shanhuiguan.

The temple has a stairwell with 108 steps, 108 being a Buddhist number representing the troubles that plague man. There was also a "looking for her husband" rock with some interesting calligraphy, a bell pavilion, a front and back hall, and the eye of the sea. Mengjiangnu Temple was built during the Song Dynasty (9620-1279), then reconstructed in the Ming (1368-1644) to commemorate this courageous and enduring heroine. Legend has it that Emperor Qin Shihuang, known as one of China's cruelest rulers, sentenced a talented young man, Wan Jiang, to backbreaking work on a the easternmost region of the Great Wall (Changcheng), near the seaside town of Shanhaiguan, for the views this man held opposing imperial pleasure. Wan's wife, a beautiful woman known as Lady Meng, traveled a long distance after months of worry to give her husband clothes for the winter. Upon her arrival, she searched through thousands of withered workers on the wall. After many months, the heartbroken lady Meng, still walking along the wall, was drawn to tears. The heavens heard her cries. The section she was near crumbled before her, revealing the bones of her husband and numerous other workers who had died from exhaustion. Lady Meng, overcome with grief, finally broke, hurling herself into the sea from a boulder. The original statues inside survived until the Cultural Revolution (1966-76). The government had them remade in approximate likeness in the late 1970s.[14]

From one of several fantastic viewpoints overlooking the mountains in the distance, Nicka and Coco and I ended up separated from the group while taking photos. In an attempt to find everyone, we continued in the wrong direction, returning to the entrance at the bottom of the 108 steps. Coco called the principal to find out where they were, but couldn't get an answer. Retracing our steps, I followed as they made a complete circle back to the beginning before taking the correct path leading us out. Half an hour passed before we joined the others waiting impatiently to move on to our next attraction.

A few miles away was "The First Pass Under Heaven," also known as the East Gate (Dong Men). Off to the east, decayed sections of battlements trail off into the hills. This Ming Dynasty structure is topped with a two-story double-roofed tower and was built in 1639. The calligraphy at the top (attributed to a scholar named Xiao Xian) reads: "First Pass Under Heaven." The words reflect the Chinese custom of dividing the world into civilized China and the "barbarians," the Manchus, who stormed the gate in 1644, enslaving China for 250 years.[15] Inside, the tower was crawling with people. With the exception of Mitchell and his grandmother, our entire group joined the crowd while the three of us waited outside. After waiting for some time for the others to return, Mitchell's grandmother decided we should walk along the battlement wall. Souvenir stands were set up everywhere, almost defeating the purpose of the history behind it.

I couldn't believe we wandered off on our own. Although we ended up being the only ones who saw the entire battlement wall, we would also be the only ones in deep shit for wandering off. By the time we walked back to the square below the tower, it was just past noon. Most of our group was already inside the restaurant. The rest of the group waited in the square for us to return. Mitchell's grandmother had the job of explaining where we were and why to the principal. Judging from the look on their faces, neither the principal or Coco were very impressed.

Inside the restaurant, the others didn't seem bothered by our rendezvous in the slightest. Jemmitt had my seat waiting next to him, immediately ordering a round of beer before lunch arrived. As usual, there was plenty of food, too much in fact, but it was excellent.

I was quickly learning, the terms "vacation" and "relaxation" in China would never appear in the same sentence. It was an entirely new experience from my perspective. Everyone was up at the crack of dawn, running nonstop until six or seven in the evening. However, I was not complaining, only merely along for the ride.

Shanhuiguan is noted for its geographical location, as it lies at the easternmost section of the Great Wall, before this fortification collides with the sea. It is a old fortification town guarding the eastern Great Wall from the wilderness of Manchuria and Mongolia, to the east and north. Four kilometers south of Shanhuiguan was Old Dragon Head, our last stop of the day. Old Dragon Head had many features of centuries long past, such as town walls, a small hutong courtyard, historic buildings, horse stalls, prison cells and wheat vats.[16] A stone maze runs along the center of the square for anyone who chooses to find the way through it.

Instead, I settle for an ice cream and walked to the top of a building overlooking the maze to catch a glimpse of others in the maze. Some dancers had collected in the large square below and were about to perform, so I joined the others to watch as they paraded around in their bright ensemble to entertain the tourists.

While exploring the remnants of the fortress, we watched waves crashing along the side of the structure through the open cavities. Every now and then, the water would hit with such a force that all observing would be drenched by the waves. While our group made its way toward a sea god temple (Hai Shen Miao), they explored barefoot along the shore, chasing waves and collecting shells. As we walked, I discovered our tour guide spoke some English and began translating what she could of the site's history. There were many dynasties attached to the Great Wall, and they were somewhat complicated to follow, yet the history behind all of it was quite fascinating.

A sea god Buddha temple ran parallel in the sea with Old Dragon Head. Huge waves rolled from beneath, pounding up and over, crashing off the side to capture its complexity. Our tour ended with a stroll through the indescribable structure before returning to our hotel.

Our last evening in Beidaihe, dinner was not included. We either had the option of staying in town and making other arrangements for dinner, or going back to the hotel. After finding I liked seafood, needless to say, I was thrilled Jemmitt asked me to join them for some shopping and a seafood dinner later. Being a seaside town, much of it was waterfront, and most of the restaurants served seafood.

Before dinner, Lacey, Heather, Zoe and her mother, Coco and Nicka did some shopping inside a small mall before strolling through some of the outdoor markets. Neither Jemmitt nor I were all that interested in shopping, so we walked on ahead. At the end of one market street Jemmitt and I waited for the others to catch up when suddenly we spotted a huge commotion midway along the market street. Smack dab in the middle of it was Nicka's bright yellow backpack, but we couldn't tell for sure if she was involved, so we walked toward them. By the time we arrived, Nicka was into a full-blown drag-'em-out scrap with one of the vendors. They were punching, shoving and kicking each other, and everyone was screaming. Soon after our arrival the fight broke up, all over a trinket worth one or two dollars.

It was getting late, so we decided to eat. Jemmitt had been checking out some seafood restaurants along the way and had picked one for us to eat at. While Jemmitt was outside choosing our food, the events of the fight became repetitive as they carried it on. Nicka called her mother to tell her what happened, and I assume asked her to come for dinner.

Shortly after we began eating, the principal and others arrived, and the fight was rehashed once more. Because I was so busy sampling the food Jemmitt had ordered, I didn't particularly care. It was probably a good thing I didn't understand Chinese, as the Chinese tend to beat a dead horse to death, so to speak. Nicka's brawl was the main topic of discussion throughout the entire dinner, continuing long after arriving at the hotel.

For the most part the seafood was OK, but far from the typical type of seafood I was used to eating, and a couple of times I could have sworn items were staring back at me.

At 7:00 a.m. the following morning, we waited in the hotel parking lot for our transportation to Chengde, a seven-hour ride through the mountains. 7:15, 7:30, 7:45 came and went, the principal pacing at the entrance to the hotel the entire time. Just before eight a small van pulled into the parking lot.

Shit! You've got to be kidding me! I thought, as my eyes almost bugged out of my head. How the hell were twenty-some people with luggage, not to mention the driver's wife, going to fit?

It was bad enough having armrests doubling as extra drop down seats, but one had to draw the line when the tiny foot-high foldout chairs where available under the seats. Luggage was stacked everywhere. Suitcases and bags were piled everywhere, stuffed between and behind the seats and doors, and stacked four deep and four high next to the driver.

Almost an hour late, crammed in like sardines, no washroom, there was no doubt in my mind it was going to be a trip I'd never forget. Ten minutes into the trip was paved road, then it was off the beaten track into the rugged wilderness of washed-out dirt roads for the next six hours. It was the most incredible ride of my life. Perhaps the Australian outback or jungles of Africa might compare; however, that is just an assumption.

Out the window was the most beautiful, green, lush countryside, filled with eight-foot high healthy crops of corn. As we passed the many tiny towns and villages, the driver stopped to take on another passenger; big surprise, considering how the trip was already going. Nonetheless, the scenery was absolutely breathtaking. Mountains surrounded us from every direction. Cows, goats and sheep wandered up and along the mountain edges and roadsides, grazing while their herder stood waiting with a long staff until they finished.

Life began to appear somewhat primitive as we passed a convoy of mules pulling prehistoric looking flat bed carts. The driver, with reins in one hand and a whip in the other, had his legs dangling over the front edge of the cart. Tractors, perhaps from the steam engine era, ran on some ancient-looking motorized pulley system.

It began to rain, then it poured, submerging the already non-existent roads. The van hit huge potholes buried in water, bottoming out and almost tipping. The driver made a turn. Finally, the bouncing ceased, but only briefly. Within a few minutes the driver turned again, and paved roads just weren't meant to be.

It wasn't long before mountains no longer surrounded us from a distance. For the remainder of the journey we were headed straight through them. In places thick, dense fog socked us in, but as we traveled through a long mountain tunnel, everything was clear once again. A vague image of the Swiss Alps came to mind as I grabbed my camera to capture some of it. What a mind-blowing backdrop of lush green peaks and valleys, with arched bridges over flowing rivers between them, yet the Chinese didn't seem to take much notice.

Being out in the middle of no man's land certainly has its disadvantages. As we made our way through many small, desolate-looking towns along the way, I noticed garbage piled in front of houses four to five feet high in some places. Living conditions consisted of rundown shacks with rotted or missing roofs. Some appeared to live in only half a building with walls, windows and doors missing, and most likely no plumbing or running water. The deeper into the mountains we traveled, the more inhuman the living conditions seemed to become. Just to see it from a distance almost brought me to tears.

It had been a few hours since boarding the van, and I wondered if we were going to at least have a rest stop. Then again, after observing the living conditions along the way, I really wasn't sure I wanted to. No sooner had the thought crossed my mind than the van pulled into a rundown roadside gas station. Ah, finally we could stretch our legs and hopefully use the restrooms.

Several people exited the van, including me, and I made my way into the building to look for the facilities. I was quickly whisked outside and steered to an area the others were returning from. Located off to the side of the main building were the facilities, behind a white stone wall. OK, how bad could it be? I thought. As I rounded the corner, the stench alone was enough to kill any rodents for a mile. Standing with my mouth gaping open, I stared at what resembled horse stalls. Open at the front, with two cement dividers, everyone was on display while doing their business. Oh man! It was worse than my worst nightmare. I could hold it, I thought, but with at least two more hours to go, I had no choice. Still hesitant, yet having no choice, all I had to do was take the next empty stall, step up on the raised cement platform directly in front of me, straddle the trough that led to somewhere beyond, and do my business. This was real-life China, unimaginable, and something you have to see to believe. No one except me seemed to be bothered by it. Personally, a spot in the bush would have been fine by me.

Once everyone had finished, it was time to board the van and carry on. For Christ's sake, I thought, can't we at least get a drink or something first? What the hell was the hurry? Nothing else was planned for the remainder of the day except perhaps sitting around the hotel room to do nothing.

To add to my misery, it was still pelting raining, and the deeper into the mountains we went, the colder it got as temperatures dropped steadily. Before I left, I had made a point of asking Hank if I needed to take a jacket or sweater. He told me I would need neither, so I didn't pack them.

The van continued along the same almost non-existent roads, bouncing and jerking everywhere. The little girl behind me, no more than five years old, was whiney and restless. The driver's crabby wife was sitting directly in front of the little girl in a flip down seat next to me, and was less than amused with the whining. Suddenly, the little girl hurled, throwing up everywhere, all over the driver's wife and her seat. Abruptly, the woman stood up and let loose a few choice Chinese words before grabbing a roll of paper towels from an overhead rack and throwing them at the girl's mother. Glancing down at her seat, she discovered it was covered in vomit, so she pulled a foldout stool from under the seat and sat on it for the remainder of the journey.

We arrive in Chengde right on schedule, at a holding station were people wait to transfer to hotels, trains or other buses. Similar to a bus station, it was furnished with chairs, snack bars and washrooms. Nicka and I went straight to the snack bar to grab a few things to munch on, then joined Coco, sitting in the lounge area with the others. It must have been the perfect opportunity for Coco to start ridiculing and belittling me in front of everyone. Out of nowhere, the crap suddenly flew out of her mouth.

"All these parents are very angry. They paid a lot of money to have an English teacher along on the trip, and you have not done your job," she boldly pointed out.

Wow! I thought, as I stood stunned and speechless while my hair began standing on end.

"You must be a terrible teacher," she added, "because you didn't teaching them anything. You can't entertain them, and you do a lousy job at holding their interest."

I could feel my ears burning as though a fire was brewing to shoot from them. I'd had just about all the crap I cared to take from her. I just wanted to smack her upside the head, but not with my hand, with my foot. I was that furious. Instead, I maintained my composure and calmly informed her the children weren't on the trip for me to hold their interest; that was their parents' job.

"You didn't do your job on the train," she persisted.

"You know what," I snarled, "my job was to play games with the children on the train. I did that."

"You only played cards."

"Is that not a game?" I challenged. "They are children, and children who, when they have the chance, want to play with their friends and each other."

"If you were a good teacher you would hold the interest of all the children," she added.

Before I dropped her right where she stood, I walked away.

After the hotel courtesy van dropped us off at the hotel, the three of us were assigned a room on the seventh floor with no elevators. Inside the room, I dropped my luggage at the end of my bed. Still steaming mad, I was ready to blow this pop stand, find the first bank and catch the first train back to Wuhan. To ponder what I was going to do, I decided to go for a walk to cool off.

"Where are you going?" Coco questioned.

"Out!" I replied.

The weather was damp, cold and still drizzling rain, and my fingers were already numb by the time I got halfway up the street, so I began looking for a place to purchase a sweater.

The more I walked, the more enraged I became. If I took the train back, I thought, I needed to know how to get to the train station and buy a ticket. If I did decide to go through with it, getting the cash was no problem, as there were banks everywhere. The chances of finding a sweater were slim, and after walking for about an hour or so, I was almost frozen, so I returned to the hotel room. Nicka and Coco were out. A few minutes later the chambermaid was banging on the door to tell me dinner was ready. I nodded and shut the door, choosing not to attend.

Ten minutes passed, and the phone rang. It was Coco.

"Sharon, dinner is ready."

"I'm not hungry," I replied.

"So you're not coming for dinner?"

"No, I just told you that!"

"OK, we'll see you later."

To entertain my mind with something else, I began writing post cards. My logical side was telling me there were only a couple more days left before heading home anyway. If I could put a safe distance between the two of us for the remainder of the trip, it would be my best and only option.

An hour had passed when Coco and Nicka returned from dinner. As I continued with my post cards, Heather, Lacey and Zoe walked in, straight to Coco's bed. The conversation was entirely Chinese, and every now and then they all glanced in my direction. Not long after, the principal showed up, trucking the remainder of the children into the room to Coco's bed. Instead of leaving, she stood at the end of my bed and gave me a hostile look.

Coco began some activities with the children, no doubt in an attempt to show me up. However, I wasn't about to play this little game with her, so instead I smiled and sat watched her execute her plan. It didn't take a rocket scientist to figure out I was the topic of conversation during dinner. Every so often they would all turn and stare at me before they continued. Perhaps it was Coco's attempt at making me feel guilty, I thought, by showing me how easy it was to entertain all ages. And for her it was because she had the option of translating everything in Chinese into English and back. All I wanted to do was shout across the room, "Why don't you try explaining everything in English without the Chinese translation, you smug witch! Let's see how long you hold their attention then." It wasn't long before the children began to wander off. She couldn't hold their attention any longer than I could; in fact, less.

Lacey looked at me and asked, "Why aren't you playing with us?"

Glancing directly at Coco, then back at Lacey, I replied, "Actually, Coco is doing a great job at entertaining everyone, so I've decided it was best not to interrupt her."

Smirking, I clenched my hands behind my head, laid back on my bed and eventually fell asleep.

Chapter 16
From Chengde Temples to Modern Beijing

After weighing the pros and cons of my situation, to leave now there was not a chance! The Great Wall of China was awaiting my arrival. Besides, everything was already paid for, and I would only be cheating myself by leaving, regretting it later.

As far as I was concerned, Little Miss High and Mighty wasn't about to ruin the rest of my trip. I wasn't going to let her. As long as I stuck to the plan to put plenty of distance between us, things would work out fine.

Our first stop was the Imperial Summer Villa, the biggest Imperial garden in China. The area, encircled by a wall, was were all the dignitaries stayed when in the area, even serving as the second political center of the Qing Dynasty (1644 - 1911 AD). The villa was listed as a world cultural heritage site in 1994. This place is part dynastic relic and part park. A lake dominates the park portion of the retreat. Lotuses and pine grow everywhere, extending into the low surrounding hills. Trails led off into the hills.[17] To take in the entire grounds in a day would require some very energetic walking, yet I was convinced it would be virtually impossible. With less than half a day to see this phenomenal setting, we would be lucky to cover one quarter of it.

Chengde was an obscure town until 1703, when Emperor Kangxi began building a summer palace. By 1790, during the reign of Kangxi's grandson, Qianlong, the summer villa had grown to the size of Beijing's summer palace and Forbidden City combined, blending in the charms of both North and South China.[18]

The palace's section, located at Lizhen Gate (Lizhen men), is where the Qing emperors conducted state affairs. Because of the "famous" stigma attached to the gate, our entire group spent half an hour exhausting every photo opportunity known to man with it before our tour guide continued through the gates into the park. Upon entering, was the front (and rear) palace (Zheng men) that contains the emperor's living quarters and the main throne hall. To the west lies the West Palace (Xi gong), where the devious Empress Dowager Cixi lived when she stayed in Chengde. The concubine and emperor's mother resided in the Pine and Crane Residence.[19]

Again, everything was in Chinese, so I began to give the parents their money's worth. I began probing the children on the history. To do this they had to translate what they could about each item or area and, in essence, practice their English skills. It was quite clever, and both the parents and children loved it. After an hour or so wandering through the halls, looking at furniture and antiques, I was becoming bored. Observing Jemmitt, it was apparent he was bored and getting very restless. A brief discussion took place between the principal and the others, and I concluded by their sudden actions the group was splitting up to go their separate ways.

Most of the group, with the exception of the principal, Coco, Nicka and a few others, wanted to take the scenic cars up the mountain along the outer edge of the grounds. Lacey motioned me to follow their group, so I did, only to learn they had all purchased tickets at a price of forty yuan to take the car. It was either buy the ticket or hang out with the principal, Coco and Nicka for the remainder of the morning. That just wasn't going to happen. I much preferred to hold onto whatever sanity I had left.

The wait for a car was at least three-quarters of an hour, but we managed to amuse ourselves after spotting some deer in the bush. The deer didn't seem bothered much by all the commotion, nor did they mind us having a closer look for some photos.

Shortly thereafter, our car arrived to take us up the mountain. There were several points of interest, with spectacular mouth-dropping views in every direction along the way. What an inspiring place to write or just sit, I thought, with the entire park at our disposal. Then, sadly, it was time to move on.

At our last viewpoint, atop the mountain and beyond the wall, was an astounding view of the temples, two of which where on our itinerary following lunch. Puning Sì Temple of Universal Tranquility, and the.Putuozongchen (Zhi Miao). Although each stop was brief, having the opportunity to tour several areas of the park was well worth the investment. To cover the same area of the mountain on foot would have been very time-consuming and difficult.

Camouflaged by mature trees in every nearby small lake and pond, exquisite giant lotus leaves blanketed the water. Across a quaint little stone bridge, we had just enough time to investigate some gardens with a small temple in the background before lunch.

Of the temples thus far, the Puning Si surpassed them all. My admiration of the incredible architecture held me in endless awe. Outside Mayhayana Hall, the main temple, Chinese tourists were lined up, buying bundles of incense to burn in the iron pit in front of the temple. At the entrance into the temple were several steps to a platform, where prayer continued while half a dozen monks wearing large pointy wicker sun hats sat playing ancient music with much more ancient musical instruments.

It was built to commemorate Qianlong's victory over the Mongolians. A Chinese-style (Hanshi) temple at the front, with a chubby Milefo, or laughing Buddha, and Tibetan-style (Zangshi) features at the rear. Inside, Mahayana Hall is the Buddhist goddess of mercy statue, Guanyin. The goddess (more strictly a Bodhisattva or a

Buddha-to-be) goes under a variety of aliases and is one of China's most incredible accomplishments, and truly a remarkable piece of work. Guanyin has 42 arms, with each palm bearing an eye and each hand holding instruments, skulls, lotuses and other Buddhist devices.[20]

Directly in front of the statue was a small fence. Just inside the entrance doors was a prayer area furnished with large red pillows on the floor. Many tourists became caught up in the prayer ritual involved, and I chose to observe. Behind the pillows were three square wooden boxes with slots in the top half filled with money. To the left of the prayer area was a monk holding a cylinder of fortune sticks, eager for willing participants to purchase. Tourists who chose one paid a fee of twenty yuan to have it matched up to a fortune card before being translated by a monk. The main objective was to receive forgiveness from the god of mercy and prayer, lots of it. For this privilege, it was mind-boggling the massive amounts of money being spent to get it.

While staring in complete amazement at the statue standing over 21.3 meters high, our tour guide introduced me to her English-speaking friend, who asked if I knew the story behind the statue. I remembered there was a huge stone statue with a write up about her I'd seen at the first Buddha Temple in Wuhan. On either side of her stood two monk statues depicted as her students. She continued, telling me many people believe there is a very strong power behind her, bringing out the goodness in them; however, I had some difficulty with that. Directly in front of her piled five feet high and four feet wide was a massive stack of flowers. Chinese were moving in a continuous flow to purchase bouquets of flowers to set on the pile before praying again.

At least an hour or more of the tour was taken up inside or around. Wandering outside, I couldn't resist a good photo opportunity. In front of the temple stood some of the younger children, not a care in the world; they had no interest in rituals. Instead, they had bought seeds and spent much of their time feeding the large gathering of pigeons at their feet.

Before ending the day, our last stop was Putu Zongsheng Temple. It was built in 1767 and is the largest of the eight remaining Chengde temples. It was designed as a mini-replica of Lhasa's Potala Palace originally built for minority group leaders from all over China to celebrate the 60th birthday of the Qing Dynasty Emperor Qianlong (1711-1799). It came to serve as the locale for religious ceremonies and as the meeting point for Qing emperors to meet minority dignitaries.[21] One could only wish for such a lavish birthday gift.

It was incredible the amount of time spent waiting for our group to finish with photo sessions. If the word "famous" was attached to anything, be it a rock, a tree or a person, the Chinese posed for photo after photo of each attraction, with each family member first, then all together. Although amusing at first, it usually cut into our time for more important things.

The main hall was housed at the very top, surrounded by several small pavilions. The view to the top was well worth the climb. The temple used to have a sacred aura but has been ruined by graffiti.

As we entered the temple it was like walking onto the set of *Indiana Jones and the Temple of Doom*. Greeted by massive buildings of inconceivable grandeur and astonishing pieces of architecture, we had virtually no time to view any of the great halls peering out from every angle. If I had a choice, with what time we had, it would have been more logical for me to go directly to the main hall first rather than follow the group.

The day ended at one of the local restaurants for dinner. Our evening was free, but with a six o'clock start to Beijing the following morning, a shower and a good night's sleep was just fine.

At the train station the following morning, I chose to follow Jemmitt and the girls when the group became separated going through the boarding gate. Once on the train, it didn't take Jemmitt and Zoe's mother long to discover some of us had no seats and would be standing for the duration of our five-hour journey to Beijing.

Not long after, the principal made her way through the cars to find all of us standing with our luggage at the wash sink near the bathrooms. A heated discussion ensued between the three of them before the principal left. She returned a short time later, leading us through several cars, passing the remainder of our group, including Coco, scattered about one of the cars and settled in their seats. As we continued, we were led into the dinning car. Aha, I thought, I was quite familiar with how this scenario worked, and knew we would be spending the entire journey in comfort. For the time being at least, I was far enough away from Coco that I didn't have to worry about taking orders or dealing with her. Life was good. Knowing there would be a charge for the luxury of dinning in, I was fully prepared to reach into my pocket and fork it over. Just then, the principal intervened, footing the tab for all ten of us, including breakfast. Now that's what I call traveling in style. Although breakfast was anything but gourmet, it wasn't entirely bad either.

After breakfast, the children began playing card games. Heather and Lacey called me to their table to show me how to play one of their card games. After playing several games, they started getting bored. To change the pace a little, I grabbed dice from my pack and a Monopoly game with English questions and dud spaces I had created for almost all ages to play. Two of the children didn't want to play, so it was just the four girls and myself. Not sure of the game difficulty level, giving it a test run was a good way to find out. Because these girls were very bright to begin with, I knew they would get most or all the answers. Nonetheless, they thought the game was great. It took some time to play two rounds, after which the girls needed a break, and all headed to the bathroom. It was a stroke of luck we were separated from the others, and that meant no pressure and no tension. It not only gave the children some breathing space, they didn't have to worry about making an impression on the entire car.

While the girls played, I sat talking about many things with Jemmitt, including Lacey and Heather. They were both very smart, very bright girls who would both do quite well for themselves in the future. Several times during the trip, Lacey's father would pull her aside for a talk. Her expression at times gave away her frustration, even her anger, as he spoke. Perhaps it was his way of staying on top of it, making sure she succeeds in the future.

In the corridor between the car doors and the dinning room, I joined the girls. Thinking of something to do, I did an impersonation of Donald Duck to liven things up, then tried to teach them how to mimic me, definitely good for a few laughs. It was time for them to have a few laughs and them to turn the tables and teach me some Chinese. Needless to say, I paid attention and followed their lead. I should have known better than to repeat everything they were teaching me. The girls and many of the passengers watching suddenly burst into hysterical laughter. It was a set up.

"What are you girls teaching me?" I asked smirking, "Why is everyone laughing?"

They all burst into laughter and told me to repeat after them and they would explain. What I was saying in Chinese pertained to me eating my rear end.

"You're enjoying this, aren't you?" I said, amused.

"Yes," all of them replied, continuing to bust a gut.

"All these people just watched you make me look stupid. Was it fun?" I asked, trying not to laugh.

"Yes, it was very funny," Lacey replied, almost doubled over with the rest of the girls.

Just then Mitchell joined us. At that point we were all having such a good time, we felt like singing, but not because we had to, because we felt like it, and it showed in their tone. These kids were amazing! They were having so much fun they were belting it out and loving every minute of it. What an incredibly entertaining five hours.

Our hotel in Beijing was out in the middle of nowhere, miles from anything. Coincidentally, the principal's uncle lived just a few hundred feet away in another building. The next day and a half was free, so I had to pick my options carefully and make the best of what time we did have. Beijing was the focal point of Chinese history, with so much to see and do, making my choice much more difficult. I wanted to visit the Great Wall, and since the principal was in our room at the time, I asked Coco if she could ask her how I would go about getting there.

"We are quite far from the town here," Coco said, "so if you want to go into town, you have to take a taxi."

"How far is it to anything?" I asked.

"Maybe one half-hour by taxi."

"Do you know where I need to go to find a tour to the Great Wall?" I asked.

After discussing it with the principal, she replied, "The principal said that Jemmitt is going into Beijing to Tiananmen Square later, and he could help you. Would you like to go into town with them?" she asked.

"Sure, I'd love to, if it's all right with them."

Shortly after the principal left, the phone rang. Coco answered, spoke briefly, then hung up. The principal had called to say Jemmitt was going to Tiananmen Square at about five o'clock and would call me before they left.

Around five, seven of us headed into Beijing and had to take two cabs. For me it was payback time for all the meals and beer Jemmitt paid for on my behalf, so I looked after the taxi rides for the remainder of the evening.

Somewhere along Tiananmen Square we entered a shopping mall. Directly inside, on the first floor below, an ice-skating rink caught everyone's attention. The girls had never ice skated before, but wanted to give it a try. The women wanted to shop, so once the girls were set up in their gear, they wandered off shopping while Jemmitt and I stayed behind with the girls.

All in summer clothes, we watched as they froze their little behinds off. It didn't take them long to discover the loose surface ice. After rolling a few ice balls they soon found a way to fill my shirt and pants. The fight was on, and we spent the next half-hour chasing each other, almost getting tossed out of the establishment for cramming ice balls into each other's clothes and causing trouble.

An hour later we met up with the women and took a taxi to another section of Tiananmen Square where Jemmitt introduced me to some local Beijing food, paying the bill. Zoe's mother delivered three bowls of what looked like soup. Its contents contained thin strips of something with a beige coating on one side. Perhaps it was squid or octopus, I thought. The second dish was a yellow rice cake with dates through it. The last two dishes included a plate of icing sugar and a plate of deep fried dough balls to dip into the sugar. It was sweet, but very tasty. Jemmitt passed out chopsticks. Leery, I tried a thin strip from the bowl. It was definitely not squid or octopus, and the texture was gross and very chewy. With such a strange coating, I then thought it might be strips of cow tongue. After gagging down another one, I finally had to ask Jemmitt what we were eating.

"Sheep's stomach," he replied.

Oh God! I wanted to hurl. Instead, I switched to eating the fruit-filled rice cakes and sugary balls.

After our snack, we wandered to a nearby famous market and walking street, another section of Tiananmen Square. Food, souvenir and fruit stands were everywhere. Tourists and locals were everywhere, swarming so thick they were almost piled on top of one another. Along the way another small eatery caught Jemmitt's attention, and we stopped for a second round of snacks. Two more bowls of the sheep stomach coming right up! The second dish was definitely a plate of baby squids. Passing on the sheep stomach, I went straight for the plate of squid, and before long I realized I had eaten an entire plate myself.

It was after ten o'clock and it suddenly struck me that I hadn't asked Jemmitt about tours to the Great Wall. After inquiring, he asked, "How early do you want to get up in the morning?"

"It doesn't matter to me, I'm flexible," I replied.

Assuming we would eventually end up at a tourist information booth or tour company, we wandered, blending in with the rest of the tourists, then Jemmitt hailed a taxi back to the hotel. With no idea where sections of the Great Wall were on the outskirts of the city, I needed to come up with some kind of miraculous plan if I was going to pull off a stunt like this one. The fact was, I didn't have the slightest clue where to even begin; how the hell was I going to tell the driver to drop me off, or better yet, where? Although I had no translator, no map and my China travel Bible was sitting on my dresser at Hank's, I did have one thing in my favor: vast amounts of determination. However, I wasn't convinced that would cover it.

Coco and Nicka were immersed in a Chinese television program with an empty bucket of KFC chicken on the nightstand. The smell of lingering chicken was much more appetizing than sheep stomach. They were both curious to know how my evening went. After telling them the evening went great, I told them I still didn't know how I was getting to the Great Wall. Out of desperation, I asked Coco if she could write down the address of Tiananmen Square in Chinese and I'd find something after the taxi driver let me off. Coco quickly put that idea to rest, informing me it would be impossible because Tiananmen Square occupied one entire quadrant of the inner city limits.

No help whatsoever, I suddenly went into an uncontrollable laughing frenzy while sharing some imaginary scenario with Coco and Nicka that was rolling around in my head. As they listened to me describe my ridiculous scenarios of how I would first get the taxi driver to take me to the square, my laughing fit had became contagious. The three of us went into hysterics and doubled over, laughing for the next ten minutes as I continued.

"Then, when that didn't work," I informed them, "I'd improvise, using body language, observing his face gestures to see if it appeared like he knew what the hell I was going on about. There wasn't any guarantee that I'd even make it into town, however, there was a slightly larger possibility I'd end up somewhere else not even close to where I needed to be. After all that, he'd let me off, big smile on his face, with his hand out, waiting, no, *expecting* to collect the last dollar I had for this delightful experience."

In the end, the reality was that I had no idea where I was going, how I was going to get there, or even where I'd end up, perhaps ending up with a total waste of a day. Maybe I should quit while I was ahead, I thought. Ah, not a chance! I had to at least try, and if all else failed, there was the entire Tiananmen Square.

Chapter 17
The Great Wall Caper

Seven a.m., packed and ready to go, I handed my luggage and room key to one of two clerks behind the desk. Check out time was noon, but we were to leave our luggage at the front desk because our train didn't depart until eight p.m. that evening. Both clerks were mystified and had no idea what I was doing or talking about. To solve the problem, I gave the woman the principal's cell phone number to call.

Within minutes one issue had been resolved. Improvising, I drew a picture on a piece of paper, taking a chance they would understand my interpretation of the Great Wall. If nothing else, they definitely had a good laugh. They must have felt sorry for me and reached under the counter, pulling out a map of Beijing. Wow! I was ecstatic, thinking they must have understood or read my mind. The map was mine now, and I would pay whatever price they wanted for it, only they weren't getting it back.

Just then, a Chinese hippie with shoulder-length hair, glasses, and reeking of alcohol, entered the hotel lobby. Excited, the women spoke with him in Chinese, then waved him to the counter. Assuming they explained what I wanted to him, they let him take it from there. Even in his inebriated stupor, he could speak reasonable English and began to explain where I needed to go and how I would get there. OK, it was something, I thought, a start, providing he didn't pass out before he finished giving me directions. His instructions weren't entirely clear. Nonetheless, I did know for sure that just beyond the hotel complex, I needed to catch one of two buses, the number one or the number four.

"The number one or the number four bus," he repeated several times. "OK?" he continued. "The one or four."

With four quadrants encircling Beijing, I knew our hotel was located in the outer west quadrant of the city. The section I needed was on the outer east quadrant, which meant crossing all four. This was going to be a walk in the park, I thought. The man had given me all the directions and the number of each bus I needed to catch. Life just didn't get any better than that. Still, just in case, I had him put everything in writing, including bus stops. Before I left, I thanked them for all their help and offered to pay for the map, but they wouldn't take it.

Just as the hippie said, outside the complex, a number three bus pulled up right behind me. After paying a ticket collector on board, I showed her my instructions and waited for her to instruct me to get off. Nearly and hour passed when she motioned me to get off, yet I still wasn't sure where to go. Nothing really jumped out at me indicating Great Wall tours or buses to get me there. I began walking, stopping people at random, showing them my instructions. Each person I stopped didn't hesitate when pointing me in a direction, so I continued.

After making a loop off the original path, I ended up around a bend, under and past a bridge, then into a large U-shaped market area. Still, nothing jumped out at me, and I stood confused, questioning why I was standing in a marketplace full of shops. Great, just great! That will teach me for listening to the intoxicated hippie, I thought. Obviously he was in some temporary land of delusion, sending me on a wild goose chase to waste my time.

Outside, a store clerk was putting items on display, so I showed her the instructions. Immediately, she directed me through an opening between two shops, across a cute little white stone bridge over the river, and then right. Under the impression I was going in the right direction, there was still no sign of what I thought I was looking for. Through the opening beyond the shops at the bridge revealed three roads to the right, all running adjacent to the river.

Christ sakes, now what? Which one was it? I thought. A guard was having a conversation with someone at the edge of the bridge, so I interrupted to show him my directions. After the two men conversed briefly, they directed me over the bridge and to the right, narrowing my alternative down to two roads instead of three. Still unclear which road was correct, I chose the one along the river, sheltered with trees. Suddenly, it began to rain, and I had no umbrella. Perfect. This day just gets better and better, I thought, grabbing a breakfast snack from my pack to take my mind off things.

Almost half an hour passed, and it was apparent I had taken the wrong road. Instead of turning around, I decided to walk a bit further, only to find the road ended. Now in the middle of Timbuc-friggin'-tu, frustrations were mounting by the minute. I had all but thrown in the towel on this ridiculous excursion when I turned to walk back. Paying little notice, I walked past a taxi parked at a T-junction. In an attempt to get my attention, the taxi driver was yelling in Chinese. Ignoring him, still walking, I rolled my eyes and suddenly stopped with nothing more than an overwhelming feeling that he was parked there for my benefit. Whatever I was looking for was nearby; perhaps all I needed was a little extra help finding it.

Upon showing the driver my instructions, he nodded, then motioned me to get in. Before I did, I asked, "How much money," using the international sign of rubbing my thumb and fingertips together. In response, he crossed his two index fingers, indicating ten yuan, which I knew was good for about fifteen kilometers anywhere in Beijing before it moved.

The driver was trying to tell me something, but what? He kept referring to the instruction sheet, then wrote something down, adamant about making me understand. What was he trying to tell me, he would take me to the wall? At that point, as tempting as it seemed, it would be at least an hour's drive. Certain I didn't have the kind of money required to cover the trip by taxi, I motioned him to take me to the address on the sheet. Taking the second road to the right would have taken me where I needed to be in the first place, the main junction turnaround for the buses. As I pulled out the money to pay the driver, he was still insistent on me staying in the car to continue on with him. The way my day was going, I didn't need any more surprises, so I paid him and got out.

When the taxi pulled away, a number one bus was parked directly in front of me. What kind of crap was this? Why would the ticket collector tell me to get off the bus when the directions I walked for the past hour led to where I was standing? My foolproof escapade was turning into a damn nightmare right before my eyes. I didn't have a choice, I had to keep going, at least until I saw something that might look familiar.

Showing two Chinese men the second part of my instructions, they directed me to the number four bus just pulling into its assigned parking space in a large parking lot turnaround not fifty feet away. Once boarded, I showed the piece of paper to the ticket collector. She nodded, then took my money and smiled. Was she smiling like all the others, I wondered, or did she actually know what I wanted?

One stop into the ride, a middle-aged Chinese woman got on and began talking to the ticket collector. The woman turned to me and spoke.

"Where do you want to go?" she asked.

"You speak English?" I asked, surprised.

"Yes, a little. Where are you trying to go?"

"The Great Wall," I answered in a frustrated tone, handing her my instructions. "A man at my hotel gave me these instructions, and so far all I've managed to do is get lost while going in circles."

The woman turned the conversation back to the ticket collector before answering.

"You're on the right bus," she said as she laughed. "This woman here," referring to the ticket collector, "will take care of you and make sure you get to where you are going."

"Thank you so much for your help."

"If you have any problems or any trouble at all, I want you to call me on my cell phone, and I will help you, OK?"

"OK, thank you very much. Are you sure?" I replied, handing her my piece of paper to write her number on.

"Yes, it would be my pleasure."

After reassuring me the ticket collector would look after me, she got off the bus.

Whoa! How odd that was, I thought.

According to my map, we were going toward the center of the city in the direction of Tiananmen Square and seemed as though we were backtracking.

A railing separated me from the ticket collector as I patiently waited for her signal to exit the bus. If the remainder my day was to continue in the same direction it was already headed, there was always Tiananmen Square and plenty to see and do.

During the Cultural Revolution, Chairman Mao reviewed parades of up to a million people there, and when he died in September of 1976, a million more people jammed the square to pay their last respects.[22] His mausoleum was constructed shortly after, surrounded with an assortment of monuments and other historical points of interest past and present.[23]

If all else failed, there was still time to change my plans for the remainder of the day. Badaling, the most popular section of the Great Wall, was at least an hour away, providing I could get there, but first there was another bus to catch. By the excited expression on the ticket collector's face, my stop would be coming up soon. In fact, anyone observing her might think it was she, not I, going to the Great Wall.

When the bus stopped at my transfer location, the ticket collector grabbed my arm and led me to the stop directly in front of us to catch bus number eight. Graciously, I thanked her and smiled, watching her return to the bus.

"What bus are you waiting for?" asked a Chinese man reading a newspaper, also waiting for the bus.

"Number eight. I'm trying to get to the Great Wall," I replied, showing him my directions.

"You need the number eight bus, then must transfer to the 919 bus right here," he said, pointing to the writing on my sheet. "The driver will know were you need to get off. Just show him your instructions. The ride on the 919 takes about an hour."

"OK, great. Thank you very much."

Just then, the number eight bus pulled up. The man wished me well and motioned me to board the bus.

Half an hour later, the bus pulled into a parking area. It was the end of the line, and everyone got off, including the ticket collector. Racing off the bus, I flagged him down, pointing to the number 919 on the sheet. He pointed across the street. In front of me, where he pointed, was a very large, old gray brick building or fort of some type. Confused, I stood shaking my head, not sure what to do next, crossing the street toward the building. This wasn't part of the Great Wall, was it? Panic was consuming me now. What the hell, this can't be happening!

As I crossed the street, examining my sheet, looking for something, anything, that would give me an indication of what I was looking for, I passed a parked van. A sign, even a number, would be helpful. Where was the bus stop? Better yet, where was bus 919?

From behind, a man shouts, "The Great Wall!"

Hanging out the van door of the van was a very large, plump Chinese man.

"The Great Wall?" he asked, excitement beaming from every pore.

"Yes," I said, giving him the sheet. "I'm looking for the 919 bus."

From behind his back he displayed the sign with the 919, then opened his arms wide, guiding me onto the van. Several Chinese tourists inside the van yelled, "The Great Wall!" in unison before breaking into laughter. Shaking my head, I took a seat at the back and began laughing right along with them.

Before putting my sheet away, I quickly glanced at the instructions, and it suddenly dawned on me what the cab driver had been trying to tell me. He didn't want to drive me to the Great Wall. He knew exactly where he was going and was only trying to save me time by driving me to the 919 bus stop.

En route, at and between every stop, our Chinese recruiter, quite a jovial man, hung out the side door of the van yelling "The Great Wall!"

in Chinese. Although very entertaining, the impression that immediately came to mind was of a jolly oriental Stay-Puft Marshmallow man. As Mr. Jolly walked by and collected the fare from each of us, I asked him how much by rubbing my thumb across my fingers. Hesitating a second, he put up two fingers, which I interpreted as twenty yuan. When he returned a few minutes later, I held up twenty yuan for him to see.

"OK?" I asked.

"OK," he replied, extremely excited.

What an odd little fellow, I thought.

Sitting back for the next hour, all I could do was observe as the van completely filled with Chinese passengers.

Across the aisle and up one sat a couple with a little boy between two and three years old, fussing and screaming the entire way. His mother was plopping him into different positions in the seat while yelling and screaming at him. When he didn't stop, she began yanking him by the arm, almost ripping it out of the socket. Once she became overly frustrated, the father would take over relieving her. It wasn't long before Mr. Jolly cut in and took over. Having no idea what he was saying, it was apparent that not only could he make the kid laugh, but all the passengers as well, including me.

There were no toilet facilities on board, and at one point Mr. Jolly bolted from the van, nonchalantly walked about twenty feet, and had a leak. When he finished, he shook his penis off, put it back in his pants, and returned to the van as jolly as ever. Taking trips with the Chinese was always somewhat educational, not to mention entertaining. Besides, I was becoming quite accustomed to it.

The van was full, and Mr. Jolly continued to hang out the door, yelling and recruiting more passengers. Where in the hell was he planning to put them? I wondered, as a family of four piled on. From under the seats, miniature folding chairs came out to quickly fill the empty spaces. After Mr. Jolly finished recruiting, which never really happened, he would also use the tiny stools for the remainder of the trip. Yikes!

Badaling is 70 kilometers northwest of Beijing on an elevation of

1,000 meters. Suddenly the mountains were zooming in on us, and Beijing had all but disappeared in the distance. The Great Wall, otherwise known to the Chinese as the "10,000 Li Wall." One li is roughly 500 meters. The Great Wall stretches from Shanhuiguan on the east to Jiayaguan in the Gobi Desert.[24]

As we ascended up the mountain road toward the entrance of the Great Wall, boulders and thick rock formations began jutting out all along the cliffs. The mountains exposed huge boulders, large rocks and stone, and endless remnants of trailing Great Wall. It was hard to fathom how it was even possible to break or cut through any of it to build anything back then. What an incredible sight to behold!

Thirty yuan for an entry ticket seemed pretty reasonable to me. After all, there was a lot of walking and climbing involved. I needed film, so I stopped to purchase a roll at a small souvenir/snack bar next to the ticket booth. Pointing to the roll, I made a "how much?" gesture to the clerk. After punching the figures on his calculator, he displayed a figure of eight-seven yuan; four times the normal price! Scrunching my face, eyes almost popping out of my head, I shook my head, spinning my finger around my ear several times to symbolize he was retarded, and walked away.

"How much you pay?" the vendor yelled, waving the calculator.

"Twenty yuan," I replied.

"No," he said, shaking his head. "Fifty yuan."

"No, forget it, you're insane," I bellowed, walking away.

"OK, OK, wait, wait. Thirty yuan," he bartered.

Pulling money out of my pocket, I walked back with my last offer.

"Twenty-five and I'll take it."

"OK, OK, twenty-five."

The exchange was made, and I continued on.

Upon entering the grounds, a tour guide appeared from nowhere, speaking to me in very broken English. The last thing I needed, especially today, was another Chinese tour or guide.

She led me and several other Chinese tourists into the building of Genghis Khan. Beijing's history really got underway in AD 1215, the year Genghis Khan set fire to Yanjing and slaughtered everything in sight.[25]

A tour would have been interesting, but the interpreter's English was not great and was difficult to understand. Before she continued, I told her my time was limited and asked her if she could point me in the appropriate direction to walk the wall. Excusing herself from the rest of the group momentarily, she led me to another cubicle to purchase a ticket. The initial 30 yuan got you past the gate, but there were two more fees totaling fifty-six yuan, another entrance fee and a cable car fee for the first segment of the wall.

"I don't need a cable car, I'll walk," I said.

"It is the same price," she argued.

Our discussion was turning into a loud heated debate when I blew a gasket.

"What? That's retarded! Why would it cost the same price for both?" I disputed.

Her English was so poor I wasn't sure I understood most of what she was trying to explain, so I paid the fees. In the end she made a point of apologizing for her poor English; however, it wasn't her English I was upset with, it was the hidden charges. One thing was clear, if I didn't pay the additional money, my initial fee of thirty yuan would have been for nothing. After putting so much effort into getting there, it would have been pointless to walk away and catch a bus back.

As the tour guide led me to the cable car it began to rain once more, and nothing about the way my day was going surprised me anymore. For those who had no umbrella, there was no shortage of vendors selling raincoats. At the entrance, I discovered it was not a cable car at all, but a sled you sit on with a hand stick brake, pulled by a conveyer track. On the way up I soon found that if neglected to keep the hand brake pulled firmly toward yourself, it would slip backward, smashing into the person behind.

The original wall began during the Qin Dynasty (221-207 BC), when China unified under Emperor Qin Shihuang. Separate walls constructed by independent kingdoms to keep out the marauding nomads required hundreds of thousands of workers, many of them political prisoners, and 10 years of hard labor under General Meng Tian. It took an estimated 180 million cubic meters of rammed earth to form the core of the original wall, and legend has it that one of the building materials used were the bodies of deceased workers.[25]

It was incredible and became quite clear as to the reason why the entire project took over one hundred years to complete. The cost in human effort and resources alone were phenomenal. Every section of the wall was congested with photo booths, souvenir stands and tourists either resting or taking photos.

Beyond the first battlement were stairs that are straight up, and the initial part of the climb is very steep. Each step, very deep and very high, combined with a ninety-degree incline, made the climb very difficult and tiring. I imagine the climb up Jack's bean stalk would be quite similar. Along my climb I ran into several people who spoke English, one who told me the steps were built that way for horses to carry materials to different sections of the wall.

It continued to rain. The steep climb was very exhausting and took a great deal of effort. Why would anyone want to pay money to do this? I thought. Nevertheless, there were hundreds of others who obviously did not share my opinion. As I continued to climb, mesmerized by the phenomenal trailing walls in the distance, it became clear. The first kilometer of the wall trailing over the mountains has been restored before it began to disintegrate into ruins. Many chose to walk the entire distance, although from several sections of the battlements, much of the wall was visible anyway.

It was not possible for me to walk the entire wall, as time had run out and I had to make the steep climb back down. It was an entirely new outlook to the climb up, and a sure-fire way to pop a kneecap out of its socket! It was very easy to lose your grip on the metal railing, especially in the pouring rain, and dangerous. Except for the metal hand railing, there were no real supports in the event someone fell. If they did, it would be like falling off a ladder, the only difference is that you would be bouncing off stone all the way down. To even fathom how the older people, even little children, made the climb was beyond me. The Great Wall now all but a memory, it was time for me to find the 919 bus and make my way back to the empire of Never-Never Land.

Chapter 18
Take the Long Way Home
and Away

A 919 bus was parked near the entrance. Upon showing my information to the driver, he waved me aboard. The bus quickly filled with passengers, and we were under way for the return trip back to Beijing. Knowing I needed twenty yuan for the return trip, when the young man collecting money approached, I retrieved it from my pocket and gave it to him. He then handed me ten yuan in change. Bastard! The Stay-Puft man ripped me off! That would explain Mr. Jolly's cheerful disposition when I asked him if twenty yuan was OK. Still, ten or twenty yuan was neither here nor there. It worked out to be about three or four dollars for an hour; actually quite a bargain compared to what a regular bus tour would have cost.

Less than half an hour into the ride, the man collecting money sat next to me at the back of the bus, and impulsively I handed him my instruction sheet. His expressions suddenly changed, and I had a gut feeling things were about to change. Shit! He's not going to tell me I'm on the wrong bus, I thought. I couldn't be. It was clearly marked 919, and the driver had motioned me to get on. A moment later, he turned and pointed out the back window. Behind us was another 919, perhaps a city bus, and the young man began making hand gestures indicating he wanted me on it. When both buses stopped, he rushed me off the bus, signaling the driver behind to wait until I had boarded.

What the hell was going on? I wondered. Having no idea as to what was taking place, all I could do was board the bus, hopeful it was taking me back to the 919 stop where I originally got on. If it didn't, then I would be literally screwed and end up missing the train back to Wuhan. Another three yuan was required, so I handed him the money and the instruction sheet, pointing to the section with the number 919. I knew for sure the 919 picked me up there, and a number eight bus would be within close proximity to return me to Tiananmen Square.

An older Chinese gentleman sitting in front of me, and the young man, were discussing my instructions. I was not sure why I was on that particular bus, and whether or not it was even going to take me to the location I needed. All I could do was hope for the best, trust that everyone except me knew what was going on and everything would work out fine.

There was nothing that looked even remotely familiar, although why would it? I had never been to Beijing in my life. The only landmark I knew was the large gray brick building at Deshengmen, the 919 pickup and departure point I caught the van from. It seemed longer than half an hour passed before I was being motioned to get off at the next stop. It was just before three p.m., and as I looked around, there was nothing that caught my eye. Panic ensued, similar to being in the middle of a desert and seeing nothing for miles.

Within minutes the bus rounded a corner. There it was, my big beautiful landmark, and I was never so happy or so relieved to see an ancient old building than I was at that moment. I did it! I just pulled off the most amazing adventure ever with little or no English translation, and nothing more than a Chinese map! How I did it will remain a mystery forever, but what an incredible rush!

From there it was a piece of cake. I'd catch the number eight bus parked in the lot returning to Tiananmen Square. I was home free and still had time to do a bit of sightseeing. A block or so before the bus turned the corner at Tiananmen Square, I got off and walked. Rounding the corner, it was the most incredible sight, like nothing I'd ever seen, as I stood watching in disbelief. The largest urban square in the world, with a capacity to accommodate 10 million people, thousands swarmed the entire area like locusts, filling every space and every nook and cranny in sight.

I had already seen one of two places on the top of my list of important things to see in Beijing. The other was the Imperial Palace, better known by its unofficial title, the Forbidden City, home of two dynasties of emperors, the Ming and Qing. For five centuries, and through the reigns of twenty-four emperors, ordinary subjects were forbidden from approaching the palace walls of the largest and most complex preserved palace in China.[26] Of the impression it was also outside the city limits and unable to translate my map, I chose to improvise my way to the Great Wall instead, discovering later it was located just opposite Tiananmen.

Tiananmen is a national symbol. The gate was built in the fifteenth century and restored in the seventeenth. There are five doors at the gate, and in front of it are seven bridges spanning a stream. Each of the bridges were restricted in its use, and only the emperor could use the central door and bridge.[27]

The front gate sites on the southern side of Tiananmen Square. The front gate actually consists of two gates. It guarded the wall division between the ancient inner city and outer suburban city, dating back to the reign of Emperor Yongle in the fifteenth century. With the disappearance of the city walls, the gate sits out of context.[28]

The Great Hall of the People is the National People's Congress. It's open to the public when congress is not sitting. These are the halls of power, many of them named after provinces and regions of China.[29]

The Mao mausoleum is a monument of national importance for China. However history judges Mao, his impact on its course was enormous. Easy now to verify his deeds in excesses, many Chinese show deep respect for this man.[30]

North of Mao's mausoleum is the Monument to the People's Heroes, completed in 1958, and it stands on the site of the old outer palace gate. The obelisk, made of Qingdao granite, bears bas-relief carvings of key revolutionary events (one relief shows the Chinese destroying opium in the nineteenth century).[31]

It didn't take long to exhaust what time was left. There was so much to see and learn while wandering the square. Looking down at my watch, it was five-thirty and time to either catch a cab or have one last venture by bus. What the hell, I might as well complete the journey and find a bus. If time ran short, I could always catch a cab.

At that moment, turning the corner was a number four and a number two bus, so I knew there had to be a bus stop nearby. Within twenty minutes of boarding bus number four, I was outside the hotel complex, with half an hour to spare before we departed for the train terminal.

No one could enter the hotel complex without being a resident or being met by someone at the gate to confirm it was OK to enter. Jemmitt had just ordered dinner for him and his group when he was nominated to retrieve me. Exiting from a different gate, he had to walk a short ways to get me. When we returned to the very same gate, he was denied entry into the compound, and we both began laughing. He had to make a call to get us back in. Within ten minutes a resident showed up and told the guard to let us in. Needless to say, Jemmitt missed dinner. Everyone, especially Coco, Nicka and the principal seemed somewhat surprised to see me, and they were even more surprised I made it to the Great Wall.

Everything on schedule, we boarded the train for the thirteen-hour ride back to Wuhan. Everyone's sleeping quarters were staggered throughout several cars, but I was once again put with Heather and Lacey's group. It was after eight when everyone finally settled for the long journey home. I couldn't tell if Jemmitt was uneasy or if he just needed a cigarette. The girls were all but tucked in when Jemmitt asked me if I would like to join him in the dining car for a beer. Having enjoyed his company the entire journey, I wasn't about to say no, and having a beer seemed like a perfect end to what ended up the perfect day. My mouth dropped as we entered the dining room.

In comparison to previous trains, the train was fairly new, the restaurant resembling a five-star resort. Secured overhead at each end of the dining room was a big-screen TV. The adjoining lounge was furnished with crystal glasses behind a half-moon-shaped sit-down bar with leather-covered bar stools. A few feet away, two more round tables covered in beautiful red linen were facing another big-screen TV. Now this is luxury, I thought.

Jemmitt knew I had missed dinner, and because he didn't want to eat alone he ordered something for both of us while I grabbed a table. The entire dining car was ours for the next hour and a half to sit in peace and quiet, enjoying our meal and each other's company over a couple of beers before retiring to our bunks for the evening.

Our train arrived in Wuhan at 8:00 a.m. Instead of catching a bus home, Jemmitt offered me a ride, with a detour for breakfast before being dropped off.

Barely twenty-four hours had lapsed, and only half of my laundry washed, Hank called to tell me I was leaving for Shanghai that afternoon. Another fun filled twelve hours by train, then I would take a taxi directly to the corporation's head office to begin the course within the hour. Hank had given me 1,000 yuan, more than enough to pay for expenses, and instructed me to find Margy, a woman who was going to look after my passport when I arrived.

Day one of the course was somewhat redundant. We had three coordinators, a South African and two Chinese, Brian and Jill. Jill was born in China, but had spent six years working in Ottawa, so she understood fully the problems and frustrations most foreign teachers were facing.

In my opinion, the course was very beneficial for me, yet had the two-day course been a prerequisite prior to continuing on to Wuhan, it would have been much more valuable. Some of the schools are franchises, and some are run independently. There is a cost for the course, but the schools are under no obligation to have their new teachers take part.

Kevin, the Canadian from B.C., was also attending the course, so there was at least one person I had something in common with. For lunch, several of our group wanted to check out a quaint little spaghetti restaurant across the street on Xi Kang Lu. After discovering it was full, we opted for a traditional Japanese restaurant across the street.

We arrived late for class, and Brian was waiting to get class underway. The course was to provide us not only with information teaching various aspects of the different books, but also how to handle children, telephone and other related tests, and translators. Both Kevin and I pointed out we hadn't been involved in the telephone testing, and one of two English books were only taught by the Chinese/English teachers. Kevin and I pointed out that occasionally we were instructed to review sections of the book, but trying to fill an entire fifty-minute class teaching two pages from the phonics book was very frustrating, to say the least.

Our feedback didn't seem to be going over well with head office, yet we were all learning valuable information about the rules and regulations that none of us were aware of. For most of his classes, Kevin had an interpreter in the room with him so "bad" children weren't as much of an issue for him. On the other hand, it was an issue I was dealing with. Jill asked me if the interpreter was having problems handling the classes.

"Interpreter?" I asked. "What interpreter? I go round up a staff member when there's a problem."

None of the instructors could believe I was placed into the classes with no help provided, and was never given an interpreter. It was the main reason I was running into so much difficulty. A larger picture was beginning to form, so I made a point of asking Jill not to make a big issue of it, because I had been in the system teaching for several months. It would have been pointless to stir up trouble, but more so, the aggravation was something I could do without, and she agreed.

Classes ended at five-thirty that day. Mark collected me, Kevin and a South African woman into a taxi, taking us to a hotel five minutes away. On the way, while making conversation with the South African woman, she suddenly turned to Mark, laughing, and for the remainder of the ride began speaking in a South African dialect. Kevin, who was sitting in the front, picked up on it and turned around briefly, giving me a look.

After checking in, Kevin and I went to locate our room, but we were back in the lobby shortly thereafter due to a mixup with my key. I was in possession of someone else's room, already occupied, and had to exchange rooms.

On our way out, the African woman was still sitting on one of the lounge chairs in the lobby, talking to Mark. As I walked toward the door with my bags, she paused her conversation, asking me to call her if I wanted to go for a walk later.

Outside, Kevin asked, "You're not going to call her, are you?"

"What do you think? Shit like that really irritates me. It's rude. As far as I'm concerned, it says a lot about her true identity, and I didn't care for it."

"You're right," he agreed. "It's very rude, and I don't care much for people doing that either."

"Do you think I'm being irrational?" I asked.

"No, I would have done the same thing," he said,

My new room was the nicest of any excursion around China so far. The bed was comfortable, with nice, thick, fluffy pillows, and the shower was an actual stall with a shower curtain, not a pipe between the toilet and sink draining into a clogged drain in the floor. It was wonderful.

Kevin and I decided to have dinner, then take the subway to People's Square to do some sightseeing. Having no success for lunch, we returned to the spaghetti house for dinner and lucked out. We started off splitting a quart bottle of Chinese beer. Each of us tried a different pasta dish, and I had almost forgotten what "real" food tasted like, it was so good.

Following dinner, we caught the subway to People's Square, three stops away near the waterfront. Although inhabited by thousands of tourists shopping for silks and souvenirs, at night it could be mistaken as a mini-Las Vegas.

We made our way toward the Bund, an Anglo-Indian term meaning "muddy water embankment on the waterfront." On the west side of the

Bund tower various buildings of different architectural styles, including gothic, baroque and Romanesque, once known as Shanghai's version of Wall Street to the Europeans. The combination of these creates a unique boulevard, which resembles the Liverpool docks and 1920s New York.[32]

Between 1920 and 1965, the city sank several meters, and water had to be pumped back into the ground. Shanghai, still threatened by the Venetian syndrome, has many high rises set on concrete raft foundations to hold the spongy mass.[33]

Shanghai was built on the trade of opium, silk and tea. By the 1930s the city had 60,000 residents and was the busiest international port in Asia.[34]

Along the main street running adjacent to the river were many historic buildings. Across the river stood the Oriental Pearl Tower, a much brighter lit, much smaller version of the Toronto's CN Tower, apparently hosting sensational views of Shanghai from its lookout halfway up. The city and buildings looked brilliant all lit up at night, so we continued along the continuous waterfront before returning to the motel.

Before classes the next morning, Kevin and I went to the Jade Buddhist Temple (Yufo Si) a few blocks away from the motel on Anyuan Lu. The outer yellow entrance walls stopped both of us in our tracks. Inlayed in dark wood within the wall were several exceptional animal carvings.

The temple was built during the Guangxu period of the Qing Dynasty (1875-1909), but was burnt down in the early twentieth century. In 1918, the jade temple was rebuilt on Anyua Road with magnificent architecture from the Song Dynasty. Monks currently live in the temple, and the temple houses the Shanghai Buddhist Institute. Here many ancient statues, paintings, a complete set of Buddhist scriptures (printed in the Qing Dynasty), and over 7,000 other rare scriptures are housed.[35]

The centerpiece is a white jade Buddha around which the temple was built. The story goes that a monk from Putuoshan traveled to Myanmar (Burma) via Tibet, lugged the Buddha back to its present site, then went off to alms to build a temple for it. The seated Buddha, encrusted with jewels, is said to weigh 1,000 kilograms. A smaller Buddha from the same shipment reclines on a mahogany couch.[36] For five more yuan we could view the Buddha; however, we opted to make our way back to the school.

On our way to class, we stopped for some fruit, a half-apple and half-pear combination. The vendor told Kevin it would cost five yuan for two.

"You're ripping us off, aren't you?" Kevin asked, nodding.

The woman nodded, then smiled.

"You're robbing us blind, aren't you?" he continued, still mocking her.

She continued to nod as I handed her the money for the fruit, then we broke into uncontrollable laughter.

Before the course started we returned to the motel to check out. Kevin and I were next in line to check out when a Chinese man suddenly barged past to be served, pushing Kevin out of the way. The cocky soul he is, Kevin body-checked the guy, knocking him off balance, sending him to the far end of the counter.

"I can't believe you just did that!" I said as I laughed.

"That shit really irritates me!" he said.

"You can't do that. Do you have a death wish?"

"No, it's rude, and I don't like it."

"I noticed you just body-checked the poor bastard."

"He might think twice about doing it again," he replied.

"He's probably afraid you'll beat the crap out of him."

"Good."

The Chinese man never made any further movements, and Kevin was served first.

We spent much of the second day discussing how to handle children, what games to play, and the things we all needed to cover that we were having problems with. Jill explained how the Chinese rules work, but also the problems they were having finding foreign teachers to fill spaces in their schools.

Near the end of the course, Jill and I had an opportunity to talk. She told me the corporation had many schools desperate for good English teachers. She knew my contract finished in a couple of months, and they were anxious to recruit me.

"You don't even know if I'm a good teacher," I said.

"Yes, I do. I've been observing you on camera for the past two days. You are the type of teacher we are looking for," she said, persuading me to return to Shanghai should I decide to return to China and teach at a later date. Wow! That was something I really needed to hear.

Brian spent most of the day looking after my passport, my return train ticket and hotel reservations for another night. At a corporate rate of three hundred yuan, Brian booked me into a lavish room on the sixteenth floor of the Yin Fa Hotel a few of blocks away.

After checking in, I went for a walk, eventually ending up at the spaghetti house again. Although more expensive than Chinese cuisine, the food was excellent, and it would be a while before I'd get to eat food like that. On my walk back, I encountered a Starbucks. Ah, a real cup of coffee! Viewing the prices through the window, my craving came to a grinding halt. One regular cup started at twenty-five yuan, or five dollars.

Checkout wasn't until noon, and I had been told Shanghai's Yuyuan Gardens were well worth seeing. Getting up at six a.m. gave me plenty of time to walk, and my map was pretty self-explanatory anyway. An hour into the walk, I was at the edge of FuYou Lu and JuanChang. So detailed, so exquisite, it was a maze of small streets and old buildings. After seeking directions to the gardens from a few locals, I was still unclear if I was actually looking for a botanical garden or something else. Not realizing I was in Old Shanghai City (Yu Yuan Chang Cheng), I continued.

The area surrounding the gardens make up the Old City God's Temple Area, known in colonial times as the "Chinese City." What is nice about the area are the numerous antique markets and small side streets, which have not been renovated by the authorities.

Hungry, I spotted a vendor selling steamed vegetable dumplings, and I bought breakfast before continuing on to watch some women doing their morning exercise routine, gracefully snapping their large red fans open to music. A strong smell of incense lingered everywhere as I walked through long mazes of narrow alleys leading in every direction. Although overflowing with souvenir shops, as I ventured through each alley, it was as though I had just entered some ancient time warp. It was so peaceful, so serene. Exiting the alley, I stopped, staring in awe. Surrounded with old Chinese-style architecture, separated by a white stone bridge across a charming little pond, there was the famous Huxingting Tea House. Although something of an institution around those parts, and while quaint and interesting, it is extortionately overpriced.[37] By 8:30 all the serenity came to an end, as clusters of tourists, clinging to their cameras, were glued to their tour guides and began pushing their way through.

The gardens themselves were completed in 1577 by the Pan family. The original gardens were destroyed twice in the 1800s and have now been restored. The gardens cover a significant space and include a few halls, springs and other buildings of interest.[38]

The Chinese have a saying: "Jiuade buqu, xinde bulai" (If the old doesn't go, the new won't come).[39]

Chapter 19
Always Calm Before a Storm

Before making my way back to the hotel, I detoured back to the Huungpu Jiang for one last stroll to view the marvelous architecture of the many old buildings encompassed within the Bund. Tourists were jammed everywhere along the hazy, smog-filled waterfront, making it difficult to see even the Pearl Tower across the river.

I tried making the most of what time I had left before flagging down a taxi to head back to the hotel. During the ride the driver was weaving in and out of traffic like a maniac. It felt as though we were making our way through a maze as he zipped up and across one street and down another. I watched as a scooter sped past me on the passenger side of the car and cut in front him. Suddenly he slammed on the brakes, creaming the scooter, hurling me backward into the seat.

A car following too close from behind immediately smashed the taxi from the rear, catapulting me forward with a jerk. Within seconds of the driver getting out and inspecting the situation, a policeman on motorcycle was on the scene. The driver reached across me into the glove box, speaking Chinese, communicate something using hand gestures, only I had no clue as to what. The meter read ten yuan and was still running, but I suddenly had a bad feeling remembering I had no passport. Being detained by police with no passport was painting less than a positive image in my mind. It wasn't the time to stick around to find out or wait to be questioned and possibly miss my train. My only option was to exit the car and make a quick get away and get out of sight. Once I was far enough away, I hailed another taxi.

After checking out of the hotel, I caught a taxi to the train station and was dropped off in the underground parking. While paying the fare, a Chinese man appeared without delay in possession of my suitcase and backpack. At times naive, I assumed he was a helpful employee, and I followed him through masses of people to put my belongings through an x-ray machine at the terminal entrance. Insistent I could take it from there, he quickly maneuvered in front of me, once again collecting my belongings. What was he doing? I thought. Was he trying to steal my pack? At that point I knew it was unlikely I was dealing with a Good Samaritan, and began to panic as he led me into the train to my assigned sleeping quarters. After he set my bags down I offered him ten yuan for his help. He pulled out a calculator, showing me the number 50.

"No, I don't think so," I retorted.

He sat on the edge of the bed, determined to con the fifty yuan out of me. In my pocket I had thirty yuan, so offered it to him and he left, less than happy. A Chinese man within earshot spoke.

"How much did you give him?" he asked.

"Thirty yuan."

"Five is the standard fee," the man informed me.

"I offered him ten, and he insisted on fifty."

"Because you are a tourist who didn't know."

An hour into the journey, my assigned bunk was occupied by a Chinese man. Not sure what to do, I located the man I spoke with earlier, showing him my ticket. According to him, I was assigned the bunk in compartment 12, not 16. However, that bunk was also occupied with someone. After comparing the two tickets, both had been assigned to the same bunk in the same compartment. The man left to find an employee member who could help. The thought of being on the wrong train was the only thought going through my mind before panic set in. Three train personnel and the man returned to check the tickets to discover the man occupying my bunk had been assigned the opposing bunk. I didn't care to switch bunks, so claimed the undisturbed bunk for the remainder of the journey.

When the train arrived at Wuchang station in Wuhan, I walked to the road where several cabbies were lined up. Because I didn't have the address on me, I indicated to the driver on the map where I needed to go. Many drivers refuse to take passengers to various sections of the city if it is out of their jurisdiction and usually can't get a return fare.

After being refused by several drivers, a man parked on a motorcycle nearby called to me. Paying no attention, I began speaking with another cab driver. While pointing out my destination on the map to a driver, a man on a motorcycle approached, engaging in conversation with the driver and the man with the motorcycle. The taxi driver would not take me, but signaled me to go with the man on the bike. Oh man, not again.

Before getting on the bike, I needed to know how much it was going to cost. The man responded with a peace sign, meaning twenty yuan. Agreeing with a nod, he removed a helmet for me from the back compartment and stuffed my backpack into it. Once I was securely on the bike, he laid the suitcase across my lap between him and me. The ride was very smooth, and his driving was very safe and courteous, never speeding once. Although I didn't mind, it appeared he took the scenic route, but we had already agreed on a price. Within twenty minutes I was dropped off and met by the security guard just inside the compound gates, knowing there would be no renegotiating the price.

Shortly after I walked in, Hank was up and wasted no time informing me he had volunteered me to be a judge in the singing competition. The competition was to take place at 7:30 a.m. the following morning. Several students attending our school were entered and had been practicing for well over a month. I asked him if he had considered it would be a conflict of interest for me to judge because I taught at the school. He didn't answer, and perhaps didn't understand what I meant.

When Hank and I arrived at the school, it was already bustling with people. Under the impression, after speaking with Elly, that the actual competition wasn't to start until two, unclear as to why I was required to be there so early. Up until that point, I hadn't been brought up to speed on anything, only that I was a judge. About fifteen minutes passed when Hank summoned me to follow him into a room where fifteen Chinese people where already seated. Before being seated, Hank introduced me to the coordinator, who greeted me in English upon entering the room. In front of me, on the desk, was a form containing numbers and columns in Chinese. The coordinator gave me a brief two-minute rundown of what the form entailed and what was to take place. For the remaining half hour, she translated the rules and instruction to the rest of the group in Chinese.

Each room was assigned two judges, and I was paired up with a judge named Chad who volunteered me as his partner. He studied esthetics at the university and spoke English quite well, so while we waited for the competition to begin he explained the rules a little more clearly.

The competition got underway as small groups of children began to arrive. Chad was under the impression we would receive a sheet for each team, yet neither the instructions nor checklist we were given related to what was actually taking place. We were given words to songs the children would be singing ahead of time, but had no idea what songs each child would sing. For the most part, many sang songs we didn't have the words to, and their English was so bad we couldn't understand what they were singing anyway. According to our marking instructions, we were both under the assumption the children were being judged in groups, marked in specific categories, then added up for a final mark. On the contrary, each child was marked individually and no score was to be less than seventy percent. Each child would sing two songs, and we were to mark them individually accordingly. After hearing several children, seventy was a bit too generous.

Kevin entered the room, accompanied by his wife and several

children from our affiliate school who were also entered in the contest. Not long after they sat down, someone came in and asked them to leave. Because Kevin didn't take orders well, he asked if all the other spectators in the room also had to leave. When the answer was no, he informed them he wasn't bothering anyone by being there, refusing to leave.

While judging one of the groups, the coordinator came in and spoke briefly to Chad. When she left, he told me we were to give the higher mark to entry number three, a boy. Kevin overheard our discussion, and the three of us began to mull it over. All of us agreed it was wrong, not to mention inappropriate protocol for a competition. Another little girl competing against the boy had a much better presentation and costume, so we ignored the coordinator's request, giving the little girl the higher mark. Chad didn't seem anxious to change the mark, so I put him at ease, telling him it wasn't fair to the others, and I wouldn't do it. When the coordinator returned to collect the marks, Kevin and his wife had left. After she spoke with Chad, his facial expression seemed very peculiar.

"What did she say?" I asked, curious.

"She suggested again that the little boy was better than all the others. We are to give him the higher mark."

"Are you serious?" I asked in an angered tone.

He shrugged before he replied. "She told me the boy's father put a lot of money into the competition."

"So what? I don't care if he put his house up for sale for his kid to come here. If this is how the competition is going to be run, what's the point of having judges? Let's just give the rich kids the prize up front and send the rest home."

Chad shrugged in agreement, now torn between what to do.

"Look, it's up to you what you want to do. This isn't my country, so I'll go along with whatever you decide, but I don't play by these rules," I finally said. "What do you want to do?" I asked.

To keep peace, we gave the higher score to the boy, but adjusted the marks so it looked as though the point spread between the two were very close, yet in reality, the girl's original score was much higher.

Kevin returned a short time later, and I told him what happened. He immediately bolted out of the room, saying nothing. At one point I heard yelling and someone arguing in the front office area, and recognized the voice to be Kevin's. Things really began to heat up while Chad and I stood in the hall, waiting for more competitors. Coco flew around the corner, immediately tearing a strip off me.

"Your friend the foreign teacher is very angry," she said. "Do you know why?"

"Why are you asking me why he's upset? Ask him!"

"He was sitting beside you in this classroom, and he's your friend!" she bellowed.

"First of all," I bellowed back, "I met him briefly a couple of times, and we attended the same course in Shanghai, but that does *not* make him my friend."

I was well aware of the problem and understood exactly why Kevin flew off the handle.

"Do you have a problem with the children?" she prodded.

"No, I don't have a problem with the children." I refused to discuss anything with her. Although she may have thought otherwise, it was none of her business.

"Then what is wrong with him?"

"If he had a problem, I'm sure he must have told you. Weren't you listening?" I questioned.

"He was very angry, and I think he went home."

"Oh well." I shrugged, walking away.

A few minutes later, the coordinator showed up, pulling Chad to one side, conversing in Chinese. He didn't look very happy. I wasn't sure what was going on, but had a hunch it was centered around Kevin's outburst and the change in marks. It seemed the air was getting thick, so I returned to the classroom to wait. When their conversation ended, Chad returned to the room and sat next to me without saying a word.

To avoid being detected by the office staff, Kevin entered the building a few moments later through the back stairwell to our classroom and was furious. He had been in an argument with the coordinator and several of the staff members over adjusting marks for certain competitors. Everyone he spoke with acted as though they didn't understand anything he was saying, including the coordinator. I knew she spoke English well enough to understand him, yet gave Kevin the impression she couldn't. When he demanded to know why she told us to change the marks, he was led down the hall to observe some of the other competitions in progress to get him away from the others.

Kevin, still enraged, stood in front of Chad and me, telling us we should put everything out in the open. Chad still wasn't talking at all, and I wasn't sure I should push the issue or my luck much further.

"What are you going to do about this?" Kevin asked.

"Don't worry about it, Kevin. I'm not going to pursue it. We're already in enough shit, and it doesn't matter."

"So you're going to change the marks?"

I looked at Chad, still saying nothing, then turned to Kevin and shrugged.

"No."

"You're just as bad as the rest of them! It doesn't matter whether it was a request or a suggestion, it's wrong, and she can't get away with it! I have told all the parents waiting outside what is taking place, and they're all fighting amongst themselves!" he yelled before storming out of the room.

Chad began eating a Twinkie Lindsay had given us earlier. After devouring an entire container of Pringles earlier, I offered him my Twinkie as a peace offering.

"Here, you can have mine if you like. I'm not very hungry."

"Thank you," he said, "I'm getting very hungry."

"You're welcome. I'm sorry about all the trouble Kevin and I have caused for you. I've had about enough of this competition anyway. I just want to get out of here and go home. Being a judge wasn't even my idea, so I don't really care," I said. He turned to me and smiled.

A few minutes later, Susie entered the room, announcing the competition was over and everyone, including the judges, were all to meet for lunch at a nearby restaurant. I was left to wonder if the competition was over because everyone was finished, or because of the trouble. Nonetheless, I wasn't about to ask.

Al, Lindsay and Elly didn't seem bothered by any of it, yet I was getting some precarious looks. As Al and I walked, I suggested it would be best if I went home for lunch. He laughed. "This isn't a very important competition anyway. No need to worry, everything is fine," he said. Less than convinced, I walked at his side into the restaurant. Between judges, teachers and staff, three large round tables were taken up during lunch. For the first half-hour, even a dim-witted person could have detected the evident chill in the atmosphere.

As large quantities of food began arriving, everyone seemed to become more at ease, as though a problem never existed at all. One of the male judges approached me from one of the other tables, held out his glass of beer and toasted me.

"Cheers," he said.

I returned the gesture, and we clinked glasses.

"Thank you for being a judge," he said.

Dumbfounded, I nodded, and another male judge walked over to make a toast shortly thereafter.

Prior to leaving the restaurant, Chad walked toward me with his beer in one hand, putting his other hand out for me to shake.

"Thank you for being my partner," he said.

Stupefied, I shook his hand, then he held up his glass of beer for me to toast, a sign everything was now OK. I couldn't help but think the events of the day were becoming stranger by the minute and perhaps the entire ordeal wasn't such an ordeal after all. The coordinator who created all the tension in the first place never did thank me or acknowledge I was even there, and nothing was mentioned about Kevin or the competition until Hank asked me a couple weeks later why Kevin was so angry.

When we returned to the school, Hank showed me the sheet for the contestants we had judged and had changed the marks for.

"Do you remember these students?" he asked.

"Yes."

"Do you remember if there were any who stood out better than the others?"

"Yes, there was one little girl in a pretty white costume. Her singing and her routine was much better than all the others. This other little boy wasn't bad, but he was not that special," I pointed out.

"OK," he said, then left.

What took place was wrong, and perhaps in a roundabout way they were admitting their mistake. More importantly, they were correcting it.

There was a two-week lull before classes were back in session. After spending a week traveling with the school, then traveling to Shanghai for the course, I was all tripped out and really didn't care to go anywhere. Jake and Mac wouldn't be returning until the middle of September, so Hank was making arrangements to have an Australian teacher, Luis, to fill in while they were away.

Hank and Luis were good friends, and when Hank was in a bind for a teacher, he would call Luis. Jake also knew Luis and had introduced me to him and his wife one day when we went for lunch together just prior to summer holidays. On several occasions Luis had taught at the school part-time, but quit each time because he didn't get along with the principal, comparing her to a Nazi. Charming.

The prospect of teaching rotten little children for the next few months with no materials didn't really appeal to me, so it was time to go on a mission. I had a plan to set my imagination and artistic skills into action. Flashcards and props were provided to the Chinese teachers for the main book they taught from. However, just for shits and giggles, the foreigners taught eight different levels of phonetics using no flashcards or props.

The Chinese teachers spent class time playing games and singing songs to keep the students interested. In theory, that was great when communicating in Chinese, if they are learning while they play. However, I was opposed to teaching fifty-minute classes utilizing two pages of a book that would hold their attention for fifteen minutes. If nothing more than to heighten one's sense of humor, in my opinion everyone should try this at least once. Well aware students could memorize words, I wanted to know if they were actually learning and could even identify anything I was teaching them from previous lessons.

My plan was to create flashcards that not only challenged their memory, but would improve their reading and writing skills as well. In my mind, hypothetically, my plan would work well. Dividing sheets of paper into four sections would supply flashcards not only be big enough to see, but also useful for a multitude of fun games and activities, reinforcing their learning skills.

For the next two weeks, I threw myself into a frenzy of photocopying and cutting and pasting pictures for each of the eight levels to coincide with the letters and symbols I drew in the center, before laminating each one. Game ideas were popping into my head like wildfire, and if nothing else, I knew it couldn't possibly be worse than what I had already been doing.

Chapter 20
Cleanup Time!

August had ended and the new school semester had arrived. With Hank out of town, the principal was in charge of things once again, including Luis's hours and class scheduling. There was definitely no love lost between the two of them, and within the first two days he knew he was going to have problems. Luis had been given mainly the disruptive classes or classes no one else wanted, so he packed everything up and walked. Because he lived on the far side of Hankou, his trip time alone to teach two classes a night was two hours each way, and he was only doing it as a favor to help Hank out for a couple of weeks. He didn't need or want the aggravation or job, making it quite clear he was going to pack his things and walk.

Things didn't change, and it was only a couple of days before Luis was in a major confrontation with Liela over his schedule. To kickstart his day, he was scheduled to do two demo classes consisting of three- and four-year-olds, topped off with most of the rotten classes. We were the only foreign English teachers there, so I had also been given four- and five-year-old students and one demo class. From the beginning I had made it quite clear I didn't want to teach the younger age groups.

The thought of teaching four year olds intimidated me, but what intimidated me even more were the parents who either sat in on the class or stood in the hall and gawked through the glass window at the entire class. After teaching them for a couple of weeks, my fears subsided and came to the conclusion that children behave and use their manners because the parents are in the room, and they are more likely to learn. The younger children were actually a lot more fun to teach; however, purchasing stickers for their books from the corner store also helped.

We both approached Liela about the demo classes and were bluntly told it was our job as foreign teachers to convince the parents to sign their kids on at our school. Luis lost it.

"I don't do demos, Liela, OK? I teach English, so revise the schedule, because I'm not doing it!" he demanded.

"But, ah," she hesitated, "you must, it is very important." She was frustrated and was glancing at me.

"Don't think you're giving them to me," I retorted. "I already have one, and three other classes of very young children as well."

Luis began packing up his stuff to leave.

"Liela, I don't need this job! I'm only doing this as a favor to Hank until Mac and Jake return. I don't do demos, I teach English. Demos are not a class. Do you understand?" he bellowed.

"But, ah, we have no one else to teach," she continued, still attempting to convince him.

"Yes, well, that's not my problem, is it? Go talk to Hank. I have seven classes Saturday and Sunday, and five of them are little children. I'm not doing them!"

After Liela left in a huff, almost in tears, Luis called Hank and everything was sorted out, at least for the time being, and Luis did do the demos.

The first week was total chaos, with Saturday and Sunday jam-packed with little kiddy classes. On top of it all, I was also expected to throw a "free" session of English Corner in during my lunch hour. That wasn't about to happen again in this lifetime.

By the time we had finished Sunday afternoon, Luis was looking forward to having a couple of beers in the park that was furnished with benches and shade trees across the street, and he asked me to join him. It wasn't necessary to twist my arm. After a week like that, a non-drinker would probably have started! Seldom indulging, or even buying beer for that matter, I was ignorant to the fact that the corner stores sold beer. Luis was treating, so he purchased three or four for each of us. Two very long, tiring days followed by a couple beers, and I was half-corked. Although Luis found it somewhat amusing, it was good to have someone to hang out with and talk to for a while.

Confrontations between Liela and Luis were becoming a daily ritual. I was starting to think that he enjoyed winding her up. Many of his expressions were quite colorful and quite foreign to Liela. Following one such confrontation, Liela stood at my desk, hesitant before speaking.

"The word 'shit.' How do you spell this word?" she asked.

Naturally, my delay in answering was due to the fact that I was doubled over in hysterical laughter.

"Why are you laughing?" she asked, angry. "What is the meaning of this word 'shit'?" she repeated. "I don't know this word. This is a very bad word, isn't it?"

"Yes, it's a bad word," I replied, still smirking.

"Um, Luis is very angry. What does this word mean?"

"It doesn't really have a meaning. It's a word people use instead of saying what they mean. Luis isn't angry at you, so don't take it personally." I continued, "He doesn't like the classes, so he referred to them as shit. Don't worry about it, Liela. He's only here for a short time," I reassured her.

Later, when Elly, April, Liela and I walked to the bus stop, Liela asked another loaded question.

"Sharon, what does it mean, 'you don't know shit'?"

Caught totally off-guard, I broke out laughing. A Chinese female using an unfamiliar word like shit in a sentence was worth the price of admission. It didn't help that Elly and April were also laughing. Liela, almost crying, pummeled me in the arm, convinced I was making fun of her, so I put my arm around her and continued walking.

"It means you don't know anything," I explained.

Her expression went blank as I continued. "There are many expressions using this word, such as, This is Bullshit! What kind of shit are you trying to pull? Do you have shit for brains? You stupid shit! They all mean nothing."

She was still upset, but it was enough to get her laughing.

"Liela, don't take it personally. Jake and Mac will be back soon."

"You, Jake and Mac don't use these words."

"Oh, yes we do, just not in front of you. When I'm angry, you'll know."

Liela smiled. "Yes, and I don't like when you're angry."

"I don't like when I'm angry either, Liela."

"I think Luis must be very unhappy man," Liela concluded.

"Perhaps you're right, Liela."

The following Sunday began like any other day; however, that was about to change. On my way to the bus, an endless steam of students in military attire four rows deep were carrying books and a tiny foot-high stool, walking from East Lake toward Wuhan University.

After boarding the bus, traffic was suddenly gridlocked for the next ten minutes at the traffic lights to the entrance of the university. Students dressed in military attire were running in formation, four wide, toward the campus from their dorms, through the intersection in formation. The reality, thousands were passing, a partial army in fact, and the world could be in serious trouble, I thought, if a war broke out and they weren't on our side.

Drivers were getting impatient, wailing on their horns, even as police were directing and controlling the traffic. Our driver was on a mission, putting the pedal to the medal, aggressively shifting gears and bulldozing his way into and through the intersection, barely missing the officer directing traffic. In the center of the intersection he suddenly slammed on the brakes. Out my lefthand window, the whites of the taxi driver's eyes were clearly visible when the front end of his taxi scarcely halted under the tire of the bus. On my right, another taxi was within an inch of the bus's front bumper. Our driver punched the bus into high gear, honking the horn with no sign of letting up. Weaving in and out around traffic and through red lights like a maniac, we grabbed whatever we could to hang on. Turning the corner a few minutes later, he was pulled over by an officer on a motorcycle and got out. When the officer finished writing the ticket, he handed it to the driver, coolly put on his sunglasses, got on his bike and sped back toward the university.

As the day progressed, it remained on the same continuum, one disaster after another, and it was about to change. With two classes still remaining, it was time to turn the tables and take charge of these classes.

Ten minutes into my second to last class, Bill walked across the room and began pounding the crap out of a girl almost half my size. Naturally, I wedged myself between them, grabbing Bill by his shirt collar and twisting to break them up. He had at least thirty pounds on me and was determined he was going to finishing what he started. His eyes were full of rage as he grabbed me by my shirt collar and necklace, twisting, almost chocking me as I pushed him backward across the room. As he tightened his grip, I lost it, tightening my neck muscles to prevent him from choking me. He suddenly felt like a rag doll in my hands as I continued to push him, hurling him into his chair before letting go. No one moved, and for the next ten minutes Bill stared into oblivion with his arms crossed while I continued with class. Ten minutes later, I included Bill and things were back to normal.

B07 was not only my last class that day, it was my worst nightmare. The atmosphere in the room hit me like a sack of potatoes. After teaching them the previous week, I knew they had no intention of learning. The boys and a few of the girls were an absolute nightmare. As it was their last class, I was to review the entire book. However, they couldn't identify one sound or picture, much less answer any questions. Completely out of control, perhaps they decided it would be more fun to disrupt the class and tick me off.

It was cleanup time, and this class was no exception. Holding up the book, I flipped through the pages, indicating they had finished the book. The girls seemed to know some answers, so I thought it time to play a game, girls against the boys. To sweeten the pot, I held up a bag of candies before pulling out a stack of flashcards for review. The boys continued playing amongst themselves, laughing and ignoring me. In my backpack I had my Chinese-English dictionary, so I pulled it out, emphasizing the word "fail" with the number zero, indicating they were going to fail.

Mike, one of several instigators, had the class at his disposal and began pushing my buttons. Pointing to the door, I requested he leave. When he laughed, I yanked his five-foot-seven ass out of the chair, escorting him across the room. Suddenly, he planted his feet firmly on the floor so I couldn't move him, and he crossed his arms, laughing hysterically with his classmates. Looking down, I instantaneously kicked his foot out from under him, setting him flat on the floor, then crossed my arms, staring down at him. He sat on the floor, staring up at me with a blank expression while the class laughed. Perhaps he would run straight to the principal and tell his parents a woman half his size took him out, but in all likelihood, the chance of that was pretty slim. After he got up, I escorted him back to his desk and told him to sit down, then immediately picked up his book, opened it, and slammed it down on his desk.

"If you open it," I yelled, "you might learn something!"

He glared at me, fear written all over his face, and the tone of the entire classroom changed at that point.

I continued with the flashcard review game, girls against the boys, stacking ten flashcards for each team face down on two chairs at the front of the room. Each team had to turn a card one at a time and write on the board what each were. In no time flat, the boys began cheating, using their books, so I collected all the books to see just how clever they really were. Needless to say, the boys were spelling words that didn't exist, and the girls ended up kicking their cocky little behinds.

It was discouraging, and there was no doubt in my mind all of them would advance to the next level regardless. I would not be disappointed. At least half the class should have failed, yet everyone had been moved ahead. One more opportunity was staring me right in the face, a chance to make a difference. With less than two months left on my contract, I had two requests and was determined to go on one last mission, one last challenge, so I requested to take over B07, the new class from hell. After all, I had turned the Spitter Bob class around, so I had to at least give it one more try.

Neither Liela nor Elly could understand why I wanted to take on the task of regrouping this horrible class. It was simple, really. There had been several Chinese/English teachers teaching B07, and all had nothing but problems. There were too many teachers, in my opinion, no structure, no routine and, therefore, no control. How could any learning take place when patience had obviously run out with this group long ago? Hopefully I could teach these kids to speak, write and maybe even understand some English before my departure.

My second request was to have someone else take over B14, the master's class from beyond hell. In China it is a known fact that students who come from the most money are like a god in the classroom. The master was it, still in control, and I didn't want any more to do with it. For weeks I had tried everything in my power to reach this class, but it was like talking to a wall each week, and an absolute waste of my time. Luis also had nothing but problems the few times he had taught them, yet agreed to take over the class. Giving someone else the pleasure of setting them straight, especially the master, was a relief and seemed to put a glow on Luis's face.

That Sunday I entered my first class, a level six class. Not one of my regular classes, all the faces were unfamiliar, all but one: Pat, a Spitter Bob class original. He was excited to see me and made a point of greeting me at the door. Although Pat got off to a slow start from day one, he began to make a great deal of progress once Bob and Billy were gone. The change and progress in Pat and the other boys throughout the semester was phenomenal. They were learning, speaking and making sentences that made sense. Tony, Jack, Frank, also rebellious in the beginning, had jumped ahead in the participation category, advancing to the next level. It took Pat a little longer to get involved, and there was a fifty-fifty chance he would also move ahead. However, he didn't quite make it and was repeating the level.

As class got underway, it didn't take long to discover the entire class, with the exception of Pat and a couple girls, was identical to B07. Pat was the only one who could or even attempted to answer any questions correctly. When class ended, Pat was walking ahead of me, and it occurred to me that I had made a difference, and Pat was living proof. I caught up to him and asked him to follow me to my office. In my desk I kept a stash of suckers, so I pulled one out and gave it to him. His expression was one of confusion, but he said, "Thank you."

"You're welcome," I replied before putting my arm around him to let him know how proud of him I was.

As he walked away, he hesitated, turned back, smiled and said, "Thank you, Teacher," and left. What an incredible feeling! Pat had become my child prodigy, and I was really proud of him.

My request had been granted, and I officially had the class from hell, B07. Mike thought it might be fun to try and push a few more of my buttons, but it was nothing a couple of looks and a change in my tone wouldn't fix. Well aware there was more than one troublemaker in the class, I fully expected to have a Mike clone take over, and wouldn't be disappointed.

Dan, a chubby, evil boy who could care less about learning, took right over. He pulled out a container of goop, stretching it and rolling it while talking with his friend Jeremy. Approaching his desk, I politely asked him to put the goop away. He stuck it behind his back, and the moment I walked away he began playing with it again. After asking him the second time to hand it over, I took the lid and he gave me a look that clearly implied, "Who the hell do you think you are?"

Dan was getting angrier by the minute, yelling in Chinese as I walked away, ignoring him. The third time was the last straw. Dan and Jeremy continued playing with the goop, laughing and talking so loud they were disrupting the class. I stood in front of Dan with my hand out, asking him in a firm voice to give me the goop. He stretched the goop, laughing, then rolled it up and smacked it hard, smearing it all over the back of my hand. Whatever the substance was, it didn't remove easily. The class was in hysterical laughter as I stood calm, cool and collected in front of his desk, smiling while I peeled it off. Once off, I rolled it into a ball then smacked it firmly on Dan's forehead, smearing it, then backed away. As he attempted to get the goop off, he wiped upward, smearing it into his hair. He then took a tissue and tried to wipe it off, resulting in a combination of goop mixed with tissue stuck in his hair. The entire class went into hysterical laughter. Rage began jetting out of every pore in his body as I continued teaching the class. Jeremy approached me, asking if they could go to the toilet with Dan. It would definitely take both of them to get Dan cleaned up, so I let them go. When they returned, Dan still had remnants in his hair, and seemed more pissed than ever.

After classes finished, Luis and I went downstairs to Hank's office for coffee, and I told him what happened with Dan. He laughed, then asked what he was like when he returned to class.

"He was very angry," I said, "giving me dirty looks, refusing to participate."

Hank finally told me he intercepted the two boys on their way to the bathroom, asking them what happened. When they told him the story, Hank became very angry with them and said if they ever did that to another teacher, foreign or otherwise again, he would call their parents in and they would be informed of what was going on in the classroom. If Hank had not intercepted, Dan would have told his parents an entirely different story, to benefit him to reverse the tables. In my defense, I explained to Hank that everyone in the class saw what happened and, no matter what the situation, there are always a select few who insist on telling the truth. The best I could hope for was Dan's crap to end. Less than convinced that taking over the class was a good idea, I decided I had set a goal and would prevail no matter what.

Sunday, just one week later, my day ended with B07. When I entered the classroom, eight boys were missing, two of them returning five minutes into the lesson. The school had a rule of no food and no drinks in class. When students or parents brought food into the classroom, we were instructed to have them wait until break or eat in the hall.

Four of them, including Dan and Jeremy, returned from the

washroom ten minutes later. Instead of coming in, Dan took out a stash of junk food and they all proceeded to sit on the window ledge in the hall, eating it. When I instructed them to come into class, Dan smirked and pointed to his bag of candies to indicate they couldn't eat in class. With a smug grin, he looked directly at me, then began pouring out more to share with his friends.

I left to get Elly, and they had all returned to class by the time we got there. Elly spent a couple of minutes tearing a strip off them anyway, only to have all hell break loose the instant she stepped out of the classroom. It wasn't five minutes later that the last two stragglers returned and things became progressively worse. The entire class had no interest; however, Dan had already set the pace.

Standing at the front of the class with my arms folded, I said nothing, waiting for silence. Two minutes, three minutes, five minutes passed, and they continued, so I pulled up a chair and sat down. Dan finally stopped talking, then glared at me briefly before he continued. This was payback for him, and his evil facade was glowing, growing by the minute, with no intentions of stopping. I approached him, asking him to leave the class. He shook his head, smirked, crossed his arms, then began talking again. Any patience I had went out the window the moment I yanked him out of his chair to assist him across the room. As we reached the door, he jammed his feet into the wall to prevent me from throwing him out. At that point it was simply a matter of opening the door to heave him out into the hall.

The class broke into laughter, and nothing changed as they all resumed talking. Whatever composure I had managed to hold onto, I lost, throwing my book across the room into the middle of the floor. Elly arrived at the window just in time to observe my display. Standing with her arms crossed, glaring at the children, she was seemingly unconcerned with what I was doing.

"I will call each one of your parents in. I don't care!" I yelled.

Knowing full well they understood the words "mother and father," I tried once more.

"I will call your mother and father and tell them you don't want to learn English, and you can tell them why," I finished.

Perhaps they were beginning to clue in that I was not a Chinese teacher or someone they could walk all over, and if they so desired, I in turn could become their worst nightmare, if that's what it took. They understood, and for the moment I had their attention and asked one last question.

"Do you want to learn English?" I bellowed.

No response.

"Do you want to learn English, yes or no?"

The answer was yes. For the remainder of the class their books were open, and they began to learn. Dan, on the other hand, had disappeared and did not return to class that day.

Elly and I were both well aware of my situation with B07 and had one last card up our sleeve. The "three strikes you're out" action plan was to commence after the mid-autumn festival.

Chapter 21
A Visit to Mulan Lake During Mid-Autumn Festival

The mid-autumn festival is also known as Harvest Moon. Each year on the fifteenth day of the eighth month of the lunar calendar, the Chinese celebrate what is—outside the lunar new year—the biggest event of the year. It is a time of reunions, where families get together to feast and also snack on moon cakes. Moon cakes symbolize the full moon, and the most famous legend associated with it dates back to 1368 AD. In the fourteenth century, China had been overthrown by the Mongols. The Chinese used moon cakes to hide messages with plans for the rebellions. The Mongols, who did not eat moon cakes, were unaware of the subterfuge. Families were told to eat the cakes on the day of the festivals, and it is then the revolt happened. A traditional moon cake is filled with lotus seed paste with a salty egg yolk in the center, which represents the moon, but they are now made with many different fillings. They are very high in calories, and therefore are usually cut into quarters to be shared.[40]

All the staff members, including me, were given a gift box filled with various types of moon cakes. My assorted cakes were made of flaked pastry stuffed with a wide variety of fillings. Egg yolk, lotus seed paste, red bean paste, and coconut were most common, but walnuts, dates and other fillings can be found as well. Each cake had characters for longevity or harmony inscribed on the top. It is a celebration of abundant harvest that in some ways I found similar to our Thanksgiving holiday. Traditionally it is celebrated outdoors under the moonlight, gazing at the moon, eating moon cakes.

Hank would be in Taiwan during the festival, but I would be moving into a three-bedroom apartment in the same complex, to be joined by two new roommates, Damen and Angel, from Canada. Two years earlier they taught English at the same school, but left due to the SARS outbreak. They were to arrive within two days from an Australian working holiday. However, before their arrival I had my work cut out for me. It definitely needed a woman's touch, and took two entire days of washing and scrubbing to clean it up.

Since I was never big on roommates, I wasn't entirely sure my new living arrangements were going to work out, but the day came and my cell phone rang. They were at the train station, and within the hour were waiting at the front gate, loaded down with backpacks and bags.

Much to my surprise, the three of us hit it off great. To have a normal conversation in English without analyzing content and structure was such a treat. It was wonderful to have someone to hang out with or just eat with.

Later that evening, the three of us met up with Jake and Damen's friend Josh at a nearby outdoor barbeque. Jake and Josh were awaiting our arrival with a couple bottles of beer. At two yuan per liter bottle, we couldn't go wrong. We ordered almost everything available to be barbequed: cucumber, mutton, mushrooms, potatoes and chicken feet. While we waited for our food, we drank beer, and Josh, a very unique and very smart black South African fluent in Chinese, English and some African dialects, told us his story.

Five years earlier, Josh and his best friend left a small village in Africa and traveled to China to enroll in Wuhan University to study to become doctors. However, his friend only made it through one semester. The problems with the Chinese, the ridiculing he encountered, especially from his Chinese professors, were so overwhelming that he snapped, demolishing his dorm room and smashing his brand new computer before returning to Africa. After living as a local with the Chinese for five years, Josh was still called a "black devil" to his face, and still encountered problems on a daily basis. Observing a couple of occurrences, it became clear to me that Chinese were very prejudiced toward black people.

Three younger Chinese students sat at a tiny romper room table and chair set at the end of ours. We sat at a normal table, as no normal adult could possibly sit in that position for any length of time. Angel wanted to take a picture of them eating chicken feet, so as a courteous gesture, Damen bought beer and had it delivered to their table. None of us were feeling any pain at that point, and it wasn't long before they sent a plate of barbequed corn on the cob, returning the gesture.

After a few dozen glasses of beer, Angel and I was coaxed into trying chicken feet. The huge fascination behind eating them was beyond me. Everything, including the toenails, was still in tact. They are repulsive really, containing very little if any meat.

On our return trip to the apartment, about midnight, the massage establishment was still open. We had all had enough beers by then and decided a foot massage would be just the thing to end our evening. Having had several beers, I didn't much care, but was nonetheless hesitant. Damen, however, reassured me he knew enough Chinese and could translate to the therapist to go easy on me. It was OK.

Lindsay and I had planned on visiting the famous three gorges and hanging coffins during our five days off, but the prices doubled during that time and would consume over half of Lindsay's paycheck. It wasn't a big deal to me, so I offered to cover some of her cost, but she would not accept my generosity. Instead, we chose somewhere else, a Sunday outing to Mulan Lake, the name originating from the legendary story of Mulan, China's most famous woman warrior.

An article which best depicts the story behind the Mulan legend, in my opinion, is an article by the late Amy Ling, who is beloved and missed by all, cited in "A Cultural Lexicon for Asian Pacific Studies" in Leonard, George, ed., *The Asian-Pacific American Heritage: a companion to Literature and Arts* (New York: Routledge: 1999, pp 656-657).

Mu Lan is China's legendary "woman warrior," heroine of a folk ballad in which a brave girl takes her aged father's place in the army by disguising herself as a man. Her story was little known in the West until 1998, when the Walt Disney company put its awesome cultural might behind the feature-length cartoon *Mulan*, which became a summer blockbuster. Amy Ling, who researched Mu Lan for her work, writes: "Mu Lan (variously known as Fa Mu Lan or Hua Mu Lan—Hua/Fa means flower, and Mu Lan means magnolia) is the heroine of a folk ballad that mothers traditionally sang to their children in China. When the emperor goes to war against Northern invaders, the Hu, he drafts a son from each family. Mu Lan's family has no son old enough to fight, so her elderly father gets drafted. Mu Lan disguises herself as a man and takes his place. The new army takes the attack to the Hu, high up in their snowy Yen Mountain strongholds. Mu Lan fights for over a decade without being discovered, and so valiantly that the Emperor himself, bestowing medals, titles and land grants after the war, offers to make her a minister of state. She asks only to go home. There, she reopens the wing of her house that had been sealed for ten years, puts on her woman's dress again, and emerges, to the amazement of her old comrades-at-arms.

Mu Lan's religion is Confucianism. She doesn't hear the voice of God, but of her conscience, commanding this loving duty to her father. Nor is it possible to imagine the ballad's Mu Lan so eager to regain her womanhood and, already the model of family duty, not proceeding on to marriage and motherhood. Indeed, the poem dwells on her rather amazing ability to effortlessly return to femininity, fashionable "beauty patches" and all. Joan of Arc revels in the battlefield, and it is impossible to imagine her wishing to return to village life; Mu Lan, offered a government ministry position, asks only for a camel to take her home. Though modern accounts, even Disney's, tend to present Mu

Lan's army service as a feminist achievement, in the Chinese ballad war seems (realistically) a catastrophe for everyone, men and women, soldiers and generals alike. Mu Lan's long years in the army are presented only as a terrible sacrifice to spare her father from going through them, and she resumes her peaceful former life with relief.

"A few historical reports exist of women disguising themselves as men in order to fight. Women, however, were not commonly trained in martial arts—nor educated for any profession, in fact. There are stories of women disguising themselves as men in order to be educated (for instance, 'The Butterfly Lovers'). The poem is potent myth, not history."

The translation, by George and Simei Leonard, was made from the Chinese text in *Selected Chinese Poems*, ed. Ch'en Hui-Wen (Taibei, Hua Lien Publishing Co. 1968) which Professor Ling furnished. They write, "This is the best known of many versions of the Mu Lan story, dating back at least to the Tang Dynasty (618-907AD). Even in anti-Confucian Maoist times, PRC children like Simei had to learn it by heart from their fifth grade readers, and recite it in class together.

"How old is 'Mu Lan's Farewell'? The poem refers to the emperor sitting in the 'Ming tang,' or 'Ming Hall,' but the term, our sources tell us, is no reference to the Ming Dynasty (1368-1644 AD). The word 'Ming' means 'brilliant' or even 'splendid' and the term 'Ming tang' for some hall of splendor in which imperial rituals are conducted, can be found all the way back to the Zhou Dynasty (founded, 1111 BC).

"Nor is the Hu invasion a clue. They're described as a tribe of Northern horsemen, and such tribes perpetually menaced China. The Great Wall, stretching across the tops of China's mountains from east to west, were built as a bulwark against such Northern tribes in the 200s BC. The Disney movie calls the Hu people the Huns, but without foundation. Rather, 'Hu people' is a catchall term much like the Greek 'barbarian.' China called any menacing Northern barbarian tribes the 'Hu,' and each dynasty since the Han (206 BC-265 AD) used 'Hu' for whomever its Northern barbarian opponent happened to be.

"Our best clue to this poem's age is that while this version refers to the emperor as 'the Son of Heaven,'—a standard designation—it also calls him, twice, 'the Khan.' Since no one but the Mongols of the Yuan Dynasty (1206-1368 AD) would have used that term for the emperor, this version could not be older than 1206, and was most likely written in those years. (Or less likely, set in those years.) 'Mu Lan's Farewell,' then, is probably a folk ballad from the 1200-1300s AD, nearly 800 years old.

'The parable of the rabbits at the end draws the moral. In ordinary times (it claims) you can tell a male rabbit from a female by its behavior. But in a crisis, when they're running, you can't tell which is which. The female runs just as well as the male. Hua Mu Lan's popular ballad does not so much reflect historical reality, as the reality of women's dreams and aspirations—not an aspiration to shed blood, but an aspiration to be recognized as people who, when the need arises, can do deeds as valiant as can any man. That the author of this modern-sounding moral was very likely a man, and a medieval man; that this story has been popular among the Chinese people for a millennium, and is even memorized in school—all this should be taken into account before anyone summarizes traditional Chinese culture's attitude to women."[41]

Seven-thirty a.m., Sunday, I was on the bus to Hankou to meet up with Lindsay for our excursion. It was a two-minute walk to catch the bus to Mulan Lake, and a two-hour trip from Hànkou. There was only one option, the eight a.m. bus from Hankou, returning at four-thirty.

In the northern suburb of Hankou, in Huangpi County, is Mulan Hill, seventy kilometers away. Within two hours the bus pulled into a massive parking lot at Mulan Lake. Other buses full of Chinese tourists had also arrived, and more were arriving by the minute. It was not only the birthplace of the ancient legendary heroine Hua Mulan, but a sightseeing spot. On a hill, the people built Mulan Temple and a general hall with Taoist temples and a religious site ever since. Temples, halls and pavilions on the hill are mostly constructed in the way of "overlaying" big stones alternating with small ones laid up on top of each other with mortar so that the stones overlap each other, thus reinforcing themselves and forming an integral structure.

Six kilometers north of Mulan Hill is the scenic spot of Mulan Lake, lined with luxuriant trees, bushes and crystal clear water as green as jade. The total area of the lake has one hundred and thirty-two small ponds, twenty-three small islands and thirteen springs, and approximately four thousand hectares. East of the lake is a wooded area with all kinds of birds, over one-hundred thousand in number, among which thirty percent belong to the second category animals under national protection. During the winter and summer seasons, migratory birds came and went in big flocks, an appealing landscape rarely found in other places.

From the entrance of the grounds all the way to Mulan lake required us to walk a good two hours up the mountain. However, following a multitude of Chinese tourists all the way up, at times, became extremely frustrating. We spent a lot of time stopping and waiting for the camera-happy tourists to begin moving again. Making our way to the lake at the top of Mulan Mountain was a very narrow and very steep climb. As we continued, about halfway up the mountain we encountered some small waterfalls, little pools and spectacular views.

Beyond the last hill at the top was Mulan Lake. Along the lake coming and going were many Chinese-style boats, and I asked Lindsay if she wanted go on one for a tour of the lake. The tour was a lunch cruise traveling directly to and from a restaurant on the lake, and Lindsay didn't want to go.

Perhaps we were lucky we didn't go on a boat that day. Lindsay read in the local paper the following day that one of the boats capsized, and it was quite conceivable for us to have been among the passengers. Instead of a boat adventure, I opted instead to soar across the lake hooked to a thick cable wire. At the peak of the mountain each participant is strapped into a canvas body harness contraption, then hooked up to roller device on the cable wire. After a slight push, you are sent on your way across the lake to a platform at the bottom. The line up for the adventure was extremely long and very slow. Lindsay had no intention of trying it, so she took my camera to the bottom platform to wait for my arrival. Forty-five minutes had passed before Lindsay returned to find I was still waiting and was now fifth in line. The thrill ride reminded me of something rigged up by the Flintstones. Hooked to two solid poles secured in the platform are two thick cables with plenty of play. An ancient-looking roller bar sits on top of the cables to get you from point A to point B. The concept is somewhat similar to one I had experienced in Costa Rica, only the Chinese version involved one swoop from point to point instead of tree hopping from tree to tree.

After being strapped into a heavy canvas outfit, which also combines as your seat, you are hooked into the roller bar that is then lifted on top of the cable wires and suspended in midair. Before being catapulted to the bottom, Lindsay played photographer. Once strapped in, I was given a big push for my express ride and was airborne. It was a short ride, but I can assure you it was extremely fast. What an incredible rush! As I sped across the lake for a landing, it occurred to me I wasn't slowing down, so I looked up. "No brakes! Christ, you've got to be kidding me!"

As I got closer, directly in front of me was a two-foot thick gym mat placed upright at the end of the line. Oh shit! At the speed I was traveling, if I hit face first, I'm toast, I thought. The thought no sooner crossed my mind when I came to a grinding halt, hitting two bumper stoppers located at the top of the cables to prevent me from impacting the mat. The sudden jolt threw me backward then forward, similar to receiving whiplash. After I bounced several times, an attendant put a step under me so I could get down and they could unhook me. It was a riveting experience, not to mention one hell of a wild ride.

Another ride there was grass tobogganing down the mountain, similar to snow tubing. At a high rate of speed on a hard plastic sled, you slide down a contour track made entirely of metal wiring, similar to chicken wire, and woven entirely with artificial grass. After watching, I imagined the scenario of being airborne and launched off one track only to rip my backside apart on chicken wire as I landed on another track. Not a chance!

It was time to begin our long journey back down the mountain. The trail back down took us in a different direction, a passageway through the celestial cave straight through the mountain. Inside, the cave was cold, with water running down the sides of the rock faces. Prior to exiting the pass stood a stone statue that no one really took much notice of. The exit of the passageway led to a high, open culvert tunneled out of sections of the rock in the mountain. Rocks were strategically placed as stepping-stones along shallow running water feeding from the mountain.

The final leg of the climb from the top was referred to as the Celestial Ladder, consisting of very deep, high steps on a ninety-degree incline, straight down. Lindsay lost her footing a few times, and my knees began to shake uncontrollably with every step. My kneecaps felt as though they were going to blow right out of their sockets. We were never so glad to arrive at the bottom of a mountain in my entire life. Still, our Mulan adventure had turned out great. What an amazing day, another historic Chinese journey comparable to so many other exciting adventures I had ventured into throughout China.

School was back in session after five days off, and before returning to classes, Angel convinced me to join her for a haircut and head massage at a small establishment they used to visit frequently. A two-hour visit entailed a dry shampoo head massage followed by a second head massage and rinse, then a haircut followed by another fifteen-minute full neck and back massage for the low, low price of ten yuan, about three dollars.

The three of us strolled into work at 5:30, and the principal was less than overjoyed. It didn't take long before she sent Liela to impose rules about working a forty hours workweek. It was apparent the principal invented rules as she went along, especially when Hank was gone, rubbing every single foreign teacher the wrong way, including Angel and Damen during their first teaching contract.

Within earshot, I interrupted to remind Liela about having the same conversation with both her and Hank during the summer, to which she denied having any such conversation. Angel took over the conversation, informing Liela that their contract wasn't signed, therefore wasn't binding. Angel stood her ground, setting the rules straight, letting Liela know the school wasn't going to walk all over them. Flabbergasted and frustrated, Liela left the room, and we felt bad for her, knowing she was always acting under the direct orders of the principal.

There were many schools in Wuhan, and China for that matter, that paid more money and didn't expect them to work forty hours or show up several hours ahead. Faced with two foreign English teachers who had unsigned contracts and weren't about to put up with any crap, perhaps the school was suddenly between a rock and a hard place. With my departure date arriving quickly, it was proving to be an interesting position for Angel and Damen to be in, at least from their perspective.

When you open your heart and feel,
You will begin to awaken to all around you.
When you feel with your heart,
Only then will the words begin to flow.
When you write what you feel in your heart,
The description will begin to flow
In a direction beyond your imagination.

Chapter 22
An Incredible End to
an Amazing Journey!

Curled up in the lounge chair, watching television, a sudden obnoxious pain developed in my upper right side. My legs were draped over the chair arm, so thinking that something had knotted up from the way I was sitting, at first I didn't take much notice. It suddenly began to worsen, and I was having a lot of difficulty breathing. Efforts to walk it off only increased the intensity of the pain, so I doubled over. No matter what I did, the pain worsened.

Angel began to worry and called Jake, relaying my symptoms to him. Dropping what he was doing, he jumped on his bike and rushed right over. By the time he got there, the pain had subsided, but he examined me anyway. Without doing any tests, his diagnosis was either a kidney or liver infection that should be looked at immediately. Not all that eager to go to the hospital, especially a Chinese one, I balked, reluctant to go, quickly talking myself out of it.

Jake and Angel were discussing my options when another attack struck, doubling me over once more. The pain was so bad I couldn't catch my breath, and Jake made my decision for me. He called Hank to let him know he was taking me to the hospital. After speaking with Jake, Hank was to call Elly. Because she lived in the same complex as us, Hank wanted her to accompany us to the hospital.

Fifteen minutes passed, and we hadn't seen or heard from Elly, so Angel called her cell phone. Hank left a message on her machine when he had called. Elly had returned his call four times to find out why he called, but he didn't answer. It was lucky for me I wasn't dying, I thought. Within minutes Elly met us in the courtyard out front. The two of us hailed a cab around East Lake and went over the bridge to the hospital near the school. Jake raced alongside on his bike. Elly had a friend who worked in the hospital pharmacy and had called him from the cab, asking him to meet us at the emergency entrance upon our arrival.

When we arrived, her friend was there. The two of them spoke for five or ten minutes, then I was led to a general practitioner's office to be examined. A urine test was required, so at the reception desk I retrieved a small cone-shaped container approximately two-inches high by half an inch in diameter to pee in. Upon unscrewing the lid, attached was a small sponge brush at the end of a wire. Oh, this was interesting, I thought. Just how the hell was I supposed to pee in it?

Christ, this is a recurring tour flashback, I thought upon entering the washroom. Trying to figure out how to pee in a dinky little tube I could barely see was one thing, but suddenly memories of our van ride to Chengde had returned to haunt me—there were three stalls divided by tiled walls, no doors and a slop trough below. The only difference was that the trough in the hospital flushed water through periodically.

After depositing my urine sample, I was sent to see a specialist on the second level, who then sent me for a kidney ultrasound. When nothing showed up I was sent back to reception for a blood test, where a nurse behind the counter grabbed my middle finger firmly and gave it a good prick before squeezing the bejesus out of it to get what she needed into a small tube. Much fun, I can assure you. Up until that point there had been no mention of fees for anything; however, that was about to change. Neither Elly nor I had any money to pay the initial fee of one hundred yuan. Because Elly was a friend of the pharmacist, it was only going to cost sixty, but Jake withdrew two hundred yuan from his account and gave it to me just in case.

A second ultrasound was ordered for my liver area. During the ultrasound procedure, the two technicians began flipping out in Chinese amongst themselves. Elly was in the room with me, and I asked her what was wrong.

"Big problem," she said.

"What do you mean big problem?" I asked.

"It's your gallbladder."

"I don't have one!" I said. "Jake was supposed to tell the doctors I had my gallbladder, right ovary and appendix out about fifteen years ago. He must have forgot."

Elly laughed, then rectified the misunderstanding with the technicians. As they continued talking, I observed they still portrayed peculiar expressions, including Elly.

"Now what?" I asked.

"There is a problem," Elly replied.

"Another one? What now?"

"There is, um, a cyst on your liver."

"Great! Is it really a cyst, or something else?" I asked.

"Wait a moment," she urged.

Elly spoke briefly with the technicians in Chinese, then the technician printed out the small ultrasound picture they were seeing on the screen and handed it to Elly.

"What is it?" I asked

"Wait a moment," she replied, then left the room.

While she was gone, the technicians wiped the goop off me. A few minutes later I joined them in the hall.

"You have to go see another specialist," one of the technicians said.

As we walked past the reception area, I asked him if he was going to pick up my blood test and urine test results.

"We already have them," he said. "Your white count is fifteen. Normal is between five and ten maximum, which means you have a very high infection."

My day was just getting better and better, and I could hardly wait for the outcome.

The last specialist to see me was a top surgeon in the hospital. After reviewing the results from the previous doctors and tests outlined in a notebook I was carting around, he spoke with Jake and Elly.

"This doctor doesn't believe the spot is a cyst," Jake translated. "He thinks it is a stone lodged in your bile duct, and he recommends you be admitted to the hospital overnight and put on intravenous."

"No way, not a chance!" I retorted.

"You have a second alternative," Jake continued. "Three consecutive days as an outpatient, receiving penicillin intravenously."

"No, just ask him to prescribe some pills."

"Sharon, you can't have pills."

"I'm not having intravenous."

"Listen, sweetie," Jake continued, "you have no choice. You can't leave the hospital unless you agree to one or the other."

Given I had no choice, I agreed to be an outpatient. Jake also informed me the injections would only take care of the infection, but agreed with the prognosis of the final specialist that the stone should be removed right away. To have the procedure done in China involved having a local anesthetic before a tube is put down your throat to retrieve and remove the stone. The cost was cheap, only four thousand yuan, but I declined and said I would have it checked again when I got home.

Anxiety began to take over, and I suddenly found myself wound up tighter than a clock, suppressing the tears. Having a needle was one thing, but when it came to intravenous the terror of past encounters resurfaced, and I had no desire to relive it, especially in China. Elly approached me, putting her arm around me.

"Sharon, it will be OK. I will be there with you, but you must have the first injection today," she insisted with assurance.

Jake offered to cover my evening classes, and Elly took me directly to a clinic across from our apartment complex to begin the first treatment. A further fee of one hundred and thirty yuan was required to cover the cost of the three rounds of intravenous injections. Because the school covered a portion of my medical expenses, I was reimbursed the entire amount. Before the intravenous was hooked up, a nurse approached with a syringe and a small bottle of medicine. There were two other patients in the room, and they were already hooked up.

"Elly, please don't tell me she's giving that to me."

"Yes, you have to have this," she replied.

"What? What are you talking about? You didn't tell me about this."

With a half-cracked laugh, Elly replied, "Muscle relaxant, in your hip. You must have it, but only one," she insisted.

Moments earlier I had watched the nurse give the same injections to an older couple who pulled down their trousers in the room while everyone watched, and it was no different for me. It had to be my most exhilarating experience yet. After pulling up my pants, I sat on an old wooden bench up against the wall and turned in the opposite direction with my arm out for the nurse to put a tourniquet around my wrist. While my hand was held straight out, the nurse gently slipped the IV needle into a vein before taping it secure. Wow! Why was it always a complex ordeal for nurses at home? For the next hour and a half, two bottles of medication about the size of a small pop bottle drained into me, with two more visits and four more bottles remaining.

Saturday was a full day, with six classes scheduled. It would have been just as easy to call in sick, but I chose to work. I only lasted through the first four classes. Liela found a couple of teachers to cover my classes, and Elly accompanied me to the clinic for round two. By the end, my head was pounding out of my skull, and all I did was sleep.

Sunday was a full day of classes, and one for good measure, before Elly and I returned to the clinic for my last visit. The intravenous ran its course in a total of thirty-five minutes, leaving me with the most excruciating headache I'd had since I'd been in China.

Angel and Damen met me at our regular barbeque hangout for dinner, and by the time we finished eating my head was pounding so bad I thought the top of my head was going to blow off. It didn't take much to figure out the headaches were caused as a result of the intravenous flowing too quickly, so I called it a night and went straight to bed.

Compared to North America, the treatment I received was topnotch. There were virtually no line-ups, and instead of seeing one doctor I saw three, two of which were specialists. The Chinese hospital system, to me, may have seemed somewhat unorthodox, yet it was much more efficient than home. Each doctor and technician summarized his or her findings in one notebook, and it goes with the patient. Anyone who sees the book knows exactly what has taken place, as well as any recommendations. As a patient, you know what the problem is, how to fix it and how much it will cost before you leave. Therefore, hospitals and clinics in Wuhan aren't cluttered with wall-to-wall people who didn't really need to be there. In my opinion, if our medical system worked the same way there wouldn't be so much money wasted. Such a simple, brilliant system.

Following my medical excursion and down time, Damen and Angel thought we should do something fun to get me out of the house. The three of us had been pumped up about riding the gondola across the river, so we set out to locate its origin. Having seen the cable cars crossing above the river, we at least had some idea where to start looking, but were unsure where exactly or what bus to take. Damen could speak enough Chinese to muffle his way through to at least get us on the right bus.

The bus driver let us off at the bridge over the second river. Across the river, the cable was visible in the distance, so we picked a path and followed our instinct. The path led us down some steep steps to a road along the river and through some fascinating, busy open markets before arriving at the gondola terminal building. The cables jetted out a couple stories up at the front of the building. However, getting into the actual entrance leading to the ride was somewhat of a challenge. It wasn't advertised like a normal tourist attraction; in fact, I wasn't even sure the average tourist was even aware of it.

To get to the entrance involved finding our way through an indoor/outdoor market, in and around booths, through another section that led to an enclosed square of rundown cement buildings and rubble at the back and out of the building. A man was waiting for us at a back entrance and motioned us to follow him into an elevator to an awaiting cable car and a big gaping hole outside where the cars were catapulted out of the building and across the river. It was absolutely perfect! No tourists and no wait.

Each car could accommodate four people comfortably. Being afraid of heights, Damen had a momentary spell of anxiety as the car left the building. Out the windows we could see everything below, around and over. The apartment buildings were unimaginable, like reliving many of the sights from the train to Shanghai or the van trip to Chengde. The difference was that our current mode of transportation was much slower, allowing us to see more. We saw complex after complex of slums and, from that view, some of the poorest sections I had seen in Wuhan.

The car traveled across the river and up the mountain into another building. Houseboats lined the riverbanks packed in like sardines, many with sections rotted away or missing, and scads of accumulating garbage was strewn everywhere. On several occasions I had seen poverty that extreme in other Third World countries, yet it was still one of the most implausible sights anyone should have to witness or live in for that matter. After exiting the gondola we were led to another area to pay for our roundtrip ticket. We had some time, so wandered along a trail that continued up the mountain to a TV or radio tower at the top.

Near the top were camouflaged rustic stone warrior statues fenced in amongst the tall mature trees lined each side of the road edge. Near the entrance of the tower, in the center of a turnaround in the road, was an enormous iron warrior statue on a horse. Although smog was thick that particular day, from the top of the mountain was an incredible view of both rivers. As time was running late, we had only enough time to make our way back to the gondola for the return trip back across the river.

Damen knew of a very large open market somewhere in the vicinity of the gondola entrance, but wasn't sure exactly where. Angel and I followed as Damen began walking, and we found ourselves lost on a couple of occasions. About fifteen minutes later, we landed right in the middle of it. Chinese were everywhere, coming at us in every direction, carrying loads of heavy bags or boxes on their backs; wicker baskets hung on rope from bamboo shoots draped across their shoulders; pulling carts were full of everything imaginable. They were piling over each other to get to where they needed to go.

At one point I stopped dead in my tracks in awe, my mouth gaping open, almost losing Damen and Angel as they began to blend in with the massive amounts of people. It was my first time witnessing a Chinese market setting that extreme, and it was certainly an eye opener. It was real China, exactly how I had imagined it to be, and it blew my mind.

Searching for a place to eat, we shuffled and pushed our way through, only to end up at a standstill with nowhere to go, suddenly lodged between vehicles parked in the middle of the street. Fifty-pound bags of anything and everything were stacked everywhere. People where pushing and shoving their loads and wares through the only way they knew how. An elderly man carrying a large box across his shoulders was trying to push his way past Damen, only Damen was turned away from the man and couldn't go anywhere. Yelling, trying to warn Damen the box was going to hit him, the man pushed through. As Damen turned, the corner of the box nailed him in the face as the man pushed through, and the three of us came dangerously close to holding hands before darting into a smaller, less occupied alley. We still had no idea where we were, but weren't too concerned, only hungry. Venturing through the alley, we came across a food stand and purchased some delicious bread resembling cooked pizza dough without any toppings.

Numerous times during my stay I had been wanted to take certain types of photographs, but never actually had the guts without someone else being with me. It was the perfect opportunity. At the end of a narrow alley, in full view on the corner, slabs of meat hung outside from hooks, then out of nowhere, Damen's chicken soup stand suddenly appeared. He had told us about a place in the market Hank had taken him to try the best chicken and pigeon soup in China, and the only place in Wuhan it was available. It would have been nice to try pigeon, but it wasn't available that particular day. Angel had a craving for egg and tomatoes, but most of the vendors still weren't open, so she also settled for the soup. It was the best chicken soup I'd tasted in a long time, mixed with all the trimmings: the gizzard, heart, liver and, Angel's favorite, a chicken foot. Suffice to say, she didn't eat it.

The day ended with a trip to one of the foreigners' shopping mall before catching the bus home. Angel and Damen wanted to pick up a few things they couldn't get anywhere else. Although the foreign food selection was quite pricey, there wasn't much that couldn't be purchased.

With only a few days remaining in my contract, the countdown was on. I had made so many wonderful friends and wouldn't trade them for anything. Because I was fortunate enough to get to know them that well, a special bond developed. In my experience, what North Americans would consider a normal friendship is somewhat different in China, so real and so deep. Perhaps it was an honor to know someone from a distant land, and perhaps those friendships would last a lifetime. In my entire life I had never experienced anything like it, and perhaps never will again.

The school was organizing a huge Halloween party and, as it also turned out, my send off. Approximately 1,000 spectators were expected to attend the large theater located in the school building, yet only about half that many turned out. For two days prior to the concert, Angel had been really sick with some sort of cold and infection in her chest, but girls in the office loaded her up on a bottle of Chinese medicine containing very tiny little black pills. Twice a day she was to swallow a hundred pills at once. By the time she swallowed seventy-five she was gagging and almost woofed her cookies, losing a few stray ones to the trashcan.

Damen and Mary, a Chinese/English teacher, had been volunteered as the MC's for the evening. Angel and I sat near the front of the stage surrounded by a dozen or so rambunctious little boys who began poking and sticking glow sticks in our ears and through our hair and wouldn't settle down.

During the two-hour performance, quite a few things went wrong, including microphones that didn't work half the time. The children at the front of the stage wouldn't sit still or be quiet long enough to hear what was going on, making it difficult for others who were trying to listen. Much of the evening was centered on a couple of short skits put on by some of my older students, and repeat performances from the previous singing competition. Heather and Lacey performed a couple Spice Girls songs, and that was the entire show. I will always remember them as two of the sweetest, most talented little girls on the face of the earth, who I absolutely adore.

Billy was another star performer, who Al had coached during the summer for the singing competition. While coaching him, Al would get very frustrated with Billy's short attention span. April and I would send Al on a time out, leaving Billy in our capable hands. Billy was quite good and definitely had potential. All he needed was a little direction, patience, and a break once in a while. All the hard work paid off. Billy was awesome as he performed, "I Want It That Way," by the Backstreet Boys.

Lacey, Heather, Billy and a couple others received trophies and awards for their performances in the summer. They had all perfected their routines, and on stage they all blew me away, almost to the point of tears. It was my first time seeing them perform since their final in the summer, and they were good. These tiny little children were thrown out on stage in front of TV cameras and hundreds of people, and they gave their all and didn't seem bothered by it in the least. Wow! What an incredible display to watch.

Near the end, Angel and I were asked to go backstage. We were to distribute candies to the children when the concert ended. Damen wrapped things up with half a dozen children he had asked to join him on stage, teaching them his rendition of the trick or treat chant, "Trick or treat, smell my feet, give me something good to eat." Angel and I stood waiting with a bucket of candy in hand. Before Mary took Damen's place on stage, I was sure I overheard my name in a conversation between Mary and the principal. Something was up. Sure enough, Mary went out on stage and introduced me, then brought me out on stage to give me a send off. The children were screaming and cheering, but the best was yet to come. Mary told the audience it was my last day, and I would be leaving for home in a couple of days. Heather was suddenly there, out of nowhere, presenting me with the biggest, most beautiful, bouquet of white roses I have ever received. With TV cameras and lights glaring at me, my eyes began to well up as she handed me the flowers and gave me a big hug. Lacey suddenly approached with a second amazing bouquet of flowers, similar to pansies with a black center. The tears began to stream down my face. Heather and Lacey will always remain two of my most favorites students, and two of the sweetest little girls I have ever had the pleasure of knowing.

Nothingness, as the wind lay almost
Dormant through the long summer's heat,
With the occasional exception of the
Intermittent passing of a storm.
Swiftly replacing the passing of
Summer, the breeze bears a current
Chill, as fall prepares to set in.
Like the winds of change, all is
Restless, tossing, turning in its
Presence, eager to resume, move on.
A lull, as the winds subside, sitting
Peaceful, undisturbed in that moment,
Until once again, effortlessly, a need
For change persists.
Suddenly, abound with an unsettled flow,
The wind searches for its inherent place.

Chapter 23
And So It Ends Where It Begins

No more classes and two free days ahead, it would be my last opportunity to eat food I hadn't tried, have one last encounter with the multitudes of crowds, take in the continual blaring of horns from passing vehicles and, most of all, it was one last goodbye to those I had come to know and love in the past six months.

I decided to make the most of it, settle back and enjoy the remainder of my stay with my friends. Angel and I hung for the day to do some last-minute shopping and sightseeing near the Yellow Crane Tower. Before shopping for some unique trinkets in a street market off the beaten track, we stopped for lunch at a small out-of-the-way eatery along the way. It was during lunch reality began to take hold. In less than two days I would be leaving it all behind. It dawned on me that I was truly going to miss those I had grown so close to, so fond of, but more so, I knew I might never see any of them again.

The possibility that any of them would escape the jaws of a communist lifestyle and cross the ocean to America was certainly feasible, but highly improbable for many of them. Although there would always be correspondence by e-mail, I still felt sad just the same. As the adventure of a lifetime quickly drew to a close, I had come to the realization that not only had my entire outlook on life changed, my life itself had changed. For six months I had been immersed in a cultural society of people whom, for the most part, were so far advanced when it came to technology that it would blow your mind. Yet, in other aspects of their existence they were so far behind, almost as though they were still trapped in a forgotten part of time. With such a fast-paced environment, or so it seemed at times, the people of China were always so real, so genuine, making the experience that much more meaningful. On one occasion I had been told that if a poor Chinese person was about to consume their only meal of the day, and they thought or knew a foreigner hadn't eaten that day, they would gladly, willingly, give up that meal to ensure a foreigner had something to eat.

It was obvious to me during my stay that when faced with any type of confrontation with a foreigner, the Chinese develop a nervous laugh and tend to shy away. That's not to say many of them would sit on their opinions, letting them fester or linger in their mind to the point of causing them stress. For the most part I found when they had something to say amongst themselves they let it rip, and life would immediately return to normal within short order.

The difference between the Chinese and the Western world, when it came to solving problems, was simply this: Once the problem was laid out on the table, they would hash things out until it was resolved. If they suspected it wasn't resolved to your satisfaction, they continued looking for a solution to suit both parties, or at least come close.

With each passing day prior to my departure, I seriously tossed around the possibility of extending my stay, scrapping my return airline ticket to purchase another at a later date. In the long-run, I would have only been working to pay for another return ticket. Besides, China wasn't going anywhere, and returning at a future date was certainly a realistic option. There was no getting around the fact that I learned so much while residing, learning, teaching and traveling in such an incredible country with people who knew very little about the Western way of life.

It was hard to believe that spending only six months teaching Chinese children English could make a difference, and within the first few weeks of teaching I would never have believed it possible. There would always be those inquisitive few who would grab hold of the rope leading to the future and run with it. Yet, with all the ups and downs encountered along the way, I had taken some of the worst classes and students from being destructive, uninterested and unwilling to participate to being the best students I had. Not only had they grown and changed, it was inevitable that I had also grown and changed right along with them. What an incredible achievement.

My final night was spent with friends, Damen, Angel, Elly, Jake and Josh, over one more hot pot dinner. We wouldn't be disappointed, learning that our requests for no hot spices was once again ignored. It was the hottest, spiciest dish imaginable. What a great send off. The Mexicans couldn't have pulled it off any better. We had all filled up on food and beer, and the remainders of our crock pot, firmly lodged into the hole on the table, was still simmering from the hot coal cylinders beneath the table. I didn't want the evening to end, but it was time to call it a night.

As Jake and I walked toward his motorcycle, I knew saying goodbye to him would be the most difficult of all. Before getting on his bike, he turned to me, and I could feel my eyes beginning to well up. He always had a way of making me laugh when I was wound up or just needed to vent. In fact, some of his real life adventures were funnier than mine. He had become my knight in shining armor, so to speak, always there when I needed him. We seemed to just click, and that's all there was too it. In my entire life I had never met anyone like him, and at that moment I realized just how much he meant to me and how much I was going to miss him.

Angel and Elly had walked on ahead, waiting for me to join them as I gave Jake one last hug before we parted ways. Jake pulled up alongside us on his motorcycle and stopped.

"We will meet again," he said. "Don't worry. It will be much bigger scale next time," he said.

As he sat on his bike, the sadness filled his face. It was all I could do to hold back the tears, put my arms around his neck and give him one last kiss on the head before he sped away and out of sight.

Outside our apartment complex it was time for one more final goodbye. Elly had become as close to me as Lindsay had. Over the past few months, Elly, forty-two, had led a fascinating life. For the most part, she was quite a private individual who had slowly begun to share and reveal her true identity to me. After getting to know her, I found her to be quite an intriguing individual and such a hoot to be around when she did finally let her hair down. As we embraced to say goodbye, she made one last attempt, begging me to stay. I knew she didn't want me to leave and, like Lindsay, we hugged for what seemed like forever, saying nothing, knowing we didn't have to before parting ways.

It was a restless night of tossing and turning before embarking on the next twenty-some hours traveling home. The following morning, Damen and Angel were up early to see me off by taxi. I was so grateful I had not pushed to stay in Hank's apartment by myself for my final month's stay, after my daughter so graciously pointed out that they wouldn't be part of the typical young, immature generation I was expecting, and probably had more in common with me than I thought. Besides, my daughter was about their age, and our relationship had always been better than ninety-five percent of the population. So why would it be any different with Angel? After all, they had traveled as much or perhaps even more than I had at their age. Despite my original assumptions, my daughter was right. We had so much in common it was as if I'd known them for years and was suddenly wishing I could stay longer.

It was November third, departure day. Outside the complex, the taxis began lining up upon seeing the luggage. Damen, Angel and I stood waiting while my favorite security guard started making deals for the hour-long ride to the airport. No matter which way I looked at it, there was no doubt the trip home was going to be my longest day in history. This was it, I thought, one last hug goodbye before climbing into the taxi. Just as the driver pulled away, I turned for one last look, tears running down my cheek as I waved out the back window.

Once I boarded that plane, I knew the next twenty-four hours would remain the same, and I would arrive the same day I left once I crossed the international date line. My only request, however, was to have a window seat. Not only was I fortunate enough to get a window seat from Wuhan, but all connecting flights as well.

Crossing Japan, the sky out my window suddenly lit up like a Christmas tree as lightning filled the clouds, blanketing the island below. Panic consumed me, as it always does while flying in unstable weather conditions. I had flown through storms before, but the one I was observing out the window gave me an uneasy feeling. Someone once told me a story about a flight where lightning ripped through the center aisle of the aircraft, exiting through the rear.

At that moment our plane veered to the left, away from the light show, and with it there was a sigh of relief. By two p.m. the sun was setting.

At home it was still November second, and it occurred to me the U.S. election between George Bush and John Kerry was still taking place. Being in China, I was oblivious to who was even winning, but wondered what affects, if any, would develop, or if life would continue on as usual.

It wouldn't take long before the answer to that question presented itself. San Francisco was a customs checkpoint with the usual proper documentation and passport routine taking place, only there was a line for U.S. citizens and one for non-resident travelers and people in transit. Joining the non-resident line, it seemed to be moving much slower than normal, and as more flights arrived, the line grew to an astounding size. There was sufficient time between my connections, and although I was near the front of the line, it hadn't moved more than a foot in ten minutes.

Each individual was processed by a new fingerprinting device and photo system already in place for non-residents, with the exception of Canadian citizens. Panic set in. Randomly checking the clock, I knew I still had to collect and recheck my luggage and possibly run out of time before catching my next flight. In the nick of time I made the connection, with less than half an hour to spare, and was on my way to Chicago to connect with one final flight to Toronto.

It was smooth sailing from there on in, so I pulled out the blanket and pillow and settled in for the duration of the trip, trying, without success, to get some shuteye. As I lay back, the phrase, "If you look, you will see, but if you open your eyes, you will see much," crossed my thoughts. That became the drive to help me grow and fit into a culture so vastly different from ours. I've been asked, "Do you regret going, and would you do it again?" I have absolutely no regrets and would do it again in a heartbeat. It was the most incredible experience I have ever had the opportunity to partake in, and for that I am very grateful.

The uncertainty of what I would now do with my life was still lingering over my head. I couldn't help wonder what life at home was going to be like upon my return, but more important, what I was going to do? To fall back into a life of routine, taking the first job available for the sake of making money, just didn't appeal to me anymore. Yet the pursuit of a career in writing did. It had become the only talent over my entire diversified career that, for the most part, intrigued me and had continued to do so for the longest period of time. Rather than slip back into a familiar pattern of life, or employment, for that matter, I decided to press forward down another unknown avenue to do something I enjoyed, something I also believed I was good at.

The best I could hope for was to spend a few weeks regrouping, recovering and perhaps come up with a suitable plan for my future in the meantime. So for now, to continue on a flow that seems to be working for me, wherever that may lead, with little or no resistance will be the direction I take.

Endnotes

[1] Harper, Damian and others. Lonely Planet, China, 8th edition. Australia: Lonely Planet Publications Pty Ltd, 2002. 498.

[2] Song, Richard. Xinjiang Oasis China Travel Service Co., Ltd. "The Guiyuan Temple." http://www.silkroadchina.net

[3] Song. "The Guiyuan Temple."

[4] Harper. "Other Things to See (Guiyuan Si)" 497.

[5] Harper. "Huang Shan (Yellow Mountain)" 315.

[6] Ibid. "Wuhan" 494.

[7] Song. "Yellow Crane Tower."

[8] Song. Ibid.

[9] Song. "Changchun Taoist Temple."

[10] Courtesy of Van der Woning, Randall, BWG Hong Kong. "Chinese Festivals in Hong Kong." http://bigwhiteguy.com/baskets/festivals.

[11] Song. "Changchun Taoist Temple."

[12] Harper. "Chang Jiang" 833.

[13] Song. "Beidaihe-Qinhuangda."

[14] Song. "Mengjiangnu Temple."

[15] Harper. "First Pass Under Heaven" 236.

[16] Song. "Shanhaiguan (Old Dragon Head)."

[17] Song. "Chengde-Imperial Summer Palace."

[18] Harper. "Chengde" 227.

[19] Song. Ibid.

[20] Harper. "Punning Si" 321.

[21] Song. "Chengde-Putuo Zongsheng Temple."

[22] Harper. "Tiannanmen Square—Chairman Mao" 164.

[23] Harper. "Mao Zedong Mausoleum" 165.

[24] Harper. "The Great Wall—Badaling" pp. 200-201.

[25] Harper. "History—Genghis Khan" 156.

[26] Harper. "The Great Wall—Badaling" pp. 200-201.

[27] Song. "Beijing—Tiannanmen Square."

[28] Harper. "Tiannanmen" 164.

[29] Ibid. "Front Gate" 165.

[30] Ibid. "Great Hall of the People" 165.

[31] Ibid. "Mao Zedong Mausoleum" 165.

[32] Ibid. "Monument to the People's Heroes" 165.

[33] Song. "Shanghai—The Bund."

[34] Harper. "Bund" 335.

[35] Ibid. "History" 325.

[36] Song. "Shanghai—Jade Buddha Temple."

[37] Ibid.

[38] Ibid

[39] Harper. "Old Shanghai" 334.

[40] Courtesty of Van der Woning, Randall, BWG Hong Kong. "Chinese Festivals in Hong Kong."

[41] Cited in "A Cultural Lexicon for Asian-Pacific Studies," in Leonard, George, ed. *The Asian-Pacific American Heritage: a companion to Literature and Arts* (New York: Routledge: 1999, pp. 656-657.).

9 781413 792560